EXPLORING WELFARE I

Key concepts and que

D1589199

Lee Gregory

P

First published in Great Britain in 2018 by

Policy Press   North America office:
University of Bristol   Policy Press
1-9 Old Park Hill   c/o The University of Chicago Press
Bristol   1427 East 60th Street
BS2 8BB   Chicago, IL 60637, USA
UK   t: +1 773 702 7700
t: +44 (0)117 954 5940   f: +1 773-702-9756
pp-info@bristol.ac.uk   sales@press.uchicago.edu
www.policypress.co.uk   www.press.uchicago.edu

British Library Cataloguing in Publication Data
A catalogue record for this book is available from the British Library

Library of Congress Cataloging-in-Publication Data
A catalog record for this book has been requested

ISBN 978-1-4473-2656-4 paperback
ISBN 978-1-4473-2655-7 hardcover
ISBN 978-1-4473-2658-8 ePub
ISBN 978-1-4473-2659-5 Mobi
ISBN 978-1-4473-2657-1 ePdf

Cover design by Andrew Corbett
Front cover image: Getty

I wish to dedicate this book to a few people.

First, while writing this book, my good friend Rob Cooper passed away. Despite great adversity, Rob was a fundraiser and campaigner to admire. He was able to be this because of the support he received from the welfare state: a poignant reminder of the importance of welfare provision to ensure all can not only survive but also flourish and impact on the lives of so many.

Second, I would like to dedicate this book to my grandparents: Audrey and Kazimierz (Jimmy) Bogira and Grantley (Pop) and Phyllis Gregory. They didn't get to see how far I was able to go, and they grew up in a world where there was no welfare state and lived through much of the history that this book reviews.

Contents

List of figures

List of tables

List of abbreviations

CSA	Child Support Agency
CTF	Child Trust Fund
EU	European Union
GDP	gross domestic product
HE	higher education
IGO	international government organisation
IMF	International Monetary Fund
IVF	in vitro fertilisation
KWNS	Keynesian welfare national state
LGBT	lesbian, gay, bisexual and transgender
MEW	mixed economy of welfare
MNC	multinational corporation
MUD	moral underclass discourse
NEF	New Economics Foundation
NGO	non-governmental organisation
OECD	Organisation for Economic Co-operation and Development
SID	social inclusion discourse
SWPR	Schumpeterian workfare post-national regime
TINA	'There is no alternative'
TNC	transnational corporation
UN	United Nations
UNDHR	United Nations Declaration of Human Rights
US	United States
WHO	World Health Organization

Acknowledgements

Concepts can be taken individually, but they are part of a wider interconnected debate, and trying to get this across in the pages that follow was a challenge as different approaches emerged during the writing. That said, there are a number of people to thank, and without them this journey would have been even more painful. And so, thanks go to Ailsa Cameron for commenting on my lecture material: 'There is enough here for a book'. This book starts from that comment, but goes beyond the material we were discussing; I also thank her for her comments on earlier drafts. Thanks to the Policy Press team (Ali, Catherine, Laura and both Emilys, in particular), and to Simon Pemberton, Stuart Connor and the anonymous reviewers for their comments. Thanks also to Paul Lodge, whose lectures in 2002 started me down this path; Mark Drakeford, as ever; as well as the usual 'Scooby Gang' and Kings Heath Running Club for needed distractions and stress busting. Particular thanks to the University of Bristol Social Policy first-year students of 2012 – our lectures and seminars informed my approach to teaching and the foundation of this text. Thanks also to my parents for their continued support. As ever, all factual or typographical errors remain my own.

The author and publishers would like to thank the following for their permission to reproduce copyright material in this book: Jonathan Bradshaw for Figure 3.4 on page 44; Taylor & Francis for Figure 9.3, page 216.

1

Introduction

Social Policy, perhaps more than any other social science, is preoccupied with the pursuit of human welfare. As a field of study, it looks at how social problems are constructed and what responses can be created and implemented to resolve them. Typically, introductions to Social Policy start by exploring how the discipline draws on a number of Social Sciences to understand particular topics – such as housing, education, health and income maintenance – with the implicit assumption that human welfare can be secured by addressing these specific aspects of social life.

Richard Titmuss (1971:20), the founding father of the discipline of Social Policy, highlighted the importance of this approach: 'Basically, we are concerned with the study of a range of social needs and the functioning, in conditions of scarcity, of human organisations, traditionally called social services or social welfare systems, to meet these needs.' A number of key debates can be drawn from this quote. We will be exploring these debates in this book. The central point is around the concept of social need and how this is fundamental to the concept of welfare. Need, as Chapter 3 will explore, indicates certain goods and services required to secure both individual and social welfare – items that, when missing from our lives, hinder us in various ways. Lack of food results in hunger. Inadequate housing can cause health problems. Inadequate education could result in poor job opportunities. What is embedded within this quote is the means by which societies organise their resources to meet these needs. For Titmuss, our welfare needs are too important to be left to the market (commercial organisations through which we can buy access to goods and services); their importance requires that affordability should not be a factor in satisfying them. This illustrates a broader debate between the state and the market as providers of welfare. We will explore these terms in due course in the early chapters in this book. For now, this introductory chapter has two core aims:

1. To explain what is distinct about Social Policy in understanding human welfare; and
2. To outline what you can expect from the rest of the book.

Starting your journey in the study of Social Policy

My discovery of Social Policy was unexpected. A brief comment by a tutor in college, who had convinced me to go to university, resulted in my purchasing Alcock's (1996) text *Social Policy in Britain*. When I read it, I realised this was the subject I had been waiting for. At the time, I was discovering Sociology, Politics,

Psychology, Law and a small amount of Economics, but it dawned on me that Social Policy was the main purpose of all of these endeavours. Without Social Policy, these are interesting subjects to study, but social policy is a potentially powerful tool for enabling significant change in the present and future for individuals and society. Social Policy means two related things: the field or subject of study, and the actual social policies developed to secure human welfare. For the sake of simplicity, I will capitalise the initial letters when referring to the first and use lower case for the second.

According to Titmuss (1971:22), the study of Social Policy is concerned primarily with:

1. The analysis and description of how policy is formulated and implemented, along with the consideration of intended and linked consequences;
2. The question of social needs and problems of access, use and outcomes of services;
3. An analysis of the distribution of resources and the impact these patterns have on services (focusing primarily on income, not only as the primary resource for securing welfare but also as an indicator of inequality); and
4. The study of social rights of citizens as participants in, users of and contributors to social services.

In other words, studying welfare requires considering not only the process of policy making and implementation but also how to determine what is provided, and to whom, at individual and societal levels. Points 2 and 4 above refer to the concepts of need, social rights and citizenship, which we will be explaining in much more depth in the course of this book. These concepts are wrapped up in broader theoretical and ideological debates about the pursuit (or not) of welfare. We will see how they get drawn into policy debates to generate particular rationales in support of particular policy mechanisms and welfare interventions.

The idea of rationale is an important one in thinking about concepts in relation to Social Policy. Levin (1997:32) states that, as the outcome of a rationale, a policy 'is calculated to achieve certain aims, goals or objectives. It is the means adopted to bring about certain ends', providing a framework through which means and ends are logically connected. How rationales are constructed depends on the use of concepts to articulate particular arguments about the nature of welfare, how welfare can be provided for and the circumstances in which citizens can access this provision. This book intends to help you to appreciate how these frameworks can be constructed, and to offer you the tools to critically review the arguments associated with welfare debates.

The unique contribution of Social Policy in the pursuit of welfare is not only the administration of welfare provision but also understanding the arguments for and against certain interventions, be they healthcare provision, anti-poverty income transfers or the development of a compulsory education system. My interest (and the goal of this book) is to explore, on the one hand, how concepts shape welfare interventions; and on the other, to reflect on how conceptual debates are instrumental in effecting change in contemporary society. I am reminded of Tawney's (1921:1–2) introduction to *The Acquisitive Society*, in which he comments:

> Most generations, it might be said, walk in a path which they neither make, nor discover, but accept; the main thing is that they should march. The blinkers worn by Englishmen enable them to trot all the more steadily along the beaten road, without being disturbed by curiosity as to their destination.

While the language is dated, the sentiment remains important for anyone studying the Social Sciences. We cannot uncritically accept the current path of social progress and its associated provision of welfare. We need to be aware of other possibilities, which may require we rethink the conceptual foundations of welfare provision in our society.

In my view, understanding concepts – the various definitions and debates, and their implications at social and economic levels – is essential to removing the blinkers. When you open your eyes to a wider range of possibilities, you can start questioning the path along which society is travelling. You can start considering alternatives. You have probably grown up surrounded by debates at home, at school and in the media about what the most urgent social problems are and what, if any, solutions are available. In a way, these debates can turn out to be blinkers, too, because they give a one-sided uncritical account of welfare and relevant social policy interventions required. Part of the task of this book is to help you reappraise your original viewpoints, start to appreciate the wider diversity of ideas available and engage in a more rounded and critical way with what the pursuit of human welfare means and requires.

My first ever lecture as an undergraduate in Social Policy started with two key questions:

1. What is good for society?
2. How is the good for society to be achieved?

The first question relates to the values that frame our perception of welfare. The second relates to how we deploy the available resources to design and deliver an appropriate welfare system (as we will examine in Chapters 4 and 5 in particular). Both questions remain fundamentally important for Social Policy – not only for those who study it but also for every citizen, as our subject matter impacts directly upon their lives. Bridging the answers of these two questions, you will find conceptual definitions and debates that you need to understand in their breadth and depth.

Concepts and Social Policy

Before we go any further, however, it is important to be clear what a concept is and how concepts relate to Social Policy. Let me use the analogy of tea (bear with me a moment). Now, there are multiple types of tea, each with distinct flavours, colours and aromas. When hearing the word 'tea', your mind will probably generate an image or idea of tea based on characteristics shared by all types of tea. This level of simplification allows you to consider tea without trying to capture the various nuances between the wide ranges of teas that exist. Even if we were to specify green tea, white tea and black tea, our minds still generalise a range of characteristics that allow us to understand the concept of tea. A concept, therefore, is a catch-all term for gathering together similar traits of a phenomenon, or idea, in a handy label; but this obscures the complexity under the surface. Similarly, terms such as citizenship or need are collective labels for often complex debates, which we'll be able to explore in more depth later in this book.

Whether the focus is on poverty, homelessness, drug use, healthcare or higher education provision, concepts sit deep in the bedrock of debate and policy development. At times, policy documents, political speeches and other sources can be quite explicit in the concepts they draw on and how they are being defined. Often, however, their usage is implicit. As such, students need to keep a watchful eye on the debate, and ask critical questions about which concepts are guiding it and how these concepts are being defined.

As we shall see, there was no single impulse behind the formation of welfare provision. The state may be involved in the provision of cash and services in kind to enhance the health, autonomy and quality of life of citizens. Yet today, the term welfare is easily misunderstood, as illustrated in Figure 1.1. Often, the term is used in a 'pejorative' way; that is, to express contempt and disapproval for those who receive welfare. 'Welfare' has lost its connotation of being a positive aspect of our lives and our wider society. Instead of seeking to liberate people from impoverishment, ill health and illiteracy, it is now a tool for controlling supposedly unsavoury elements of our society.

Welfare is the foundation of this book, featuring in all its chapters, so I wish to briefly outline how I am using this concept. First, it is in relation to an endeavour, be it individual and/or societal. Welfare in this sense refers to the means by which we ensure citizens have a common humanity and set of needs, which must be secured if they are to live rich and fulfilling lives. The second way I use the term is as the end product of wider conceptual debates. Rather than provide a fixed definition of 'welfare', I am seeking to draw attention to how the term is defined is open to debate and changes over time. We understand this through considering the underpinning conceptual debates. Figure 1.1 illustrates these two ways in which welfare can be expressed, and how these different expressions can alter efforts to secure people's welfare.

Figure 1.1: Meanings of welfare

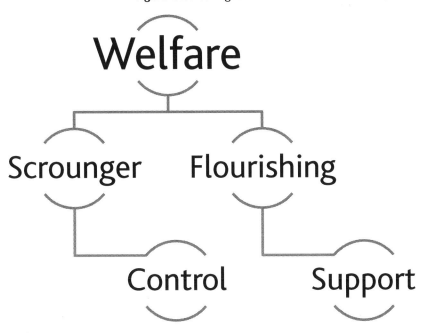

On the one hand, the term welfare can be associated with the idea of a scrounger. This is clearly a pejorative way of using the concept. Saying someone is 'on welfare' seems to imply that they don't or can't take responsibility for themselves, and more than this: that there is something morally defective about not standing on one's own two feet. A quick glance at any number of tabloid newspaper articles would illustrate this point. If social policy interventions were designed around this idea, the focus would be on correcting the perceived defect – possibly by encouraging people into employment as a way of 'getting them off welfare'. Another assumption here might be that employment will improve their living conditions. Such interventions may require individuals to act or behave in particular ways. As such, welfare interventions would have a fairly overt control dynamic.

On the other hand, the right-hand branch of Figure 1.1 presents the concept of welfare as expressing an idea of flourishing. Framed in this way, the concept suggests that we need to support not simply survival but a notion of welfare that ensures all humans have the opportunity to live the lives they wish to and to reach their full potential. This would require a form of social policy that not only ensures that certain basic needs are met (food, shelter, water, clothing and so on) but also provides a much wider range of services (for example, education provision at various levels of study), alongside interventions that create a more equal and supportive socioeconomic context. As such, we can start to appreciate how our concept of welfare will not be static; it will shift and change. This also becomes important when we consider how Social Policy, as a discipline, is concerned with the success and failure of policy interventions to secure individual and societal welfare. As I have stated a few times, we need to explore concepts to understand this change. This is one of the key aims of this book, so let me explain how it will be done.

Book structure

To help readers engage with the material, each chapter title is posed as a question, the aim being to illustrate the range of debates and the complexity of finding an answer. This is designed to encourage you to think about what *your* answer to the question would be. Of course, there are no definitive answers, which will frustrate those of you looking for *the* right answer. However, it is important to understand the multiple, contradictory debates that inform a range of different social problems and policy responses more broadly.

Chapter 2, 'What is welfare and why pursue it?', focuses on the concepts that shape the subject: welfare and wellbeing. It explores how these can be defined, and illustrates that – as with all concepts – there is no one accepted definition. It considers how the notion of welfare has been used in justifications of welfare support, and links this to the debate around social and human rights.

Chapter 3, 'Who receives welfare support, and for what?', considers the entitlement triangle of need, equality and citizenship. It explores these three concepts to understand how to construct a concept of welfare, and whose welfare will be supported, through social policies.

Chapter 4, 'Who should provide welfare support?', considers how the nation state was formed, and with it the growing recognition of ideas of citizenship, social rights and social justice. It also explores what sectors are involved in the delivery of welfare services. This chapter concludes with a discussion of universalism as the gold standard of welfare provision.

Chapter 5, 'Is universal provision sustainable?', challenges the assumed 'gold standard' view of universalism. Intentionally different debates are drawn out, which highlight challenges to universal provision and a move towards more selective provision. Concepts such as means testing, conditionality and progressive universalism are all introduced here.

The next set of chapters seeks to broaden the analysis by drawing out different narratives of welfare provision.

Chapter 6 asks the question: 'How does policy shape the experience of welfare support?'. In part, this chapter is an illustration of various policy narratives, demonstrating how debates about social problems can be constructed to identify deserving and undeserving people. It introduces the concept of stigma, but also the concept of the family. The family is essential for welfare provision; it is not only (arguably) the main source of welfare in our lives but also a unit of existence consisting of a range of social relations, which are shaped by social policy interventions. The family is fundamental in shaping our welfare experience, and how governments view the constituency and purpose of the family can shape their understanding of key policy debates regarding welfare. The concept of stigma draws attention to how certain groups are not seen as 'worthy' of support because (some would argue) they do not behave appropriately as citizens.

Chapter 7, 'Is the welfare state always in crisis?', expands the critical gaze to consider how the concepts of neoliberalism and globalisation have altered the contextual understanding of welfare provision. By this, I mean that they offer an account of socioeconomic change: we are no longer in the same sort of society as in the 1940s, when state provision of welfare became the mainstream means by which welfare was secured. These narratives create new debates in welfare provision, which fundamentally shift how concepts are drawn into debate and change the design of welfare services.

Chapter 8, 'How does risk change the welfare state?', continues with this line of argument to illustrate how there has been a sustained movement through welfare reforms to reduce state provision and relocate welfare activity onto the individual.

Chapter 9, the final discussion of key concepts, asks: 'Is social policy about control?' Particular attention is given to the concept of social control before it is explored in relation to participation and empowerment, drawing out some fundamental questions to ask of all forms of welfare provision.

Taken together, the chapters show that certain concepts have been influential in the formation and development of welfare provision, but that these have not been static. There has been considerable change in how these concepts have been articulated, which fundamentally shifts the design and rationale of welfare provision. Drawing attention to the influence of neoliberalism in this process demonstrates how certain narratives have gained influence in a process of change in welfare provision that fundamentally shifts this support away from its original aims and intentions. This theme is taken up in the Conclusion (Chapter 10), which explores how it might be possible to continue to reframe concepts to challenge some of the recent shifts that have undermined state welfare provision.

Concepts drawn on to understand efforts to secure human welfare rely on an appreciation of the diversity of different ideas, while developing a robust defence of those you hold true. Such an analysis can not only articulate a particular policy approach but also be drawn on to critique the current state of play. If you lack a clear conceptual understanding of human welfare, you will have no clear understanding of the deficiencies of existing practices in securing welfare, or of what alternatives there might be.

Finally, operating alongside the text is a website of additional learning materials. It is highly recommended that readers engage with these while working through the book, as the website provides greater versatility than the text. It not only allows various activities to be presented, which go beyond the set of questions usually found in textbooks, but also lists a number of podcasts that discuss key debates and concepts examined in the following chapters. Additionally terms in bold type in this text are explained in a quick reference, online glossary.

Studying the Social Sciences is not always an easy process. You may feel challenged on how you currently understand the world. However, the aim of this book is to provide the scaffolding to support you as you reconsider your assumptions – regardless of whether this results in significant change in your view or a more secure account of what you already thought. Some colleagues are adamant that introductory texts are unsuitable for university students, who they feel should engage with primary texts, hear the original author's own voice and then draw their own conclusions. I do not necessarily disagree; there is no better way to understand theory than to engage with original texts. But original texts do not provide the scaffolding; they are not designed to. Rather, they advocate and promote a certain perspective, idea or line of thought, which seeks to advance knowledge and understanding from a particular viewpoint.

Reading original texts is great, but it's like starting a journey without checking the direction of travel first. Some texts can be challenging to read and understand, and some general insight into the key ideas can make this easier. So, the aim of this book will be to provide you with the broad direction of travel before you engage with the original texts themselves, such as *The Gift Relationship*, *The Road to Serfdom* and *Citizenship: Feminist Perspectives* (to name a small number of examples). The intention is to help you to engage with these arguments in a way that shapes your understanding of Social Policy. And it is important that you do so. How you engage with and interpret any of these texts will be different from my own engagement and interpretation: we have grown up in different social worlds, with different political and economic contexts, which have informed those initial preconceived ideas, which we bring to our studies. Now is the hard task to find the answers that are right for you, and to learn how to articulate and defend them.

I think Dickens (1992) summed it up best in *A Christmas Carol* when the ghost of Marley visits Scrooge: "'Business!' cried the Ghost, wringing its hands again. "Mankind was my business. The common welfare was my business; charity, mercy, forbearance, and benevolence, were, all, my business. The dealings of my trade were but a drop of water in the comprehensive ocean of my business!'" As a Social Policy student, humankind is your 'business'. Understanding concepts is your first step to understanding human welfare.

2

What is welfare and why pursue it?

Welfare means pursuing your personal ambitions in life, and having the resources to do it

Welfare is for those who can't support themselves. It ensures they have the basics to live.

Key concepts in this chapter
social rights • welfare • wellbeing

Chapter 1 highlighted how welfare largely rests on provision secured through social policy. In other words, the idea of welfare has practical implications, but the scope and focus of what is practical will be steered by more abstract ideas. This still leaves us with the questions: 'What is welfare?' and 'What is policy trying to achieve in relation to this concept?'. Understanding how welfare is defined allows us to consider not only its importance but also how it is drawn into arguments that justify welfare systems. This chapter starts by exploring the concepts of **welfare** and **wellbeing** before going on to examine justifications for state intervention. This discussion will then lead into a review of the concept of **social rights**.

As such, this chapter offers our starting point into the study of concepts. As noted in Chapter 1, welfare is used both as a concept in its own right and as the outcome of wider conceptual debates. We need to understand the former before the latter, which is the focus of discussion across the majority of the chapters in this book. To start our discussion, I wish to show that a number of dimensions inform the nature of welfare. These will be presented within four components: material, non-material, eudaimonia and capabilities. We will explore each of these in the following section.

Welfare and wellbeing

How welfare is defined is open to significant interpretation. Daly (2011), for example, outlines three foundation theories drawn from Economics, Politics and Social Policy, and shows how each perspective highlights different concerns and intents. Western societies have tended to consider gross domestic product (GDP) as a proxy for welfare, on the assumption that increasing GDP will result in shared economic benefits for all in society. This economic perspective has met with some criticism. Other concepts of welfare refer to philosophical notions of 'the good life' or the pursuit of a wider idea of human flourishing (rather than the scrounger idea we explored in Figure 1.1). Generally, welfare refers to a range of different forms of security; it is predominantly used in relation to material resources such as income and housing, but also increasingly in relation to other sources such as personal relationships, health and participation. This chapter traces some key aspects of the concept of welfare.

Welfare as flourishing

The notion of human flourishing has a long history. It stretches back to the work of the Greek philosopher Aristotle, who was interested in the quest for the good life, which he termed eudaimonia. Eudaimonia was tied to people pursuing activities that exhibit 'virtue' (acceptable behaviours), so that welfare is secured through the proper development of one's capabilities. Here, we find an explicit account of a 'good life', as defined by Aristotle: in essence, that we can make an external judgement of what a good life consists of and how this can then be achieved. The aim was to ensure that citizens did not squander their capabilities on activities that detracted from the good life, thus undermining the political and social community. For Aristotle, eudaimonia was based on three aspects of happiness:

1. Pleasure/enjoyment;
2. A life as a free and responsible citizen (although how he defined a citizen would not reflect our concept today; I explore this in Chapter 3); and
3. A life as a thinker/philosopher.

As such, the work of Aristotle suggests that discussions of welfare require some articulation of an appropriate end state, which generally reflected the needs of the community over the individual.

In the more contemporary context, Sen (1999) developed the idea of capabilities to draw together what people are able to do and their freedom to choose to pursue a life that they value. Here, 'capabilities' is used to capture notions of not only income but also health, education and other resources required to achieve certain ends. These capabilities underpin our ability to function as members of a human society; they go beyond a focus on biological survival to draw attention to being a fulfilled human being. This gives us our first introduction to the idea of a 'thick' definition of welfare (Dean, 2010). A thick description of welfare goes beyond survival to also consider social embeddedness: our relationships with others, sense of self-determination and personal expressiveness. Dean uses a soup metaphor to distinguish this. A thin soup is nourishing (it maintains basic survival), but it is tasteless. A thick soup is both nourishing and flavoursome (promoting a better quality of life). It is the thick description being drawn out here in relation to both capabilities and eudaimonia.

In essence, securing one's capabilities promotes a thick conception of welfare in which individuals are able to connect with each other freely. Nussbaum (2011) suggests that the core functional capabilities consist of:

- being able to live to the end of a human life of normal length;
- being able to have good health, adequate nutrition, adequate shelter, opportunities for sexual satisfaction and choice in reproduction, and mobility;
- being able to avoid unnecessary and non-beneficial pain and to have pleasurable experiences;
- being able to use the senses, imagine, think, and reason, and to have the educational opportunities necessary to realise these capacities;
- being able to have attachments to things and persons outside ourselves;
- being able to form a conception of the good and to engage in critical reflection about the planning of one's own life;
- being able to live for and to others, to recognise and show concern for other human beings;
- being able to live with concern for and in relation to animals and the world of nature;
- being able to laugh, to play, to enjoy recreational activities;
- being able to live one's own life and no one else's; enjoying freedom of association and freedom from unwarranted search and seizure.

Some of these capabilities will no doubt be surprising to you; for example, to laugh and play, which you may think have little involvement with social policy and welfare. The state, after all, does not mandate that we all play on a regular basis. However, we need to accept that welfare does not only come from the state. There are multiple sources of welfare: income, state services, commercial services through the market, voluntary organisations and our own families. The state need not provide all of these, but it can help to ensure a context in which these are possible. Imagine, as an example, that you play a sport or musical instrument. For you, this is an important source of joy; perhaps a means of socialising with others and developing your own sense of identity. But imagine you could not do this because the level of poverty you lived in limited your opportunities to do so. A part of your wider welfare would not be met. Through income support to lift you out of poverty, however, the state can enable you to pursue those aspects of your life that form part of your personal welfare. The key point here is that wider elements of human life can be compromised where human welfare is not adequately protected.

Welfare debates, however, need not be so encompassing of different aspects of life. As Dean (2010) notes, some forms of welfare attempt to define welfare through a notion of an abstract, calculative actor. An illustration of this can be found within the debates on happiness as the basis for welfare.

Welfare and happiness

Early thinking around welfare drew upon the utilitarian philosophy to emphasise the centrality of happiness (or utility). This is an early economic framework for understanding welfare through the personal satisfaction of a person's preferences, which result in the attainment of happiness. As an economic theory, satisfaction is reflected in the price people are willing to pay for the good or services to satisfy their preferences. More broadly, utilitarian thinking seeks to secure the greatest amount of happiness for the greatest number of people. Influential in the early 1900s, these ideas have underpinned the development of welfare, as governments started to respond to welfare needs as a consequence of **industrialisation**.

Thus, utilitarianism became a key strand of thought in early welfare debates. This drew together the philosophies of Mill and Bentham. Bentham argued that all human action pursues pleasure and the avoidance of pain, and so whatever maximises pleasure over pain within the population is good and therefore right. This underpins the 'greatest happiness for the greatest number' argument found in utilitarian thought: the happiness principle.

Refining this, Mill presented a concept of happiness that shares some of the same argument as Aristotle. Flourishing refers to the ability of the individual to become a complete and consistent whole human, the maximum of their potential. As such, our understanding should be our own, as should our desires. Taking this further, Mill adds the harm principle: that the actions of individuals should only be curtailed where they cause harm to other individuals. Thus, intervention into individual actions is only acceptable where it is a cause of harm to another. Minor interventions are acceptable if they prevent the attainment of a simple pleasure (and this denial ensures the happiness of others); but harm is significant if it hinders or prevents happiness (or individual flourishing). In terms of welfare provision, therefore, this theory suggests that state interventions should be framed as ensuring justice in how humans interact with each other, and not the direct provision of goods to secure welfare. Such provision should be received through self-help and charity, not the state.

Similarly, the economic theories of Adam Smith argued that human nature was inherently self-seeking in the pursuit of pleasure/happiness. Smith argued that humans are anxious to promote their own individual interests, but also inclined to be interested in the fortune of others. As such, happiness is best met through the free market. Rather than try to establish general principles of welfare that could guide action, individuals would pursue their own desires through the market. These desires are termed preferences within economic theory. The assumption is that happiness is pursued through preference satisfaction, which can be secured only through the free market. Such markets are free from central state intervention and planning, offering a mechanism for individuals to satisfy preferences through a reliance on the price mechanism (referred to as the 'invisible hand of the market') to respond to people's needs. The invisible hand responds to demands for goods, allowing an aggregate of individual preferences to be efficiently met and thus securing the welfare of the majority. Happiness is therefore best pursued through market mechanisms, and the market would regulate itself, so that goods are produced not only in quantities that individuals desire but also at prices that individuals are prepared to pay. Goods and services are bought using the wages earned through the market by the employed (and charity for the unemployed).

There has also been a focus on happiness as a measure of welfare in the contemporary context. Stiglitz et al. (2008) reignited some interest in 'happiness' (Bartolini et al., 2016; Davies, 2016) to capture a multidimensional idea of welfare (a move away from measuring welfare in terms of GDP), and there has been some promotion of the relational aspect of social policy; that is, a focus on improving personal relationships (Muir and Cooke, 2012). This modern take on happiness is less concerned with preference satisfaction than earlier attempts to define welfare. Rather, it draws attention to a wide range of factors in people's lives: job satisfaction, health and longevity, social relationships and civic participation. For example, the UK government of 2010–15 required the Office of National Statistics to develop measures for 'subjective wellbeing' built around four measures of happiness, which were based on self-rated satisfaction with one's life. Questions focus on satisfaction with life, feeling that things in life are worthwhile, happiness yesterday and levels of anxiety yesterday. Yet such measures, Taylor (2015) suggests, risk separating individual factors from the social context: an excessively individual focus, which pays little attention to the context in which we live.

Paying attention to happiness and measuring it through preference satisfaction are not without challenge. Preferences reflect personal choice or desire; they are based upon things we *want*. This is problematic, as a want may not always enhance – and can even be detrimental to – our welfare; for example, smoking, drinking to excess, having a diet that consists mainly of saturated fats and so on. Additionally, these preferences are not objectively defined. Rather, they are subjective; that is, they are personal preferences but are susceptible to a range of influences. This might indicate that happiness defined in this way is an inappropriate measure of welfare.

For example, one such influence could be advertising. Here, marketing of certain goods and services can encourage people to desire certain products, which then form part of their own perception of their happiness. The purpose of advertising is to influence you; to encourage you to want to purchase goods, with little regard to your actual welfare and great concern for the profit motive that drives commercial activity in the market. As such, we should be critical of attempts to define welfare in terms of happiness when this is based on individual preferences, as such preferences can be misleading. Reiterating this point, White (2014) explained that how we react to information can reinforce our misconceptions. Our individual decisions can be misinformed by the information we receive. He provides the example of choosing to drive rather than fly after hearing news of an aeroplane crash, despite flying remaining the safest mode of transport. Finally, preferences change. The career we wanted as a teenager may not be what we end up doing as an adult, because we change our minds. But which preference do we use to measure happiness? The early preference of our teenage self, or the new preference of our adult self? Determinations of welfare need something less fickle than preference to inform our debates.

As White (2014) concluded, happiness as a concept for informing welfare debates is too vague and multifaceted. Yet Fitzpatrick (2001a) suggests that happiness can, in a shallow way, refer to an emotional state; but in a deeper sense, it emphasises faring well (welfare) and being well (wellbeing – this is the focus on *being* in the **ontological** sense – the nature of our existence). But for Fitzpatrick, happiness is just one of six elements that underpin a concept of welfare; the others are provided in Table 2.1.

Table 2.1: Fitzpatrick's components of welfare

Component	Definition	Debates/issues
Income security	Sufficient income to have the wherewithal to live (eat, clothe oneself, maintain a roof over one's head and so on)	How do we define 'sufficient income'? Do we need to consider the source of income and how it is distributed within household units, for example?
Preferences	Ability to choose and pursue goods and one's own life goals	These can change over time and are subject to external influence. So we can ask to what extent should changeable preferences inform how we determine a minimum level of income to meet human welfare.
Needs	Those things that are essential aspects of survival and participation in society	How are needs best defined? (See Chapter 3)
Desert	Rewards based on the contributions people make	How do we define people's contributions to society? (See Chapter 3) How do we determine the kind or scale of reward? What moral/ideological frameworks influence these decisions?
Relative comparisons	Similarity or dissimilarity in standards of living across a given society	Who are the comparison group – people we know or people we do not? Can we balance similarity with desert?

Table 2.1 demonstrates that welfare is made up of a number of elements, none of which have clear distinctions or unambiguous consequences; each component raises its own set of questions. So, even with these six characteristics, it is not possible to untangle some of the contradictions that might be generated when we think about how to pursue welfare through policy interventions.

Beyond happiness

Attempts to define welfare (as illustrated by both Aristotle and Fitzpatrick) do not simply focus on people pursuing happiness and 'faring well', but can also become embroiled in a broader philosophical debate about the nature of a good life – with all of its moral implications. Subsequently, on the one hand, some theorists offer a conceptualisation of welfare that refers to how people should live their life and how to define a 'well-lived' life. On the other hand, it is about defining those items and activities that make this life possible. Fives (2007) examines a range of philosophical traditions that have informed this debate. He suggests two general approaches that are useful here: perfectionists and non-perfectionists.

From a perfectionist perspective, the 'well-lived' life can be determined only by adopting a disinterested, objective position from which to make judgements about the good life; this cannot be done from a personal perspective, because our own experiences (and preferences) prevent a more universal notion of the good life. This illustrates the objective/subjective distinction within debates about welfare. Objective approaches suggest it is possible to investigate the human condition and develop an account of the good life, which can then be measured and monitored. Such ideas suggest that health, wealth, honour and pleasure (Fives, 2007) are the foundation of moral goodness, but that we squander these if we do not live the good life. Seeking to remove subjective valuations from such decisions, there was a move towards objectively judging the worth of different activities and the contribution they make towards the good life. Here, it is possible to see a potential blurred distinction between individual and social welfare (discussed briefly below). Such an account allows for consideration of the function of different activities. Tawney (1921:8) defined a function as: 'an activity which embodies and expresses the idea of social purpose. The essence of it is that the agent does not perform it merely for personal gain or to gratify himself, but recognises that he is responsible for its discharge to some higher authority.' Put simply, function is used to express a means by which we can determine the social worth of an activity and how it enhances welfare. If an activity creates wealth for all, then it has a function; if it results in extortionate wealth inequalities that are detrimental to welfare, then it is a functionless activity and its value to society should be questioned – and, potentially, challenged and changed.

In contrast to the perfectionist accounts, the non-perfectionists offer a framework less concerned with the *ends* of an activity (or collection of activities). Ends are the particular goals we each want to achieve for ourselves; they are based on our preferences and desires, and should not be exposed to debate about their moral validity. Rather, consideration is given to the *means* (provision of a set of goods that all need to achieve their ends).

Yet, Jordan (2008) has offered a critique of the term 'welfare', suggesting it has become dominated by economic theories, which limit social interventions. This economic framing focuses efforts around the notion of utility, and pushes aside social values around social interdependence and the common good. For Jordan, the term 'wellbeing' must therefore be used to recapture a focus on support, recognition, esteem and solidarity, and this renewed notion must be placed at the core of social policy. In a similar way, Heins and Deeming (2015) argue for a move away from GDP as a measure of welfare; expanding GDP does not mean enhanced welfare. This returns attention to the aforementioned notion of subjective wellbeing, a more holistic view of which is illustrated in the European Commission's *Quality of Life* measures and the Organisation for Economic Co-operation and Development's (OECD) *Better Life Index*. Thus, in efforts to define welfare, we cannot and should not be limited to a dominant economic framing of our core concept.

This returns the debate to a consideration of 'happiness'. While utilitarian theories sought to present this in terms of satisfaction through market activity (an economic perspective), Jordan in particular offers an analysis that seeks to encompass a wider range of factors (many listed in Table 2.1), which may not be secured through market interactions. This reiterates an earlier point: there are multiple sources of welfare. We could not, for example, secure love and belonging through market interactions; and yet these are fundamental to any sense of personal welfare we may hold. Family, friends and our communities therefore provide these forms of welfare. As such, we need measures that capture the diversity of welfare and do not restrain our discussion to economic considerations.

And so we return to a discussion of human flourishing, hinted at in this chapter and in Figure 1.1. Flourishing is often presented individualistically (as is happiness) as the result of individual actions, choices and desires. However, as Greco and Stenner (2013) argue, in order to flourish we cannot separate the individual from the wider social world. It is not enough to focus on the individual pursuit of happiness; we must also focus on the socioeconomic conditions that shape and inform this. Burchardt (2006) suggests that there is some advantage in this focus on happiness: it draws attention away from income factors. This is not to diminish income as a source of concern, but to allow for greater recognition of non-material factors that influence wellbeing. However, Social Policy remains concerned with issues of distribution, the solution to which must be (according to Burchardt) embedded in a theory of social justice (we will explore this concept in detail later), which is incompatible with approaches that recognise happiness as the objective value through which to value our lives. Although Burchardt both welcomes and warns against the development of a happiness perspective for Social Policy, her ideas reflect a shift from welfare to wellbeing.

A move towards wellbeing

This move towards wellbeing does not foster a new set of ideas. Rather, it draws on some of the foregoing, especially the recent developments in the happiness debate regarding subjective wellbeing. Thus, for Stiglitz et al. (2008) and the National Economic and Social Council (2009), it is possible to draw out six or eight (respectively) domains which should be considered in any measure of wellbeing. These include:

- economic resources
- health
- education
- relationships
- care and social connections
- participation and work
- political voice and governance
- community and environment

As with the ideas of Jordan and Heinz and Deeming, we see efforts to move beyond a materialistic definition of wellbeing; to move away from 'faring well' (achieving a minimum existence) in favour of 'being well' (living an engaged and fulfilling life of one's choosing). There is no predefined morally good life here to which we should aspire. Some of Stiglitz et al.'s recommendations rest on a move away from economic measures (where increased GDP does not mean improved living conditions for all; social inequality influences who benefits from improvements in a nation's economic performance) to focus on income, consumption *and* wealth, alongside the aforementioned non-economic factors. For others, such as Sen (1999) and Nussbaum (2011), it is possible to draw on similar ideas to focus on capabilities (see the earlier list of capabilities, as well as the discussion of need in Chapter 3).

The New Economics Foundation (NEF) similarly puts people and planet first, and their *Happy Planet Index* (2012) draws out three elements:

- the subjective experience of people to determine their wellbeing;
- expected life expectancy;
- the ecological footprint as a measure of sustainable futures.

The aim here is to take a future-orientated approach and consider 'how well nations are doing in terms of supporting their inhabitants to live good lives now and in the future. It points the way towards sustainable wellbeing for all' (NEF, 2012:4). Focusing on the whole collective takes precedent over considering individual components. Social Policy, as Titmuss (1971) has illustrated, is concerned with the individual and the societal. Many of the debates about welfare/wellbeing relate as easily to a broader societal focus, and the work by NEF highlights the centrality of this. Failure to look after the social, and (for some) the environmental, will result in significant damage to individual wellbeing. As such, Social Policy cannot ever be just about individuals; it must also cast a critical eye over the 'good life' for wider society.

This discussion illustrates the journey that Social Policy has travelled. Policy interventions seek to intervene in society and the economy to produce an effect.

The effect being pursued has to be articulated in relation to a notion of welfare, which is very much alive and unresolved. A number of competing ideas have been presented, and (intentionally) no comment has been made about which set of ideas should guide policy makers – or students of Social Policy. What should be noted is that Social Policy as a subject is concerned with how policies succeed or fail in securing welfare (however it is defined). Additionally, as Dean (2012:11) notes, it 'is the systematic study of how societies of different kinds can ensure, so far as possible, that their members enjoy good health, that they can freely participate in society and that they are able to think for themselves'. These themes and topics are revisited throughout this book.

Despite its complexity, the concept of welfare is essential for comprehending the intent and purpose of policy. As Daly (2011:5) explains: 'The concept helps to provide ways of understanding the connection between welfare related rationales and institutions as they are embedded at a systematic level, especially in social policies and programmes, and the resources and levels of wellbeing that people obtain in real life'. First, this definition illustrates the centrality of welfare as a concept. It shapes how policy makers envisage the intent of a policy and the institutional format this will take, and offers a guiding framework. Second, it provides scope for defining what people need in order to secure their welfare. Third, as Daly goes on to discuss, this concept is not inactive; it is in a constant state of flux, responding to changes in economic, political and social contexts. As such, the concept allows us to consider the 'what' and the 'how'. The 'what' refers to the number of competing ideas and objectives of welfare, whereas the 'how' (considered in the next section) highlights the provision of services to secure welfare.

Summary

As depicted in Figure 2.1, a number of different debates underpin the concept of welfare. These overlap in various ways, which cannot be easily depicted – theorists will draw from a number of different theoretical frameworks to define the concept of welfare they put forward. However, four broad areas can be drawn out, against which welfare can be defined: material concerns, eudaimonia, citizen capabilities and other, non-material concerns. Each of these highlights different components of welfare, which are drawn (to various degrees) into debates about the systems of support created to secure welfare.

The justification of welfare

Efforts to explore human welfare inevitably lead to efforts to generate a list of items essential for life. This in turn poses the moral question of how to respond to those who lack these essentials. Regardless of how welfare is defined, there is an automatic discussion of whether or not the state should be involved in provision of welfare services; we saw this briefly in the discussion of utilitarianism and

Figure 2.1: Elements of welfare

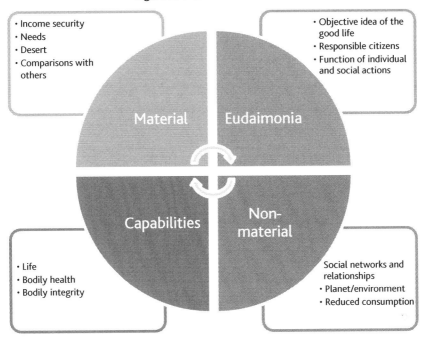

- Income security
- Needs
- Desert
- Comparisons with others

- Objective idea of the good life
- Responsible citizens
- Function of individual and social actions

Material

Eudaimonia

Capabilities

Non-material

- Life
- Bodily health
- Bodily integrity

Social networks and relationships
- Planet/environment
- Reduced consumption

the claimed importance of the market in satisfying preferences. Consequently, a number of liberal philosophers during the early stages of industrialisation started to develop arguments that advocated the need for some level of state intervention in people's lives to secure welfare.

Before exploring some of these arguments, it is worth noting that the following account draws heavily on the UK welfare context and historical development to explain the case for state intervention. This should be considered as an illustration of why states become active in relation to the provision of welfare. It is not a claim that this development occurred in the same way across different nations. Rather, we need to be aware that different nations have developed a number of approaches to meeting the welfare needs of citizens. This will become clearer as you progress through the chapters of this book and start to appreciate how concepts create different arguments for and against state provision of welfare. Additionally, while I illustrate many of the debates with UK examples, different histories of social policy within a number of national contexts indicate variation in state involvement in welfare services (for example, Pilisuk and Pilisuk, 1976; Karger and Stoesz, 1990; Jencks, 1992; and see Ginsburg, 1992; Mason, 1993; Hort, 2014; Ngok and Kwan Chan, 2015).

However, we are able to review how concepts have been drawn into debates in two important ways with regards to welfare: first, recognising the importance of welfare provision in the face of socioeconomic change; second, recognising the importance of concepts in shaping different types of welfare provision across the western world. Taking the first of these as our focus, this section starts by considering the influence of early liberal philosophies, which sought to move away from some of the earlier utilitarian ideas to suggest a need for state provision rather than reliance on the market alone. Philosophers such as Green promoted a number of key justifications for state intervention, which recognised disadvantage resulting from industrialisation but were resistant to significant levels of centralised state provision (Green and his contemporaries were referred to as 'reluctant collectivists'; see George and Wilding, 1976). Green suggested a need to consider the 'common good', which referred to the facilitation of each individual to pursue self-realisation for the benefit of him/herself and others. But this could not be achieved alone; it required an element of collective action and support. Central to the common good, therefore, is mutual interdependence: we might all be individuals, but we have to rely on each other to produce food and clothing, educate ourselves and so on. Second, there are social duties; an individual has the right to expect assistance from others (via the state) in efforts to achieve self-realisation, but has a duty to respond in a similar way to the efforts and needs of others. Third, equality of opportunity refers to the equal chances of everyone to fulfil their own abilities, and for Green was to be pursued for societal benefits. In his view, some inequalities can be justified, but only where they serve the common good. Consequently, for Green and his contemporaries the interventionist state became permissible, because moral behaviour was to be expected of citizens only if they benefitted from the material and spiritual progress of society.

Similarly, Hobhouse (writing at the same time as Green) accepted the existence and potential of capitalism rather as an economic system, but rejected collective state action. What we find in these debates is a growing recognition that unregulated capitalism was socially destructive and eroded people's ability to satisfy their preferences (to return to the earlier language of happiness). Thus, a small amount of state intervention was permissible. As such, Hobhouse proposed that the state had a duty to remove obstacles that impede a person's self-development, requiring the state to stimulate self-help, individual effort and enterprise. In addition, Hobhouse suggested the need to provide conditions in society that enable citizens to live as full members of that society: full employment, a living wage, a benefits system for those who cannot work and public service provision of education and municipal gas/water to provide a national minimal for all. These reluctant collectivists sought to distinguish themselves from earlier utilitarian thinkers in emotive terms by suggesting that hope and confidence are better motivators than the fear and insecurity that result from the unregulated market of **classical liberals** (this is important for our discussions in Chapter 6). Thus, a broader argument in favour of state intervention is built on a number of key concepts (common citizenship, equalities, duties and need) that determine entitlement to support. Such ideas have found contemporary significance in debates between the economic theories of Keynes and Hayek (Wapshott, 2011).

Such debate draws attention to the roles of the state and the market in efforts to secure welfare (we explore this in detail in Chapter 4). For now, we need a quick review of this debate to understand how an overt focus on welfare as an activity of government gained popular support. The core of this debate rests on the different theories of the market offered by Keynes and Hayek during the 1930s and 1940s. For Keynes, capitalism is the best economic system for industrial societies, but is not self-regulating. Thus, when it causes social harms as a consequence of production, or generates unemployment during an economic crisis, there is no protection of citizens unless there is some form of state intervention and regulation. For Hayek, the central planning suggested by Keynes was the first step towards totalitarianism and stifles individualism, self-help and private enterprise. However, Keynes's classical theory suggested that underemployment and underinvestment result from a competitive market; only through state action can employment and investment be secured. Such views found support in the UK with the influential William Beveridge, who was tasked with a review of early welfare provision during the Second World War that resulted in the 'Beveridge Report': one of the most influential documents to inform welfare debates.

Keynes's economic theory therefore suggested a revised analysis of how people's welfare could be secured. Employment in a regulated market would create the stability and security required for citizens to meet their needs and allow them to contribute to society through employment, earn additional rewards through their individual effort (linking to the idea of desert) and ultimately allow them to pursue their own preferences for their lives. Keynes and Beveridge were wary of the state's ability to promote and not threaten freedom (through interference in people's lives); they remain reluctant collectivists. Consequently, state action was only justified where necessary to achieve a healthier and happier nation: the state had to compensate for failures in market provision.

Keynes's limited commentary on welfare provision results in a pairing of his work with that of Beveridge. Sharing a similar argument – a need for the state to foster full employment – Beveridge was also concerned with unemployment resulting in a perceived lost sense of usefulness to the nation. This provided a starting point for his analysis of 'five giant evils' that had to be overcome in post-Second World War (British) society. These giant evils were idleness, want, ignorance, disease and squalor (unemployment, poverty, (lack of) education, ill health and poor housing conditions), which were detrimental to both individual and societal welfare. These problems formed the foundation of social policy activities by governments and other actors, and provided the initial core fields of the subject. They provided a set of predefined areas of welfare provision, into which the state was able to intercede and take precedence over the market.

The rise of the welfare state

Growing scepticism of the market as a provider of welfare was founded on the Keynes/Beveridge argument, which outlined the characteristics of the market that reflected its failure to, or incompatibility with, efforts to secure welfare. These forms of market failure are outlined in Table 2.2.

Table 2.2: Market failure in welfare provision

Form of market failure	Explanation
Public goods	Certain things are too expensive for individuals to be expected to pay for, and even if they did, those who haven't paid for them can't be excluded from using them too (for example, clean air and roads)
Negative externalities	Production and market activity can have negative consequences for welfare; for example, water pollution from the disposal of chemicals or sewage
Psychological externalities	Distress caused from the social harms observed by members of society; for example, visible homelessness or crime
Information failure	Markets rely on information symmetry between purchaser and provider (both sets of actors have adequate information to facilitate a transaction, without either actor holding anything back to unfairly advantage themselves within the transaction). In relation to welfare, this is not possible; welfare professionals have specific information that citizens do not, and citizens have information about their lives that professionals do not.

Market failure analysis offered an explicit critique of market functions. It suggested that leaving welfare to the auspices of the market and people's preference satisfaction failed to adequately address the inability of the market to provide certain goods and the inappropriateness of certain market mechanisms for securing welfare for all citizens.

Summary

As noted earlier, debates regarding the nature of welfare cut across a number of different divides, but this in turn leads to an automatic debate about how best to satisfy those needs. Figure 2.2 illustrates what the foregoing has argued. The market was initially left to provide for people's welfare needs, but as processes of industrialisation significantly changed the socioeconomic life of whole populations, there was a growing awareness that markets could not adequately address those needs. Nor could markets respond to broader societal needs, because they were focused upon individual preferences. There was therefore a reluctant acceptance of the need for the state, and the identification of certain deficiencies in market practices that limited the market's potential to satisfy welfare. Early arguments that the price mechanism facilitated welfare satisfaction, and a concern that state provision would intrude into people's lives and foster a dictatorial government, gave way to new philosophical debates. These debates suggested a need for state intervention to strengthen common humanity, which unites us all. Need, citizenship, equality, empowerment and freedom then became concepts that came to define and justify state intervention. These concepts are explored and challenged in subsequent chapters; as noted earlier, they shape how we define welfare. The remaining focus of this chapter is how this justification for state provision of welfare was generated around claims regarding social and human rights. It is through these rights that other concepts associated with welfare were articulated.

Figure 2.2: Welfare provision: the state vs the market

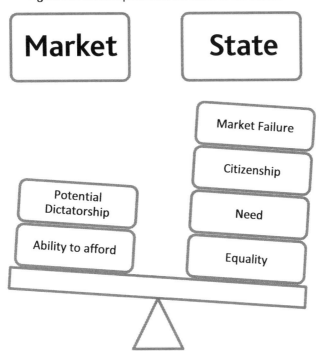

Human and social rights: framing welfare entitlement

Despite the breadth of analysis regarding the meaning of welfare, it was possible to argue that the central state needed to be involved in its provision. This was articulated through a sense of common humanity encapsulated in the idea of social rights. These rights sought to encapsulate both a definition of welfare and how this justified state provision of welfare support. Such rights, and how they are defined, shape the entitlement of citizens to secure access to welfare support at appropriate moments in their lives. Thus, the study of Social Policy requires an understanding of social rights. However, I wish to start with the more contemporary focus on human rights. While this breaks with the previous historical focus, human rights offer an easier route into the following discussions, and emphasise the common humanity that underpins welfare debates. Social rights, as we will see, are rights that are specifically associated with particular nations; human rights exist across these national boundaries.

Human rights

Freeman (2011:7) suggests that rights are 'not mysterious *things* that have the puzzling quality of not existing, but *just claims* or *entitlements* that derive from moral and/or legal rules' (emphasis in the original). Equal treatment within the law, the ability to vote and the ability to marry are all examples of rights that can be found in the United Nations Declaration of Human Rights (UNDHR). Such rights must be *universal* (they apply to everyone), *inalienable* (they cannot be taken away) and *indivisible and interdependent* (a government cannot pick and choose which rights to respect). Thus, as Flanigan and Hosie (2016) explain, human rights are not given or endowed by nation states; rather, they are respected and protected, or not. It is worth noting that human rights were introduced in a way that ensured the United Nations (UN), as an international organisation, could not directly interfere in states' efforts to promote human rights; how rights were protected would be up to individual nations. The UN could apply significant political pressure through other states and external actors, but how these rights are pursued (if at all) remains within the auspices of each nation.

For Carr (1949), implicit within rights is a notion of duties. The state cannot protect human rights if individuals fail to provide the necessary resources required to promote and protect rights (for example, through paying taxes to fund state activity). Thus, there is, for some, a precondition of discharging certain duties in order for rights to be protected. Alongside this are suggestions that respecting others' human rights forms part of these wider duties to fulfil moral and social obligations. How these obligations are defined is open to debate and interpretation.

Certain duties/obligations may be determined within the social body as being required before a right is accepted. This emphasises how human rights do not exist in nature but are social constructions. This led Freeman (2011) to suggest that human rights must follow from a theory of the good society; they cannot precede it. The earlier discussion of welfare is therefore a prerequisite for determining rights. However, different conceptions of what makes the good society (and a good life) result in different concepts of rights, and no universal standard can be easily achieved. Often, human rights are the result of political power, pragmatic agreements and limited moral consensus. However, Freeman does draw out some key characteristics relevant to our discussion.

Freeman (2011) points out that the UNDHR contains several Articles that refer explicitly to the topics of Social Policy:

- Article 21(2) refers to equal access to public services.
- Article 22 outlines the right to social security in accordance with the organisation and resources of each state, linked to economic, social and cultural rights indispensable to dignity and the free development of one's personality.
- Article 23 refers to protections in relation to work and employment, including equal pay.

- Article 25 outlines the right to a standard of living adequate for the health and wellbeing of the individual and their family, and even identifies certain goods and situations to be provided/protected against. It additionally offers protection to mothers and children.
- Article 26 refers to access to education.

The declarations, however, are not easily interpreted. For example Article 22 suggests that everyone should have access to social security *as a member of society*. This, Freeman highlights, is not access *as a human*; those not considered members of society – such as asylum seekers, refugees or migrants – may not be protected in the same way as those who are. It is important to note that human rights are associated with being human – a universal attribute. As such, they are not subject to the cultures and customs of any particular nation. Thus, Freeman (2011:67) suggested human rights are 'rights of exceptional importance, designed to protect morally valid and fundamental human interests, in particular against the abuse of political power. They carry special weight against other claims, and can be violated only for exceptionally strong reasons.' They contain three key characteristics: they are universal (everyone has human rights), everyone has them equally and they are the rights of individuals.

However, how rights are protected is left to the auspices of the nation state. Thus, while the human rights outlined in the UNDHR are to be protected and respected, the nature of entitlement is a separate matter. Flanigan and Hosie (2016) suggest citizen rights are *given* by states, which makes them different to human rights. States define and shape what rights are to be provided, influenced by a number of factors, such as cultural expectations and financial restrictions. As long as such parameters meet the broader UNDHR Articles, a state can be seen to be respecting human rights while controlling the shape of citizen rights. This also highlights the close association between citizenship and nationality. Nationally determined rights of citizens are developed and pursued, often, as noted in Chapter 3, as part of a wider nation-building project. Citizen rights and duties are defined in a way which achieves national objectives. However these are often associated with particular gendered and racial assumptions about the 'type of person' to be granted citizenship status.

Social rights

The most influential account of the development of citizenship is found in the work of Marshall (1992), who suggested that citizenship consists of three sets of rights. First, civil rights developed, securing the right to liberty and equality in law. These were followed by political rights, which granted the right to vote and participate in political processes. Students of politics or history will be aware of the development of the right to vote, which was not automatically granted to all but has been gradually expanded from the right of a few to the larger population. For some groups, such as women, this only happened due to hard-fought campaigns for the right to vote. Finally, Marshall suggested that developments in the 1940s constituted the third and final stage: social rights, which granted the right to basic welfare and full participation in society. It was suggested that these rights had followed an evolutionary path, although this is a very 'British' view of the development of rights; other nations have experienced different trajectories. Regardless, within Social Policy, his account has been influential. Importantly, the endowment of rights came with specific requirements around citizens' duties; but also, welfare is provided as a right. What should be apparent at this point is that, while social rights are granted by states, they are also shaped and determined by these states.

While human rights are broader and have been deemed to be universal, citizenship rights – in particular social rights – are different; they are more fluid in their form. Social rights are often defined in relation to access to social security, employment protection, housing, education and health and social care services (Dean, 2010). Such concerns underpin state intervention into welfare provision; but this is not without some theoretical diversity. From a utilitarian perspective, policy interventions could be supported to implement a number of social reforms even if this compelled citizens to act/behave in certain ways, provided it secured benefits for the greatest number in society. For example, in Victorian England, requiring the impoverished to comply with the dictates of the workhouse to secure relief was acceptable within a utilitarian framework. Dean (2015) notes that this embedded the notion of social rights being conditional on behaviours considered necessary for the greater good of society. As such, the development of social rights has an element of conditionality at its genesis, which is explored in Chapter 5. However, as the previous section illustrated, a broadening concern with citizens' welfare was fundamental to securing the freedom of individuals to pursue a life of one's choosing. Removing the impediments generated by the market system would facilitate the full flourishing of the individual. As such, for some there is less concern with the individual per se than with the individual within and alongside society – the welfare of both are inseparable and mutually dependent. Thus, as the state increasingly involved itself in securing goods and services considered integral to welfare (which were lifted out of the auspices of the market), social rights became a central focus of state activity.

Social rights are, in essence, an attempt to capture a notion of welfare that can guide the action of welfare providers. How social rights are defined, therefore, suggests that there are certain 'things' that humans need to secure their welfare. We will shortly explore this in relation to the concept of need (through which we can potentially identify the contents of social rights). For now, we need to keep this at a more abstract level.

If we accept that social rights reflect those items fundamental to our welfare, then there is a need to ensure that these rights are decommodified (Esping-Anderson, 1990). **Decommodification** refers to the ability to satisfy certain social rights without reliance on the market; essentially, that the ability to afford should not dictate satisfaction of essential welfare goods and services. Decommodification is vital because, if affordability dictates access to these goods/services, employment is given greater importance. Employment results in an income (wage), which allows us to purchase certain goods/services. But if the conditions of employment deteriorate, we cannot easily seek out other employment if we have no other means by which to satisfy our welfare. Consequently, our welfare is eroded because we are essentially trapped in a form of employment that no longer secures our welfare. Social rights, therefore, are the label we attach to items that cannot be left to the market alone; to do so could actually damage our welfare.

Yet, Dean (2015) notes that decommodification should not be confused with the removal of labour as a commodity; rather, it reflects the degree to which individuals can maintain socially acceptable living standards independent of market participation. In turn, Esping–Anderson (1990) suggests this is the route towards an equality of status. Decommodification undermines class inequalities because the tripartite notion of citizenship (civil, political and social rights) prevents people from being treated as 'things' to be purchased and sold. However, different types of welfare system accept various levels of decommodification, as shown in Table 2.3. Securing welfare via social rights has therefore drawn upon acceptance (or lack thereof) of decommodification in various ways across different nations. Principally, the idea of decommodification has suggested that there are certain aspects of human life so fundamental to existence that they should not be left to the market to provide, because people with insufficient financial resources will lack access to those goods. Subsequently, Twine (1994) suggests these rights are interdependent.

Table 2.3: Welfare regimes

Type of welfare system	Decommodification and rights
Corporatist	Cautious of commodification Encourages self-help and occupational welfare
Liberal	Zero or limited decommodification Social rights are means tested (see Chapter 5)
Social democratic	Full decommodification Social rights based on emancipation, equality and reduction of stigma

He argues that, without social rights, the political and civil rights of workers and their families are more difficult to uphold. Without the decommodification of labour and certain goods/services, citizens will remain dependent on employment, which fundamentally informs and limits their sources of welfare. Consequently, social rights should grant access to material resources to secure 'wellbeing', but should also draw attention to the need for inclusion in society. Basic survival is not sufficient to secure 'welfare' in the broader, 'flourishing' sense (or in any meaningful sense) if it does not realise that citizens are not only individuals but also part of a wider, interdependent social network. Basic survival may be acceptable, but citizens must also participate in the accepted lifestyles of their societies; exclusion results in stigma and harm or shame, as we shall go on to see later in the book. Access to social rights, and entitlement to those rights, can thus be based on a number of different ideas.

Social rights and entitlement

There are characteristics that generate entitlement, and there are income-related entitlements (Twine, 1994). The former are linked to status, such as unemployment, sickness, disability, old age and childhood. These are groups that often need support securing welfare, so provision is made for them. However, these can relate to the second notion of entitlement, as state insurance schemes to pay for welfare may require contributions while in work to pay for welfare services when need arises. Thus, income-related entitlements that rely on contributions one makes while in work can dictate the level of support one receives. Those without a contributions record will often rely upon a safety net provided at a lower level of support. While social rights might exist, this does not instantly imply access, or similar access, to welfare services. Taylor-Gooby (2016) suggests that entitlement and access can be shaped in three different ways (see Table 2.4). Each of these perspectives can inform entitlement through social rights, but each offers different justifications of why such rights are to be protected and enforced by the state.

While Table 2.4 indicates types of people or situations to be supported, Twine (1994) also draws attention to the reliance of social rights on resources, reiterating the intricate link between market and welfare state. Resources are required to provide social welfare; however, this relies on not only economic growth but also a willingness to secure public expenditure for these efforts. As noted in Chapter 7, various crises narratives illustrate the problematic nature of this relationship.

Table 2.4: Entitlement and access

Type	Explanation
Needs-based	Implies government obligation to secure, but dictates that those able to demonstrate a need have an entitlement
Capability-based	Associated with comparisons between different groups, with state intervention where this is not the case
Desert-based	Where a certain quality of life or activity imposes an obligation on society to offer support; for example, support to parents (especially mothers) who take on caring responsibilities for children

Similarly, Oliver and Heater (1994) suggest that civil and political rights are necessary for the market to function; capitalism requires these for protecting free-market transactions. Social rights, however, focus on addressing the inequalities generated by free-market activity; for supporters of the free market, such inequalities are a legitimate outcome of free trade. Civil and political rights are therefore based on individual freedom; but social rights require collective action, in line with egalitarian liberal ideas. Consequently, it is suggested that social rights are different because they have a cost – unlike political and civil rights – as fiscal policy, referring to the use of the taxation system, influences entitlement, whereas the other sets of rights are not impacted by financial concerns, and as such are 'true' rights. As O'Neill (2005) argues, welfare rights do not place corresponding duties on citizens in the same way as other rights. Rather, they are borne by institutions, which are not found universally across different societies. Consequently, it is suggested, social rights are not human rights.

Plant (1992) challenges these arguments, which he suggests are misguided, as social rights are no different from civil and political rights. Civil and political rights, for example, do have a cost. Using the example of security and upholding the law, Plant suggests that enforcement of both sets of rights requires courts, the provision of the police force and so on, which have costs. They are therefore similar to the reliance on professionals to deliver social rights, as civil and political rights often have professional services attached to them, which come with cost implications. In a similar way, Ashford (2006) argues that all human rights may need institutions to be effective. This in turn means that social rights are associated with human dignity, and that institutions – and the costs involved – are required to ensure people realise these rights. Without the relevant institutions, these rights do not exist.

Other arguments have also been presented as to why social rights cannot be considered as rights per se; for example, the suggestion that social rights have *vague* duties attached to them, while civil and political rights have *clear* duties: the duty to abstain (do not kill, rape, steal). This makes it is easy to identify when a duty is not met. Social rights duties, however, are open to (re)negotiation and therefore change, and it is harder to define when they have not been met (how much tax should be paid, for example?). But Plant argues that this ambiguity applies just as equally to civil and political rights – how much police provision should be available to secure personal safety, and what budget should be provided to do so? Just like social rights, this is open to political debate.

A third critique of social rights rests on the notion of need. As illustrated in Chapter 3, need is tricky to define and heavily political. Needs are open-ended and vague, resulting from political demands and party-political desire to win elections. Additionally, technological developments alter needs. This infiltrates the debate and drives expansion of the demands under social rights – expansion not experienced in the cases of civil and political rights, or so it is claimed. Plant suggests that technological changes can impact on civil and political rights. He retains a focus on personal safety and technological change in policing, the development of street lights, changes to airport security and internet safety – all of which alter the provision of civil and political rights. We can add to this the expansion of equalities legislation to cover in vitro fertilisation (IVF) treatment for same-sex couples, or technological changes that better facilitate disabled people's interactions with society. All of these have cost implications for civil and political rights, as welfare needs have cost implications for social rights.

However, some theorists that we would label libertarian liberals (I'll revisit this term in more detail later; for now, think of them as the pro-market theorists) would suggest that social rights are unclear, politically debatable and have a cost, which implies they are not technically rights. They require state expansion and interference in the free market, disrupt market function and seek to impose a political view of social justice that is not shared or agreed by all (see Chapter 3). The consequence of such an approach is a move towards totalitarian state power. But, as Plant has illustrated, such views do not hold up because the debatable and costly nature claimed of social rights also applies to the other sets of rights. All three form part of political debate, and are open to changes and reinterpretation over time.

Consider the struggle of women to secure the right to vote (a political right), or the lesbian, gay, bisexual and transgender (LGBT) movement's efforts to secure equal marriage rights, or the development of anti-terror legislation generating new costs for claimed personal safety against the arguments that many measures infringe on individual liberties (civil rights). Similarly, some social divisions are susceptible to human rights violations but do not have special rights to protect them (although social divisions are explored throughout this book, see Best, 2005 and Payne, 2013 for a more detailed account). In all of these examples, these changes in social rights can be reflected in human rights. The gradual granting of women's right to vote through significant campaigning by the Suffragette movement (in the UK) is an example of successful social change, although further afield Saudi Arabia only changed its law on this in 2015, and Vatican City is now the only state with no voting or electoral rights for women. Or consider, as of 2016, how 73 countries still criminalise same-sex relationships and 13 retain the death penalty (www.ilga.org). Both social and human rights are complex, nuanced and change over time. The focus here has been to illustrate how, despite efforts to separate out social rights from other citizen rights, such arguments contain significant flaws; they require overlooking not only similar claims for all types of rights but also the interdependence of the three sets of rights: political, civil and social.

Summary

What does this mean for welfare? Determinations of how to define welfare lead to justifications for various levels of state intervention to decommodify those elements considered integral to human welfare. This in turn is linked to a set of social (and human) rights, whereby rights-based approaches to welfare support have developed. More recent debates, however, draw attention to human rights and their significance for policy debate. Lister (2004) illustrates this in relation to anti-poverty policy, while Wronka (1998) presents a considered account of how human rights encapsulate Marshall's (1992) triad and as such have significant importance for the study of Social Policy. However, as Dean (2008:9) notes:

> The broad concept of welfare [social] rights that had been developed within Social Policy is under threat as the basis of the capitalist welfare state has come into question. At the same time, it is not a concept that has entered to any significant extent into the prevailing human rights debate. That debate has struggled to give substance to ideas of economic, social and cultural rights, but has never ventured to forge a notion of welfare rights that might have purchase and meaning as much in the global south as in the developed capitalist world. Recent attempts to define a human rights approach to global poverty reduction would seem to embody a managerial rather than an emancipatory ethos.

This quote contains a number of issues worthy of consideration, some of which inform the wider argument of this text. First, that social rights may not feature significantly in human rights discourses. As Dean notes, social rights offer a new discourse for justifying state intervention into welfare provision, the contents of which we might express through a notion of need (see Chapter 3). Second, there is a global dimension that should be considered within our analysis. Finally, and relevant to the wider debate of the book, the concept of social rights is under threat; as will be suggested in later chapters, this relates to the rise of neoliberal ideas and their fundamental challenges to key concepts of Social Policy.

Chapter summary

This chapter has set out key issues and debates in relation to welfare and the gradual development of justifications into welfare support, paying particular attention to the development of social rights. Figure 2.3 draws out, in a basic way, some of the different ways in which decisions about how to define welfare shape the forms of welfare provision that follow. In part, Figure 2.3 acts as a brief introduction to a number of debates explored in the following chapters. It serves as a prominent reminder that discussions of key concepts require policy makers to adopt particular definitions of various ideas that underpin the pursuit of welfare. These decisions, in turn, shape how welfare services and income maintenance policies are designed to pursue particular conceptions of welfare. In the following chapters, similar figures are used to try to illustrate the various decisions that can be made, and their consequences for the design and delivery of welfare services.

Figure 2.3: Welfare: framing the debates

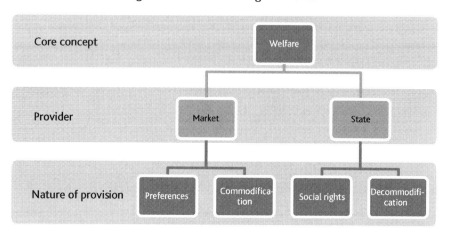

Critical thinking activity

Outline the key arguments for and against state welfare provision, and assess their relevance to the construction of social rights.

Further reading

Dean, H. (2015) *Social Rights and Human Welfare*. Oxon: Routledge.

Fitzpatrick, T. (2001a) *Welfare Theory: An Introduction*. London: Palgrave.

Fives, A. (2007) *Political and Philosophical Debates in Welfare*. Basingstoke: Palgrave.

Don't forget to look at the companion website for more information.

3

Who receives welfare support, and for what?

It's fine for people to receive welfare support if they've made a contribution to the system.

Welfare is based on rights, and rights are universal.

Key concepts in this chapter:
citizenship • equality • need

The previous chapter presented the broader debate around welfare (its definition and justification), which led to a discussion about human/social rights. It was suggested that the content of social rights was defined in terms of what people need to secure their welfare. We can therefore appreciate that social rights are central to welfare debates, justifying state intervention. We now need to consider how these rights are constructed to not only facilitate access to welfare support but also define the forms of support to which we are entitled – and who has that entitlement.

We start by exploring the concept of **needs**. How we define a need is a point of significant debate; without a concept of need, it is not possible to identify what is lacking from people's lives and causing harm. Also, are needs universal or relative to the society in which people live? Either way, the concept of **equality** becomes important to consider, for this reflects how people are treated in relation to their welfare and subsequent needs. Alongside need and equality, **citizenship** forms the third aspect of entitlement to welfare support. This final concept encapsulates in policy debates the notions of need and social rights, alongside the implicit assumption of equal treatment.

Figure 3.1 depicts the 'entitlement triangle' of needs, equality and citizenship. These three concepts are key to determining welfare in a practical sense to guide social policy interventions. Using the idea of a triangle allows us to grasp the relevance of the three concepts: each point underpins our concept of welfare. Needs refers to the specific items required to secure welfare. Equality refers in part to the universal nature of these items, as well as access to them, but it also refers to the ability to pursue opportunities for advancing and attaining our welfare. Citizenship identifies who is entitled to the social rights that have been used to justify state intervention, and therefore also who is excluded from this group. Combined, they establish entitlement; that is, the right to have these welfare items satisfied, but also the extent to which they should be satisfied by the state. For now, we need to be aware of the way in which entitlement is shaped by these three concepts. Triangles are the strongest shape, because any added force is evenly spread through all three sides. The entitlement triangle is therefore a firm foundation upon which to provide welfare. However, there are also diverse types of triangles; as later chapters will explore, pressures on welfare provision have changed the shape of welfare entitlement in relation to these three key concepts.

Figure 3.1: The entitlement triangle

Working out what citizens need

If we accept that social rights are an essential way in which we frame welfare debates, we need to pay attention to what these rights are entitling us to. Thus, for Dean (2010), social rights can be understood as articulations of human need. But how we define 'needs' is open to considerable debate and contestation. For example, Dean (2010) explains that social rights originate at a particular moment in historical development – early industrialisation – which drew attention to particular forms of harm: Beveridge's five giant evils, each of which identified a particular need to be met. Post-Second World War, the Allied Nations Atlantic Charter promoted four freedoms: of speech and religion, and from want and fear. United States (US) President Roosevelt (1944) said: 'Necessitous men are not free men. People who are hungry and out of a job are the stuff of which dictatorships are made' (cited in Dean, 2010:16). It is clear that welfare, as the basis for survival or the promotion of human flourishing, requires that a certain standard of living is achieved through the ability to meet certain needs. Expressed as social (or human) rights, these become the accepted needs of citizens (the role of governments in accepting rights is explored in the next chapter); thus, needs are the basis for the construction of rights. But the challenge remains as to how these are justified and defined.

How can we identify needs?

Any definition of welfare has to have something of substance attached to it that allows welfare to be operationalised into more practical terms. This is essential for guiding policy intervention to secure the welfare of individuals and society at large. Such criteria allow us to identify what people need, and whose responsibility it is to provide for those needs. We started to explore this debate in the previous chapter, where we saw how certain challenges were identified that resulted in (initially reluctant) state intervention into the welfare of citizens. This was framed within the notion of social rights. We then explored how these rights suggested that certain items should not just be accessible if you can afford them; rather, we suggested, it is necessary to decommodify certain items deemed essential to welfare. We must now start to move away from the abstract use of the term 'items' to explore how we can identify these and provide some practical insight into what is required to secure welfare. To help with this, Goodin (1988) draws out two key distinctions, outlined in Table 3.1.

Table 3.1: Types of need

Volitional need	We need x for y, but desire y	To purchase the latest tablet device (y), I need money (x)	Not a priority for the welfare system
Non-volitional need	We need x for y, and need y	In order to eat (y), I need money (x)	Should be provided by the welfare system

It is not the providence of the welfare state to remedy every shortfall between aspiration and attainment. Rather, as Table 3.1 demonstrates, there is a distinction between need and desire, which informs debates around need. For Mac Cárthaigh (2014), this is the implicit element of any needs statement: the need for food carries with it the implicit end state of nutrition for survival; the tablet device does not.

More broadly, this has been characterised by the difference between wants and needs. Wants, as the name implies, is something highly desired. Food can be a want when someone is hungry, just as the tablet device can be a want. However, there is broader justification of why food is not considered a want in the same way: it has that moral difference alluded to in relation to needs. Yet, in some instances, we may not aspire to meet certain needs. For example, the *need* to change one's diet to manage type 2 diabetes does not automatically generate a *desire* to change one's diet. Thus, distinguishing between wants and needs is not always so clear-cut. We could simply suggest that failure to satisfy a need would result in death, and distinguishes a need from a want. Yet participation in society, as part of wider human social experience, suggests that this is too narrow a distinction. What about a sense of belonging, or having enjoyment in life through social interaction? If I do not eat I will die. If I do not socialise I will not die, but the impact on my mental health could be significant. Consequently, the focus of welfare around survival or flourishing will inform how definitions of need are constructed.

As such, the identification of needs is the first step in a broader argument suggesting that such items should be available outside of market exchange: the ability to afford these needs should not determine access to them. However, this still isn't clear-cut. Education and health, for example, can be provided through either public provision or the market; how do we decide which? Governments can provide income support for people on low incomes, but at what level is this determined? Income support is important, as noted in Table 3.1; money is often a resource for accessing needs and wants, but sometimes we rely on the market to satisfy both.

Take the example of food. We know food is vital to survival, but should the government directly provide us with food to meet this need? As Glennerster (2003) notes, the market is perhaps a better provider here, because it allows individuals choice about what we eat – we all have different tastes, diets and preferences. The government cannot provide for such diversity, but the market can. Yet market flaws in food provision can occur, as demonstrated by the global rise of food aid and hunger in the western world (Riches and Silvasti, 2014). The identification of food as a need, distinct from a want, carries a moral imperative that the state should supplant the market – or, perhaps more realistically, ensure everyone has sufficient income to purchase the food they need to survive. Although the rise of food aid may imply the state is not seeking to provide for this need (Gregory and Joseph, 2015), it is clear that there are challenges in identifying needs to facilitate the attainment of welfare.

Consequently, while on the surface welfare debates are often presented as polar debates (it is either x or y), in practice the dividing lines are blurred. Thus, where the market may be the preferred provider, this does not mean the state is not able to intervene. There may be the need to provide support, in terms of subsidy for certain foods or the provision of vouchers, so that those with low incomes can buy food. Alternatively, the state may facilitate income support, so that individuals always have the means by which to buy food.

Can the idea of harm distinguish between a want and a need?

One approach to distinguish between a need and a want, which Goodin (1988) explored, relates to harm. There is a difference between being harmed (becoming worse off than previously) and being benefitted (becoming better off than previously). The former tends to draw attention to the role of market mechanisms in causing harm to the individual and their family/community, and forms part of the moral justification for supplanting the market for certain items. However, the idea of being harmed can be problematic (as illustrated in Figure 3.2). Assume, for a moment, that the present state of two households is as follows: Household 1 lacks sufficient income to afford food, and Household 2 can afford food. Now, imagine both of the main workers in each household become unemployed. Household 1 is not in a worse situation (it still cannot afford food), while Household 2 is now unable to afford food (a worse situation than its previous state). Unemployment support would provide both households with an income and return them to their previous states. Yet, while Household 2 could now afford food, Household 1 still could not. This illustration demonstrates how allocation by need can help to avoid harm by preventing a worsening of a situation. But if the present situation is causing harm, there may be no impetus for intervention and change. The idea of harm may, therefore, be insufficient if it facilitates only a certain group of citizens to have their needs satisfied and if harm is defined in relation to a change in the status quo.

Figure 3.2: Can allocation of needs avoid harm?

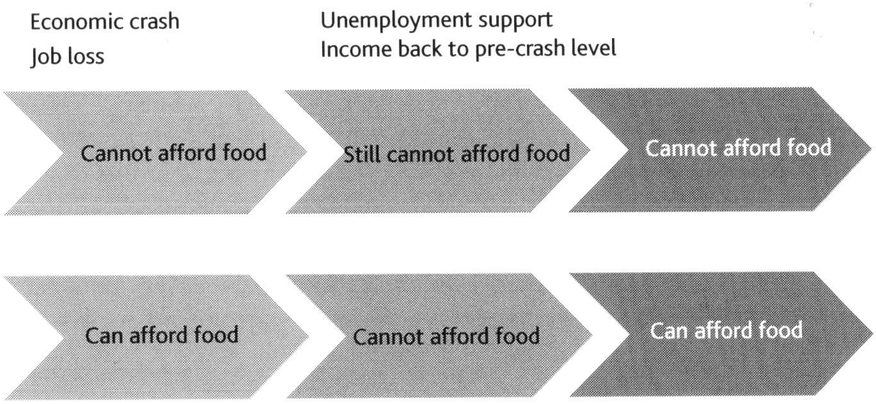

Economic crash
Job loss

Unemployment support
Income back to pre-crash level

Cannot afford food

Still cannot afford food

Cannot afford food

Can afford food

Cannot afford food

Can afford food

This does not mean the idea of harm is not useful in helping to identify a need. We could use the idea in a slightly different argument, regarding acceptable income levels linked to needs, which is the foundation of poverty debates in Social Policy. Alternatively, it can be used to refer to how society itself is organised or structured (Pemberton, 2015). Essentially, the ways in which social structures have formed generate harms, which cause disadvantage, and social policies are required to tackle and rectify such disadvantage. The idea of social harm shares more with the idea of diswelfare. As Titmuss (1967:120–1, emphasis added) explains:

> The emphasis today on 'welfare' and the 'benefits of welfare' often tends to obscure the fundamental fact that for many consumers the services used are not essentially benefits or increments to welfare at all;

> *they represent partial compensations for disservices, for social costs and social insecurities which are the product of a rapidly changing industrial urban society. They are part of the price we pay to some people for bearing part of the costs of other people's progress*; the obsolescence of skills, redundancies, premature retirements, accidents, many categories of disease and handicap, urban blight and slum clearance, smoke, pollution and a hundred and one other socially generated disservices. They are the socially caused diswelfares; the losses involved in aggregate welfare gains.

Thus, the identification of need is about not only those items we require to secure welfare in daily life but also how the wider social contexts of our lives impact on our ability to 'fare well'. From this perspective, the 'present' situation of Household 1 – unable to afford food in either situation – becomes a need to be addressed.

However, Titmuss relates diswelfare to employment-related activities: a class-based analysis, which could draw attention to biased analysis that may marginalise the experiences of some citizens (such as women and minority ethnic groups). Thus, how harm is defined and constructed, and the needs required to alleviate the harms generated, should also be mindful of diversity in citizens' lives (see Chapter 4). Even within this broader view, the construction of social relations and institutions will generate multiple harms, some of which may be within the providence of welfare systems to rectify; others may require changes to legal structures or political rights. While important considerations, these broader debates have not truly developed a definition of needs; rather, it has shown us the context in which needs are generated. We can now turn our attention to definitional debates.

Are needs inherent or interpreted?

The foregoing discussion did not explicitly define need, but set out the broader debate relating to how we enter this discussion. In our earlier discussion of welfare, attention was drawn to survival and flourishing, which Dean (2010) distinguishes respectively as thin and thick (as discussed in Chapter 2). Seeley (2015) summarises these as subsistence (thin) and participatory (thick) needs. The former refers to those items required to avoid serious harm or death. However, this adds to the complexity of definitions rather than making things clearer. Food, for example, would be a subsistence need, while education may be a participatory need or fall between the two, depending on one's personal view.

Seeking to cut across this distinction, Sen (1999; see also Nussbaum, 2011) put forward the idea of capabilities (mentioned in Chapter 2). This concept highlights two connected ideas: what people are able to do and what they are free to choose, thus leading a life that they value. Material needs are relative to the social and economic contexts in which we live. However, our need for capabilities – the freedom required to function in our society – is absolute. It is worth reminding yourself here of Nussbaum's (2011) list of capabilities in Chapter 2.

Essentially, capabilities theory suggests that if people lack the resources or processes by which needs may be satisfied, they are not free to access those things. This is more than opportunity; it relates to people's ability to choose and to act. To pursue this aim depends on individuals converting commodities and their own characteristics into functionings: the end state that we wish to achieve. This transformation of commodities and characteristics relies on our capabilities; thus, policy needs to enhance people's capabilities so that they achieve their desired ends. While such debates provide further distinctions between types of need, and we can start to question whether people live within socioeconomic and legal contexts that allow the attainment of these needs, they are underpinned by a range of theories that Dean (2010) divided into two groups: inherent and interpreted needs.

Inherent needs are those that form the basis of life as a human subject: what actually constitutes the living and embodied human actor. Inherent needs are found in all humans the world over; they are a set of needs fundamental to human existence. These items refer specifically to what humans, as a species, require to survive regardless of socioeconomic or cultural context. One example of an inherent need theory is Maslow's hierarchy of needs (Maslow, 1943, 370-96; see Figure 3.3), which claims that there are different levels of needs (from basic needs such as food and shelter up to the need for self-actualisation) universal to all humans.

This hierarchy sets out a series of different needs, which are shared across all humans, while recognising that they have potentially different importance. The lower levels consist of general items shared by all – although there will be some

Figure 3.3: Maslow's hierarchy of needs

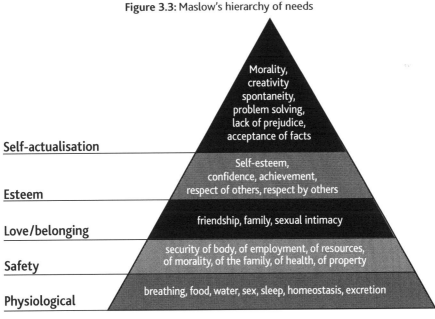

Source: J. Finkelstein (CC BY-SA 3.0).

variation in relation to personal tastes, cultural influence and so on. Further up the hierarchy is a range of needs with greater variation, based on personal preferences and desired end states. In a way, this theory bridges the survival/flourishing debate suggestion; both are essential, but we need to secure the lower survival needs before the higher flourishing needs. Opening up the debate, this can also draw attention to whether the socioeconomic, political and legal framework of the nation allows these needs to be met. This can cut through a range of debates, as indicated in Table 3.2.

Table 3.2: Debating sufficiency of needs

Need	Example	Debate
Physiological need	Shelter	In Scotland the definition of 'priority need' with regard to homelessness has been abolished, whereas England retains the priority need test, which considers, age, pregnancy and cause of homelessness.
Belongingness	Marriage	Marriage is an implicit assumption for many in their lives, but across the globe certain groups of people have only recently been granted, or are still denied, the right to marry; for example, lesbian and gay people.
Self-actualisation	Education	What level of education should the state support all citizens to attain in order to satisfy this particular need?

Definitions of need cannot be separated out from the existing frameworks, which not only shape social life but have also fostered historic social attitudes and beliefs that may exclude (intentionally or not) certain people from attaining needs that others take for granted. Thus, Maslow's hierarchy highlights needs that are universal to all cultural norms, and values will influence how these are pursued, which in turn informs political debate around the policy and legal structures which facilitate needs attainment.

The second group of theories, interpreted needs (Dean, 2010), takes a very different approach. The focus here is on how needs are socially constructed within the social context. Dean offers a number of warnings about this approach:

- needs can be falsely interpreted;
- interpreting needs entails observing the effects of social processes;
- interpreting needs entails arbitrary choices concerning the criteria or conventions that may be used.

These theories suggest that needs depend on the customs of the society you live in and the things we have become accustomed to. This relates to Adam Smith's distinction of necessities (generated by the culture and customs we live with) from luxuries (or wants). However, some luxuries, where their absence can generate shame for the individual, become necessities. We saw this argument in Chapter 3, and briefly in the previous section. Analysis along the lines set out by Smith suggests that there is no common idea of a good life; it cannot be objectively defined. Rather, this good life is individually generated by a range of cultural tastes and personal preferences, which are generated through social interaction. As such, it is not possible to have a 'list approach' to need, as suggested by the inherent approach. This is because human needs are fluid and ever-changing as a result of an ever-evolving human culture. We can identify the non-perfectionist accounts of welfare in debates of this nature, which require the free market rather than the state to provide welfare support. But this is not a position held by all theories within the interpreted approach. Rather, and it is worth reiterating, these ideas focus on human interaction as a process for defining needs.

Both inherent and interpreted definitions of need have been influential in shaping welfare debates. Within Social Policy, we can see these ideas drawn out first in the work of Doyal and Gough (1984) and then in the work of Bradshaw (2013). Adopting an inherited position, Doyal and Gough seek to establish a universal account of human need that refers to both the category of goals, which apply to all people, and the strategies for successful achievement of goals (Table 3.3). They argue that:

> While it may be true that all human goals are specific to particular cultures, in order to achieve these goals people have to act. Furthermore, it follows that there are certain pre-conditions for such actions to be undertaken – people must have the mental ability to deliberate and to choose, and the physical capacity to follow through on their decision … Survival and autonomy are therefore basic needs: they are both conceptual and empirical preconditions for the achievement of other goals. (Doyal and Gough, 1984:15)

Underpinning survival and autonomy is a series of intermediate needs that have to be satisfied to achieve these two basic needs.

Thus, the foundation for a universal theory of human need can be applied across all societies, but recognises that how the basic needs are achieved (through intermediate needs) will likely vary across time and space. Intermediate needs provide a set of preconditions for the attainment of basic needs, which are determined by personal autonomy: the end state of the individual's own choosing. Additionally, this theory recognises that the social context influences not only attainment of needs but also how intermediate needs are defined, in terms of survival and participation within society. Therefore, social policies designed to protect welfare should ensure universal preconditions, which seek to avoid serious harm to people and allow them at least the minimal participation necessary to act as human beings. Policies should establish the preconditions necessary for critical autonomy and the ability to live a life of one's choosing.

Wetherly (1996), however, is critical of Doyal and Gough's work and argues that their theory remains embedded within relativist thinking. Through a discussion of how to operationalise Doyal and Gough's definition, he suggests that the theory remains open-ended: at what level do we meet need? How do we define an adequate standard? This reflects some of the debates outlined in Table 3.2. For example, it could be argued that education is an essential need; without an education one is unlikely to secure employment, and therefore an income to access certain needs, but will also be denied the education required to live a fulfilled life pursuing one's interests. Yet does this mean all should pursue their studies until they complete an undergraduate degree? Or perhaps even a PhD? Where do we draw the line in terms of the level of provision provided as a means of meeting basic need? This retains an individual focus, which we could broaden to include the social need; but again, is this to degree level? Even objective measures of need can only be developed so far; there is a need for some boundaries to what is offered.

Table 3.3: Human needs suggested by Doyal and Gough

Basic need	Physical health
	Personal autonomy
Intermediate needs	Adequate nutritional food and water
	Adequate protective housing
	A non-hazardous work environment
	Appropriate healthcare
	Security in childhood
	Significant primary relationships
	Physical security
	Economic security
	Safe birth control and childbearing
	Basic education

Source: Dean (2010:26)

Here, the interpreted accounts of need gain relevance, because we are entering a debate about the extent to which needs are met. This is the outcome of social interaction; essentially, debate about the level to which the state provides welfare provision. Bradshaw's (2013) taxonomy of need provides a clearer indication of how limits to provision are drawn. He suggests that there are four types of need: normative, felt, expressed and comparative. Different policy responses will draw upon different combinations of these needs, which in turn influences the level of provision offered. Table 3.4 summarises Bradshaw's (2013) four types of need, and adds a fifth.

This theory is deemed interpreted because the original four types of need suggested by Bradshaw provide different lenses through which various actors engage in debates around need. This influences the policy-making process; different debates and ideas around need, utilising the original four different

Table 3.4: The taxonomy of need

Type of need	Description
Normative	Expert judgements about what people might 'normally' and legitimately need
Felt	What people might subjectively believe they need
Expressed	What people both feel and demand; this does not distinguish between need and demand, but rather focuses on what people ask for
Comparative	Arise when there is a shortfall or deficiency in services reviewed by a person/group and those of a similarly placed person/group
Technological (Forder, 1974)	Where new provision is invented or existing provision is made more efficient, resulting in a revision of felt, expressed, normative and comparative need

positions, create particular articulations of need, which are adopted into the policy design. As such, it is not simply a matter of an objective determination that x is needed to secure y, and y is needed. Rather, y is determined through debate from different points in the typology, and this in turn also determines how x is defined.

It is least problematic when all four needs are present: there is a clear need for policy intervention. But situations may arise where there is felt, normative and comparative need, but no means by which this need can be expressed; for example, problems with accessing a social care service due to perceived stigma or geographical location (such as living in a rural community, isolated from a service). Alternatively, experts may state there is a need (normative) and others may be experiencing it (comparative), but the individual neither feels nor expresses their own need. Thus, the four original aspects of the typology offer different combinations, which Bradshaw illustrates with a discussion of a researcher exploring housing need (Figure 3.4).

Like a Venn diagram, the four types of need in Figure 3.4 are constructed as overlapping, with markers used to indicate where different interpretations of need meet or are absent. The plus (+) and minus (–) symbols indicate where each of the four arguments is present (+) or absent (–) from consideration. As such, '++++' indicates that each form of need is present in the articulation of social need: felt, normative, expressed and comparative, as found in the centre of the figure. Similarly, '----' indicates that none of Bradshaw's forms of need can be identified, whereas the '+--+' arrangement suggests that professionals and a comparative sense of need are present, but the need is neither felt nor expressed by those receiving the service; for example, unwanted postnatal visits. As such, Figure 3.4 reiterates how need is interpreted and constructed through the presence (and absence) of different parts of the typology.

However, this is not unproblematic. Clayton (1983) raises some interesting challenges to the use of the taxonomy. For example, she suggests that the taxonomy is well suited to expressions of individual need, but does not adequately encapsulate group expressions through voluntary organisations or tenants' groups. Such articulations might be fundamental for marginalised groups to develop a voice

Figure 3.4: Interaction of different types of need

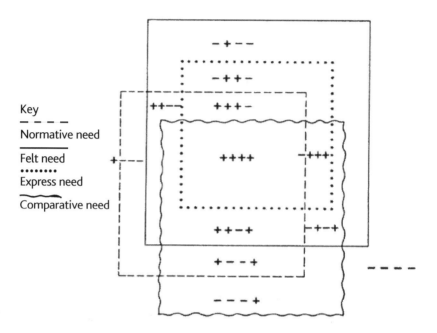

Source: Bradshaw (2013). Reproduced with permission.

and a claim for protection of social rights (consider, for example, the disability rights movement). She suggests that there are also problems with identifying felt need. First, the way in which questions are asked, respondents' perceptions of the services and the way the services are described will influence the response. Second, perception is central here; some respondents may not distinguish the difference between a want and a need, or may not perceive their situation as deprived and in need of change. Perception fundamentally shapes how people might respond to investigations of felt need. Similarly, in relation to normative need, the perceptions and views of experts are rarely questioned in terms of how they approach an understanding of the situation and needs being identified. Some have been critical of the role of experts and expert knowledge, highlighting the important contributions to be made from the subjective experiences of those in need (Williams and Popay, 2006). Thus, a number of different ideological and political influences will impact on how needs are defined and drawn into policy construction (see Langan, 1998, and Chapter 8). The challenge here is that Bradshaw's (2013) taxonomy does not adequately account for such theoretical considerations, which have a significant role in the formation of welfare systems.

Finally, we must consider whether the articulated need is the problem to be addressed or a symptom of a deeper social problem. The response to increased hunger in the western world has been to rely on food aid, but this does not address the problem of insufficient incomes; while hunger in sub-Saharan Africa has less to do with income than with harmful economic systems, conflict, environmental factors (drought and climate change) and population growth. Poverty is at the core of both, but the causes of the problem will be different. As noted earlier, it is this deficiency that indicates the existence of a particular need.

Shaping policy design

The foregoing illustrates some of the key theoretical debates around the concept of need. But as with the concept of welfare, we need a less theoretical and more practical framework for informing policy efforts to secure welfare. One key way in which need has been operationalised is determining an adequate level to be met. Liddard and Mitton (2012) relate this to establishing a basic minimum: a level below which no one should fall. Such work illustrates how an association between poverty and need has formed the bedrock of much Social Policy, but may inadequately theorise the relationship between need and poverty (Mac Cárthaigh, 2014). Early measurements sought to establish an absolute poverty line. Rowntree (2000), for example, sought to determine a level of spending required for survival and express this as a level of minimum income. Townsend (1979) sought to establish an alternative that looks beyond survival and adopts the relative position of considering what items and activities are required to participate in the society in which you live. This then becomes the basis for establishing the minimum, and an income level can be determined as a proportion of average incomes.

Developing this work further, the Poverty and Social Exclusion Survey in the UK is one example of a consensual approach to determining levels of need. A consensual approach to poverty first asks the public to identify items they consider necessary for daily life, and then asks people if they lack these due to low income or their personal choice not to have that item (www.poverty.ac.uk). In a similar way, the Joseph Rowntree Foundation has sought to update Rowntree's earlier work by asking the public to identify goods and services that different household types should have access to, and then costing these into a level of income required to access them (www.jrf.org.uk/topic/mis). The consensual approach seeks to find out what the public thinks make up the list of needs against which living standards should be measured. The Poverty and Social Exclusion survey uses a predetermined list to collect the public's views, asking them to determine if things are a 'necessity' or a 'luxury': something nice to have but not essential to participation in the accepted lifestyle of your society. Items that secure 50% or more of the public's support are drawn into a final list and used in a survey that asks people if they have, lack due to inability to afford, or lack due to not wanting each item. The study uses 'lacking three or more items due to inability to afford them' as one of its measures of poverty.

Cutting through these debates, however, are similar problems to those already identified. There is a level of arbitrariness and relativism to each set of judgements. While efforts have sought to be objective in drawing up these definitions,

Wetherly's (1996) critique of Doyal and Gough can be applied: an adequate minimum will change over time and space, and will never remain constant. There is also the need to consider the extent to which research on poverty pays attention to those who fall below a certain level of income, but does not always consider the quality of living standard achieved once this minimum standard is met. That is, poverty is often portrayed in relation to an income below a specified level; this is not the same as identifying an income that is insufficient or inadequate to attain a particular end state. Whether research (and policy) address this issue depends on the definition of welfare adopted, and expressed as either thick or thin needs.

Additionally, Townsend (1979) is clear in his distinction between poverty and deprivation. The former is tied to income; the latter has a wider, non-material dynamic. Poverty erodes nonvolitional needs: we need money for various goods and services: food, shelter, clothing, transport, gas, water, electricity and so on. Deprivation, however, relates to how people live. It is the consequence of a lack of income and other resources. So, lack of money might mean missing out on certain needs, but limited/insufficient income can also result in inferior goods or the inability to replace things if they break (for example, home amenities; accessing additional educational resources – from books to tutors; or certain recreational activities), while it also encompasses how lack of investment in your local area can have an impact (for example, poor-quality immediate environment; lack of employment opportunities, sports and leisure facilities). Additionally, lack of resources can impact on a number of other factors (such as the quality of one's housing, family support, health and social relations), which all form part of wider social participation and can therefore be integrated into measures of deprivation that allow for a wider focus than income alone.

The crux of the issue here relates to defining needs. Do we establish a list of items we need to secure biological functioning, or do we need our list to focus more broadly on human flourishing (or 'self-actualisation', to use Maslow's term)? Of course, this debate about how we define welfare is contentious. As Mac Cárthaigh (2014) suggests, (in)action towards addressing a need will depend on the perceived level of responsibility. If the individual is held accountable, then there may be no imperative to act. This does not deny that the need exists; just that there are no grounds for action. Additionally, there is a consideration of feasibility. In the previous chapter, the discussion of welfare highlighted a growing justification for state involvement in efforts to secure people's welfare. While this argument gained dominance, and the notion of social rights connected to a concept of need has been fundamental in this debate, this does not automatically generate state support. As illustrated earlier, it is not always clear whether the state can best provide for certain needs, such as food, or to what extent needs should be provided for. There is recognition that socioeconomic change creates potential harms to people's lives, which require some form of intervention to address the harm by supporting the individual, changing the socioeconomic context, or both. However, recognising the need to reduce harm is not the same as an automatic assumption of state provision of welfare. As such, there is a need to consider the appropriate source of welfare.

A brief introduction to welfare providers

As we saw in Chapter 2, there has been growing justification for state provision of welfare, while other sources of welfare have received less attention; but it has also occurred due to the identification of other providers' deficiencies. While we examine this in more detail in the next chapter, it is important to consider here in relation to need satisfaction. Glennerster (2003) offers an example that shows how welfare is not just reliant on the state: the state can influence and direct other providers to facilitate the achievement of welfare, while decommodifying some aspects at the lower levels of provision; but it need not provide them all. Glennerster illustrates how, in relation to Maslow's hierarchy, there may be different providers of needs; we therefore should not assume the state is the only provider. A modified version of Glennerster's work is provided in Table 3.5.

The role of the state and other providers or sectors is explored in more detail in Chapter 4. What is essential here is the context in which debates regarding needs are framed, highlighting a range of considerations for building and debating definitions. This illustrates not only the challenge in defining need (and therefore the social rights that secure people's welfare) but also the wider debate about where responsibility for meeting needs will rest. Such debates are further complicated when debate starts to engage with considerations of equality: the equal treatment of citizens and their access to needs satisfaction.

Summary

This section has explored debates involved in the identification of needs. Figure 3.5 draws out some of the overarching considerations that influence how we start to define needs. This highlights three sets of distinctions – volitional and non-volitional needs, inherent and interpreted needs, and thick and thin needs – and illustrates how these form different layers of the same debate, starting with broader theoretical concerns and moving on to practical attempts to operationalise the idea. This section has illustrated not only theoretical debates around needs and how they are pursued but also the socioeconomic and legal frameworks that influence them. These debates can be illustrated through a number of different layers:

- Need identification: is this a volitional or non-volitional need?
- Is the identified need inherent to humans, or the result of social interaction and interpretation (or a blending of the two)?
- Does this, in turn, refer to a thick (human flourishing) or thin (bare survival) notion of need?

Following this path allows for the theory to be operationalised; that is, transformed from the abstract into a practical measure. We can do this by listing the items that underpin welfare, and then determining who does and does not have these items.

Table 3.5: Meeting need by providers of welfare

Basic human needs	Market	Public finance and provision	Informal sector
Self-actualisation *Self-esteem*	Potential contribution through choice in the free market	State provision: access to basic education, support for higher education and lifelong learning	
Love and belonging	Not marketable		Main source (family and partners)
Safety Personal	Limited marketable provision State provision (police, courts, armed forces)		Close communities will help achieve this
National			
Physiological Public health	Not marketable	State provision and regulation	Public education
Healthcare	Market failures in provision	State finance	
Care of elderly, dependent, disabled	Significant market failures	State finance for major care	Large element of family care
Education	Market tends to underprovide	State finance	Parents as partners with schools
Shelter	Market mostly provides	Rent support and social housing	
Food	Market mostly provides	Income support	

Source: Glennerster (2003), p25.

Figure 3.5: Framing the theories of need

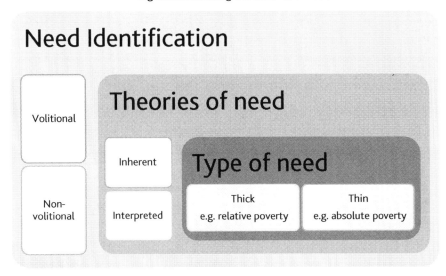

Equality and welfare provision

Social and human rights implicitly assume that such rights are equally applicable to all humans; if needs are the content of these rights, the means by which they are achieved, then they must apply equally to all humans. This draws attention to the second conceptual debate shaping entitlement to welfare support: equality. Equality is embedded in debates around welfare and entitlement to welfare support, despite the different ways in which needs may be interpreted in policy. Consider Baker et al.'s (2004) suggestion that there are 'dimensions of equality': respect and recognition; resources; love, care and solidarity; power, working and learning. These overlap with a range of needs (and capabilities) that have been explored so far. The pursuit of self-determined ends as part of the achievement of welfare, however, requires a notion of equality: equal life chances in terms of education and health, equal opportunities to access various educational degrees, forms of employment or relationships, and family formations that reflect self-determined ends. Equality is therefore fundamental to the satisfaction of need or the attainment of social rights.

This section explores different debates regarding equality and considers their influence on policy debates. Equality is highly contested, especially from different political perspectives; this relates to the idea of freedom, discussed first. The tension between equality and freedom relates to the broader justification of state intervention into welfare: equal treatment generally requires intervention to secure, but some disagree. From this discussion, it is then possible to explore equality not only more broadly but also in relation to equality of opportunity and equality of outcome.

Debates about equality start with a consideration of freedom

The starting point for defining equality is actually to consider freedom and contrast this with the idea of equality. This draws on Berlin's (1958) distinction between positive and negative freedoms and MacCallum's (1967) third dimension (Table 3.6).

Table 3.6: Types of freedom

Type of freedom	Description
Freedom *from* (Berlin's negative freedom)	Concerned with citizens' freedom from interference in their lives; for example, through limited state intervention into our lives
Freedom *to do* (Berlin's positive freedom)	Concerned with citizens' capacity to achieve ends; they are free to do x or y
Freedom *to be* (MacCallum's third dimension)	Replacing the positive/negative distinction with a single expression, based on a third characteristic, expressed as: 'x is free (*is not free*) from y to do (*not do*) or become (*not become*) z'

The premise of these arguments rests on the idea that equal treatment can potentially interfere with individual freedom. On the one hand, we should be free from interference (by government or others) to follow our desired lives. This broadly aligns with free-market ideas of social organisation and the idea of welfare as preference satisfaction. But this is challenged by the argument that reliance on the market generates different starting points for people, alongside the creation of barriers to opportunities for some, based on their social position: the decommodification argument and justification for welfare provision explored in Chapter 2. With such barriers, it is suggested, people are not truly free because they have not started from equal points in life. Thus, the positive conception seeks to promote a measure of freedom through interventions to promote equality and redistribute income and resources across the population. For some, this is the very danger of positive freedom; it is a form of interference into society, from which dictatorships and totalitarian governments are grown. Others suggest that such provision ensures there are public institutions for defending individuals from despotism – a distinction MacCallum (1967:312) suggests is misguided because it is unclear and confusing. He suggests instead one 'equation' that reflects the triadic nature of freedom: 'x is (is not) free from y to do (not do, become, not become) z'.

It may appear strange to start to explore equality through a discussion of freedom, but this is a fundamental consideration. To pursue equality, we need to ensure citizens are free to pursue their own desires without interference, but to do so in a context that does not generate barriers to that pursuit. Figure 3.6 illustrates this in relation to MacCallum's equation for freedom. If Child A is born into a poor household (the top cog), they may face barriers in terms of lower educational attainment (the middle cog), which in turn impacts on what they can later do and become (the bottom cog). Child B, however, is not in a poor household, which does not negatively impact on their education; these 'advantages' follow through into securing their future careers, when they are able to choose freely from a wider range of available options: poverty did not hold them back. As an adult, Child A has fewer opportunities and less ability to pursue their own end state as a result of their impoverished background: they have less freedom.

Figure 3.6: Freedom to be

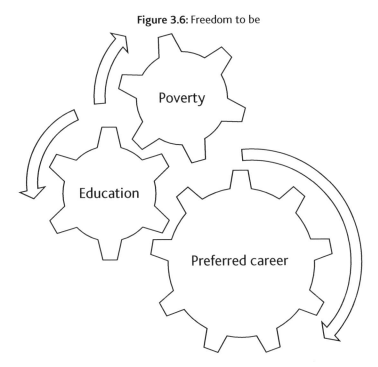

Research indicates that educational performance will vary depending on household income and resources. Certain households have higher incomes and excesses of wealth (the sources of this will be considered later). Thus, being in an income-rich and/or wealthy household may offer advantages in the early years of your life that others lack because they were not born into such a household. It is possible to use taxation (for example) to redistribute resources and ensure those less well-off have a better starting point without adversely affecting the well-off children. This would ensure that Child A and Child B have more equal starting points and can fulfil their own desires and preferences free from poverty; as Roosevelt reminded us earlier, if someone has unmet need, they are not free.

Defining equality

The aforementioned debate has no right or wrong answer. Students and academics (as well as interested members of the general public) will have their own views on how to secure freedom. Initially, the entitlement triangle emphasised how needs had to be met in line with the expression of positive freedom. This was supported by a notion of equality used to refer to equal worth of people: they have a common humanity.

Accepting this allows for a more nuanced discussion regarding equality, starting with a notion of thin and thick equality (you may already be able to predict how this will be explained, based on previous uses of the terms 'thin' and 'thick'). Thin equality refers to a minimalist principle of equal treatment by the law. Often, such views suggest that anything beyond this is a direct intervention into people's lives, which limits their freedom. Nozick (1973) supports such views, and suggests three principles that establish equality without the need to redistribute resources across people in society:

1. *Justice in acquisition*: acquiring through the market is justified, provided no one is made worse off through that acquisition;
2. *Justice in transfer*: exchanges are justified, provided they are voluntary and others are not prevented from making the same transactions; and
3. *Justice in rectification*: putting right circumstances that cause injustice, as defined by principles 1 and 2.

The aim is to ensure all can participate equally and freely in market transactions, the results of which (good or bad) are a consequence of the natural workings of the market. But there are limitations to this view. How do we define who is worse off according to principle 1? Can we be sure that all transactions are/were voluntary? In relation to principle 3, how far do we backdate the rectifications?

Thick equality, however, draws attention to social equality or equality of status. It seeks to oppose social hierarchies and privilege accumulated by some, which are the source of social divisions and differential treatment of social groups; for example, along lines of gender, ethnicity and class. However, this argument retains a moralistic framework rather than suggesting a particular form of resource distribution. Accepting that inequalities are generated by unequal resource distribution is not the same as articulating how such resources should be distributed; nor is it necessarily a discussion of legal changes to ensure equal rights. Social Policy debate engages directly with this issue of resource distribution, drawing attention to both access to material resources and the use of benefits and social services to diminish the unequal contexts between different groups of people. As such, Social Policy has often framed welfare debates in terms of distribution of resources, and this has come to influence how social rights have been conceived.

This discussion has drawn on two central concepts regarding equality: of opportunity and of outcome. These have become guiding aspects for the development of policy and the pursuit of human welfare, but they suggest very different approaches.

Equality of opportunity

Rawls (1999) provides the starting point for this debate. He developed a 'thought experiment', in which he suggested it was possible to apply a 'veil of ignorance' and adopt a position whereby we did not know who we were – nor, therefore, our social position. If we were asked about the distribution of socioeconomic resources while wearing this veil, we would seek to secure a 'just' distribution, because once the veil was lifted we would not want to discover that we had somehow disadvantaged ourselves. Thus, not knowing our social position leads us towards a notion of equal distribution of resources, based on two principles:

1. Each person to have equal rights to an extensive and total system of equal basic liberties; and
2. Social and economic inequalities to be arranged so that they both:
   (a) give the greatest benefit to the least advantaged, consistent with the just savings principles, and
   (b) are attached to offices/positions open to all under equality of opportunity.

It is clear that, while an equal distribution is sought, there is recognition that there will still be some differences in the offices and positions people enter. As such, the focus is on ensuring a fair and just distribution throughout life, especially during early-years development. This is not through the pursuit of a completely equal distribution whereby everyone has exactly the same. We each choose different lives, some of which result in additional rewards. What is important is that everyone has the chance to develop and choose without any hindrance; this requires that certain essential needs are met. This is one way in which equality debates link to our earlier discussion of needs.

However, the **difference principle** (2a) is potentially problematic. How can we know which distribution of resources will provide the greatest benefits for the least advantaged? Additionally, Rawls is critiqued for assuming that humans in the veil of ignorance would choose outright equality, rather than opt for a 'grab as much as I can' strategy and take the risk that they will end up in a beneficial position. Humans do not necessarily think in this rational way Rawls outlines.

Nevertheless, this forms the basis for equality of opportunity: the principle that each individual has the same opportunities to succeed, regardless of factors that may limit success (class, gender, ethnicity, income and so on). The focus should be on how one's ability and effort, rather than social position, allow success. Governments should promote such opportunities, usually education and employment initiatives, throughout the life-course to facilitate people's success. The concept can be presented in a narrow sense based on the idea of **meritocracy**.

Meritocracy is the idea that positions (and power) should be awarded to those who demonstrate the greatest ability/talent. Consequently, careers should be open to all, with people selected for positions based on individual merit. Young's satire *The Rise of the Meritocracy* (1979) explores a meritocratic society to highlight its potential limitations. In principle, the reliance on ability to select people for positions is a worthy ambition. But Young suggested that this leads to the formulation and solidification of a new class system, which then excludes others. Additionally, a broader definition of equality of opportunity must consider temporal and developmental ideas, which recognise people's differing histories and needs. This broadens the focus away from simply equal access to career opportunities, and recognises a need to ensure equal chances across the life-course, requiring policy to focus on early-years childhood interventions.

For Calder (2016:77–83), this situation provides an additional challenge. If we create equal opportunities for everyone born in a particular year, that generation will achieve different outcomes without bias to class, gender, ethnicity and so on. Patterns of inequality we see today would not have an impact. But in 30 years' time, the children of this group will benefit (or not) from their parents' different outcomes, creating a new source of inequality – unless we intervene in an effort to secure equality of opportunity for the new generation. As such, a focus on equality of opportunity does not negate a need to consider outcomes. There is a need for a generational focus, which potentially conflicts with the argument that different awards result from individual merit and should not be taxed or redistributed in some way.

Equality of opportunity has been a guiding principle of the welfare state. However, it has been critiqued for not actively seeking to *change* the structures that potentially cause inequality, but rather seeking to secure formal legal equality for everyone *within* existing structures. The intent is to ensure that individuals are free to choose their own political, social, educational and labour-market roles and futures. Social differentiation in outcomes is considered normal – presented as a result of choices in which equal opportunities exist – and there is no attempt to equalise people's experiences or wealth. Consequently, equality of opportunity policy offers a minimalist position that seeks to secure the fairness of *processes*. It does not impact on everyone in the same way, because people start from different social positions, and social position impacts on the ability to take up opportunities. As such, promoting formal equal access is not the same as equality – but it could be a starting point for pursuing equality, even if it is from an individualised perspective.

With regards to policy making, Rees (2006) articulated a three-stage approach to equality, outlined in Table 3.7. The suggestion is that interventions to promote equality start to gradually change how society operates and treats people, disadvantaging some while advantaging others. There is an initial need to directly intervene to offer support – and, at times, develop positive discrimination to ensure that (for example) more minority ethnic groups join the police force or more women become chief executives of major corporations. Gradually, attitudinal shifts resulting from the use of these practices influence the wider social system, and there is no further need for direct intervention because society automatically operates in a non-discriminatory fashion.

Table 3.7: Three developmental approaches to equality

Stage of equality	Description
Legal equality to access and treatment	Ensure the legal basics and minimum compliance to equality; for example, affirmative action.
Positive action	Specific service measures, family-friendly policies, training for particular groups and mentoring. A variation of this would be positive discrimination: unequal treatment, through quotas and shortlists, to promote those who would otherwise be discriminated against.
Mainstreaming	Integrate equality into the structures of society so there is no need for the various policy devices to promote equality.

As such, equality of opportunity has been pursued through the promotion of welfare, and is a standard against which many social policies are held. However, this is not without critique, including from advocates of equality of *outcome*.

Equality of outcome

The idea of equality of outcome is often presented in a mathematical sense to refer to two or more objects being equal. This is nicely illustrated in the novel *Alice in Wonderland* when the Dodo states: 'Everyone has won and all must have prizes' (Carroll, [1865] 1982). This instantly creates some reservation in pursuing this more radical approach, which looks at not starting points but end results. Indeed, the most extreme forms of this idea do argue for everyone ending up with the same level of resources (or an equitable level, reflecting family size and composition). However, the term can also encompass the general economic conditions of people's lives. This relies on the reduction (or even elimination) of material inequalities between individuals/households, blending a range of policy approaches, from redistribution of resources to early-years interventions designed to promote equality of condition.

Phillips (2004:1) suggests that the aim here is 'equalising where people end up rather than where or how they begin', and that attention should be paid to the broad spectrum of resources, roles and occupations, noting that: 'When differences of outcome are explained retrospectively by reference to differences in personal preference, this assumes what has to be demonstrated: that individuals really did have equal opportunities to thrive … moreover, these explanations reproduce ideologically suspect stereotypes about particular social groups'. Rather, the equality of outcome perspective should be at the core of society. This would cut through a diverse range of social contexts, form more diverse political representation and, importantly, separate the entanglement of personal responsibility from social inequality. Fundamentally, Phillips suggests it is a mistake to operate a notion of equality that views outcomes and opportunities as polar opposites, when the two are interlinked in complex ways. As Calder (2016) notes, equality of outcome is always implemented in arguments for equality of opportunity. Additionally, opportunities cannot be considered without a similar account of income and wealth (O'Neill, 2010). Consequently, there is a need for greater redistribution of material resources, which need not be to the extreme extent of ensuring all have and are the same.

Criticisms of equality of outcome present it as a 'politics of envy': a claim that some are jealous of others' better economic and social positions and ignore the effort and merit that caused these differences. Yet, this overlooks how inequalities can be passed from one generation to another through tangible gifts and wealth inheritance, which then (re)creates the barriers that policies seek to redress. It could be argued that people are born with different levels of ability and initiative, which are then developed through educational systems. Consequently, some individuals are predisposed to achieving better outcomes than others, making equality of outcome impossible (linking back to the aforementioned difference principle). Challenging this risks imposing *in*equality of opportunity: giving opportunities to those less worthy (based on merit) for some alternative political ambition. On the one hand, this is problematic because it depends on some judgement to determine who is 'worthy' or 'less worthy', which cannot be easily determined. On the other hand, the predisposition overlooks how existing socioeconomic positions facilitate inequalities in starting points, which have become dressed up as 'natural differences'. The capable do not always make their way to the top, and secure the opportunities this affords, if their early life is encased in the poverty of their parents. While this may appear to be slipping back into the equality of opportunity argument (investing in earlier years to tackle the issue), it also suggests a more radical idea: invest in the parents/household circumstances to remove the wider impoverished context. This may facilitate reform in the wider socioeconomic context in which people live (from the local environment to the provision of schools, healthcare and other services). Consequently, this adopts a collective perspective, looking at whole social groups rather than individuals.

Seeking equal outcomes, so that all are the same, potentially creates a stunted and boring civilisation: it does not result in difference between people. But this misinterprets the full view of equality of outcome. Incomes may differ, but should health outcomes? What about educational outcomes? In some areas of policy, we would not argue for different outcomes; in others, we might accept difference, provided it reflects ability and effort and not the advantages caused by privilege and position. Consequently, Douglas Rae (1981) suggests four ways in which equality of outcome can be achieved:

- *maximum*: maximising the levels of resources;
- *least difference*: reducing the range of inequality by limiting wealth and poverty via redistribution;
- *minimax*: reducing the advantages of the most privileged;
- *reducing the ratio of inequality*: promoting a more equal distribution of resources from the top to the bottom.

This starts to move the discussion away from equality per se and towards the related concept of social justice.

Is equality different from social justice?

Discussing social justice returns us to the freedom/equality debate. Hayek (1979) argues that people have different abilities and talents, and so equality is incompatible with personal freedom. While supportive of equal appointment, this is not about a fair distribution of wealth but the promotion of equal participation in transactions within the market. Anything more than this, for Hayek, results in the imposition of political values that manipulate the distribution of resources, which leads to totalitarianism. This is also true for the concept of social justice; we cannot develop policy to follow this principle, because it is politically contested. For Hayek, the market is the only fair distributive criteria.

However, Hayek's argument works only where the market operates in the pure form. This means no rigging and no monopolies. Drake (2001) suggests this form of market is unrealistic, and so Hayek's argument is faulty. In contrast, Plant (1984) offers the follow points:

- it does not matter what *causes* inequality, but how we *respond* to inequality;
- support for positive definitions of freedom should take precedent;
- egalitarians do not seek to impose uniformity, as is often claimed.

Equality should be based on the absence of special privilege and adequacy of opportunities open to all. It should also ensure sufficiency; that is, the satisfaction of needs secured via social rights.

For Plant, markets cause inequality; they have evolved and developed over time to protect certain interests through the operation of the wider social system. State intervention is required to ensure that all people equally have the opportunity 'to do' (the positive freedom definition), because the market does not compensate for disadvantage through an accident of birth.

There is also a moral argument suggesting that inequality is wrong, regardless of its source, and should be brought to an end. This does not imply mathematical equality of everyone receiving exactly the same (equality of outcome or condition in its extreme form), but rather everyone receiving appropriate support and resources to fulfil their abilities and capabilities, which requires a focus on individuals, social groups and wider social structures. Relating to the discussion of need, it becomes clear why certain goods and services should be decommodified. Markets cannot be relied on to provide this equal context because they do not recognise the inequalities generated by market activity.

We can now start to consider some of the links between key concepts. Debates about social justice start to draw together the discussions of need and equality with the final discussion of this chapter: citizenship. As Miller (2005) explains, the pursuit of social justice is based on the belief that society can be reshaped (through policy intervention), changing major social and political institutions to ensure a fair share of both benefits and responsibilities. He outlined four principles of social justice: equal citizenship, the social minimum, equality of opportunity and fair distribution.

Equality of citizenship recognises that there are three distinct sets of rights (civil, political and social) against which all citizens can make a claim. However, social justice does not require that all people are recognised as citizens per se. Rather, it draws our attention to the boundary debates of citizenship and who will and will not be granted this status (economic migrants, refugees and asylum seekers being primary examples of persons potentially excluded, at least initially, from official citizen status within a particular nation). Thus, support offered to citizens on a basis of equality need not equally apply to all humans. There are nuanced arguments about how we reconfigure this debate, which we cannot explore here; in essence, we need to recognise that equality is not the automatic provision of the same rights to all humans within particular national boundaries.

The second element, the social minimum, is based on the principle of sufficiency: a minimum share of resources that everyone must have. As we explored in our discussion of need, there are a number of challenges as to how this minimum is defined in theory and operationalised in practice. Consequently, there has been, and always will be, debate around the level of sufficiency. What we cannot forget is that abstract theoretical debate has an impact on people's lives. How sufficiency is designed affects people, incomes, housing, healthcare, education and so on. As with citizenship, this minimum can be linked to obligations because, for Miller, it comes out of collective resources provided by fellow citizens; as such, there is a requirement to contribute to this pool of resources when one is able. There is some recognition that a contribution need not be paid work, but this is not shared by all who argue in favour of social justice.

Equality of opportunity provides the third of Miller's principles, which suggests it should not be a person's life chances that determine their future life but their ability and motivation. There is thus a need to remove the barriers experienced by some, through anti-discrimination laws and procedures and investment in early-years education, to ensure all have the same opportunity for education and jobs (and therefore potential wealth and income). Aspiration becomes a central idea informing policy interventions, especially around education. This draws attention to the claimed ways in which families transmit moral values to young people, which young people internalise into future hopes and dreams: thus, 'poverty of aspiration' becomes a key concern for many policy makers. There is a need to be careful with this argument and ask whose aspiration and values are guiding this debate. Class-based values and aspirations are often implicitly (and at times explicitly) 'state sanctioned', while others are critiqued and stigmatised ways of being (see Chapter 6).

The final principle, fair distribution, shares similar thinking to Rawls: all should have equal resources, unless these have been gained through the personal efforts and activities of the individual, which then entitles them to a greater (or lesser, where these efforts are lacking) share. There is some luck involved here – where one inherits family wealth – which social justice cannot eliminate. But policies can be introduced to protect people from bad luck (the social minimum) or address the cumulative effect of good luck (such as higher taxes on income and wealth) to redress inequalities that may arise from such good fortune. Calder (2016) illustrated how some of the challenges with addressing family-based advantages within policy debates potentially limit efforts to redistribute the advantages of luck; the autonomy of the family is seen as too sacred for political interference (debates around inheritance tax illustrate this tension).

While understanding the broader debates around concepts is important, we must also review how these are applied in policy debates. Piachaud (2008) suggested the term 'social justice' can be used in a normative sense to assess situations, or in a prescriptive sense to guide actions of policy makers. However, highlighting the ambiguity of social justice, he drew out a number of its implications for Social Policy. First, there is a need for a fair starting point. Genetic inheritance is beyond our control, but inheritance of wealth is subject to social and economic systems, and therefore within our control. Second, there is the issue of income. For social justice perspectives, this is an insufficient measure of the ability to pay tax or be subjected to a means test for welfare support. Money income is not a true measure of one's command over resources, and it is an outcome of choices between available opportunities. Government policy tends to focus more on outcomes (people's income) and less on the opportunities available to people. Thus, changing the opportunities may be more beneficial than changing people's incomes. He concludes by drawing out a distinction between inequality and **inequity**. We cannot, he claims, suggest that all inequalities are socially unjust. Inequality refers to an unequal distribution of resources, but in some instances, this may be perfectly fair – such as additional income achieved through working overtime or a higher-salary job due to effort in school. Inequity, however, refers to unfair but avoidable distribution of resources caused by social organisation. This causes moral outrage because it reflects an unearned benefit, and here social justice requires intervention through health, housing and education (especially early-years) to prevent future inequitable outcomes.

The term 'social justice' has offered a new way of packaging some of the broader debates around equality and need in a framework that also encompasses a notion of citizenship. As such, it has become an important concept in seeking to discuss entitlement to welfare support, for it draws all three aspects of the entitlement triangle into one theoretical framework. But, as illustrated, there are often a number of assumptions as to how each element of social justice should be perceived, and we should always be critical of the claims being made. In addition, the term potentially causes a significant rethinking of welfare provision, as we will explore in our discussion of risk in Chapter 8.

Summary

This section has noted distinctions across a number of debates. Initially, consideration was given to the idea of freedom and its relevance to debates about equality. This is fundamental to an understanding of welfare; some definitions of freedom view state intervention as a road to dictatorship and curtailment of freedom, while others suggest intervention is required if those at the sharp end of social inequality and disadvantage are to have freedom to pursue their lives. Figure 3.7 demonstrates how debates around equality and its impact on citizenship can be summarised. The initial broad debate around equality and freedom shapes how we perceive wider interventions by the state into our social and economic lives. Depending on which side of the argument you find favourable, you will likely be supportive of market- or state-based interventions to secure welfare, which then requires clarity around how you define equality (in terms of opportunity and outcome), which in turn shapes how you refine the notions of needs and the social rights essential for people to secure their welfare. Linked to this will be the third concept in the entitlement triangle, citizenship, which defines not only whose social rights/needs are to be met (and whose will not) but also the duties or expectations people must fulfil to have those rights met.

Figure 3.7: Debate digest: defining equality

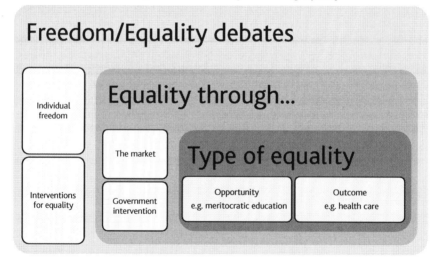

Citizenship: defining whose welfare needs are met

You should be starting to appreciate how social rights are contextualised through the definitions of need and equality. As noted, social rights are embedded within a discourse of citizenship attached to three sets of rights: civil, political and social. Subsequently, early justifications for welfare provision sought to secure a universal notion of citizenship (and the same can be said for both need and equality). In reviewing the theoretical development of citizenship (and its use in welfare provision), Dean and Melrose (1999) summarised the focus of the following discussion. Citizenship has been presented as a totalising concept: often gender neutral, universal and ahistorical. As will be shown, its development has been associated with a particular male, able-bodied and heterosexual assumption about citizens, which obscures the diversity of citizens' lives. This section outlines broad debates regarding how 'citizens' are defined, and then explores some of the debates around the duties citizens discharge to secure their rights. Subsequently, the concept is opened up to a broader critique, which recognises greater diversity and challenges the original, totalising conception of citizens.

Philosophical foundations of citizenship

Citizenship is a label that links the state and the individual (explored in more detail in Chapter 4). It also implies membership of a community, and is a status that allows claims to be made against the state. As such, citizenship is often portrayed as an agreement between the state and the individual, or social groups, which outlines certain rights and duties. Consideration must therefore be given to how citizenship itself is defined. This requires tracing the development of the concept through a philosophical aetiology.

Essentially there are two philosophical traditions to citizenship: civic or republican thinking, and liberalism. The former draws on three Aristotelian ideas regarding what being a citizen entails:

1. Involvement in making and obeying laws;
2. Public interest is paramount; and
3. These public-spirited acts will foster good government.

This was a form of patriarchal citizenship that relegated women to the private sphere and only included certain men as citizens (slaves and 'outsiders' could not be trusted). Such ideas, however, embedded the notion that citizenship entailed a performative element in terms of duties to be discharged. Thus, there was no public/private divide. As a citizen, you had obligations, embedded in the day-to-day collective life of the (then) city-state. Citizens discharged duties to the wider political and social body as part of their attainment of the 'good life' (Aristotle's aforementioned eudaimonia). This entwined public/private life retained influence across a range of civilisations until the 18th century, when liberal philosophies gained prominence. Liberal ideas argued that individuals should live their lives free from the interference of an overbearing state; public and private should therefore have a degree of separation and, through the promotion of civil and political rights, individuals would be protected from an abusive monarch. Thus, the emphasis was upon individual rights and preferences, not the duties that entitled you to certain rights and privileges.

Liberal theories continued to be explored as western societies progressed through industrialisation. This fostered a distinction between **libertarian liberalism** (briefly mentioned earlier) and **egalitarian liberalism**. Libertarian theories, such as those of Novak, envisage a limited role for the state, attached to the maintenance and protection of the civic and political rights necessary for the operation of a free market. The state has some limited role in providing public goods that a market would fail to produce (sewerage is one example), but ultimately individual freedom must be protected against state interference. Citizens should be free to pursue their lives, provided this does not infringe on the lives of others.

Egalitarian liberals, such as Rawls (1999), promote a sense of distributive justice, which takes into account the equality of different claims to basic needs and determines how those needs are to be met. There is a tension to consider here. On the one hand, citizenship can be conceived in an individualistic sense; it is a label embedded with certain rights, to which the individual is entitled and which should be protected, provided a number of duties are discharged. This can foster protection from an overbearing state or the inequities of the market. On the other hand, the notion of duties can be used to emphasise a community-focused citizenship narrative, which draws attention to social interconnections between individuals within a society and the discharge of duties in pursuit of a common good. Within both traditions, however, the idea of a citizen is associated with legal recognition of being a member of a particular nation, with the rights and duties associated with that status. It is the nature of those rights and duties that is open to debate and reinterpretation. Thus, exploring the concept of citizen is important for two reasons: first, it determines who is entitled to have their rights provided for and protected; and second, it offers insight into explicit and implicit moral and social obligations that should be discharged.

The duty to work

An integral aspect of citizenship and its associated rights has been the focus on duties to be discharged as part of this identity. Drawn out of Aristotelian and more recent communitarian ideas, there is support for citizen rights within a broad social context, focused on the unity and cohesiveness of the whole of society. Communal rights come first; there are obligations on citizens to protect, promote and conform to the values and practices of their community. However, such views can be phrased in either a conservative or radical framework. The conservative approach values such obligations as part of an ethic of moral order and duty. A more radical communitarian tradition pursues an image of the common good, often embedded at grassroots level, and promoted and campaigned for through radical community action. Thus, the former will likely pursue policies that promote 'traditional' morals and behaviours (such as support for marriage via the tax systems), while the latter will facilitate local people to collectively determine a common good and how this should be achieved. The discussions of rights in

Chapter 2 gains prominence here; efforts to balance rights and duties cut across all theoretical divides, but have gained a renewed focus in recent welfare debates, which seeks to lessen the importance of social rights.

Civil and political rights are presented as a fundamental aspect of citizenship; social rights are not automatically accepted. For some, the promotion of social rights fosters a reliance on the state to secure basic needs, which in turn generates dependency and erodes responsibility. Welfare provision to meet social rights is therefore seen as a threat to individual freedom (Mead, 1986; Murray, 1996). Thus, there are certain obligations to be met in order for social rights to be discharged by the state – often expressed in the move towards conditional access to welfare support (discussed in Chapter 5) – with the primary duty being work/ employment.

A range of social commentary, from classical texts such as Marx (1990) and Weber (1946) to contemporary accounts (such as Frayne, 2015), maps the centrality of work in modern society. Contemporary society requires work to be central for capital growth; expansion and sustainability of the economy (and, for some, social life) rests on this activity. Wrapped up in a moral narrative, work has become an imperative, an economic necessity, a social duty and a measure of achievement and worth (recall GDP was an early measure of welfare). The 20th and 21st centuries have seen a gradual intensification of the obligation to work.

As Levitas noted, in the 1980s, a moral underclass discourse (MUD) developed that suggested non-workers were somehow inferior to others. During the 1990s, this narrative shifted towards a social inclusion discourse (SID), which required employment as the main mechanism to secure inclusion in society (see also Chapter 8). This differs from Marshall's (1992) view of the duty to work, which advocated putting one's heart into one's work, promoted during the 1930s/1940s when full employment and state planning were the dominant economic theory (Keynesianism, or demand-side economics, whereby the state would directly create demand for employees). Conversely, the 1980s saw a shift towards supply-side economics, which focused on the education and skills of employees rather than direct job creation. It was suggested that this focus would upskill potential employees, making them an attractive investment for corporations to employ.

Despite (or perhaps because of) its prominence in citizenship theory, gendered assumptions regarding work have remained. Men would discharge their duties through 'gainful' (paid) employment, while women would discharge theirs through care activities. Through employment, men would contribute to the social security system, not only to protect themselves from the poverty of unemployment but also to maintain their dependants – their wife and children – who had limited entitlement to support in their own right. Assumptions about men and women, and the implications of these for their social rights and citizen status, are important here. Such assumptions not only failed to recognise that the nature of employment was fundamentally changing (increasingly, women entered the labour market) but also reflect a universal assumption that men work and women care. Such attitudes became embedded in a number of assumptions regarding welfare debates; hence Dean and Melrose's (1999) suggestion that citizenship, as a concept, has a particularly masculine perception.

Challenging such assumptions begins with developing a definition of work that encompasses a wider range of activities, including personal and family care, community activism and volunteering, and the pursuit of one's own interests to secure personal flourishing and self-actualisation. A focus on employment as the primary obligation of the citizen marginalises these activities while reconfiguring our lives towards predominantly employment-based activity. Policy plays a key role in facilitating this shift. Yet, care in particular illustrates an important aspect of citizenship. Because of the gendered nature of citizenship, women continue to carry out the majority of care duties within the home (and beyond). As such, important care functions carried out by women support the ability of men to be employed, while women are expected to manage employment as well as to discharge care. Pascall's (2012) discussion of time use illustrates this continuing issue.

For Bryson (2007), there is a need to reposition care as the primary duty of citizenship; care should be central to a reconfiguration of citizenship, and should subsequently alter policy and welfare provision. Attention has also been given to the ways in which citizens' use of time outside of their employment still relates to paid employment; as most leisure activities rely on consumption, income is essential for pursuing leisure pursuits and personal interests. Additionally, such 'free' (non-work) time (both care and leisure) essentially focuses on preparing people for recommencing work; activities both reflect work practices and facilitate recuperation prior to returning to work (Adorno, 2001). This highlights the complex interplay between work, income and citizenship, while illustrating how work (as employment) and citizenship status are inextricably linked.

The diversity of activities that underpin social functioning is not the only source of difference that needs to be recognised within our conception of citizenship. There must also be an appreciation that groups of citizens have different social characteristics, which questions the universal assumptions embedded in the concept of citizenship.

Difference, diversity and citizenship

The universal assumptions that underpin social rights and citizenship can be problematic. Freeman (2011) draws attention to the concept of social divisions: different categories of people, many of whom are often denied certain rights; consequently, their universal human rights are violated, and they do not receive any particular rights or protections attached to their difference. The totalising concept ignores difference, and in doing so makes assumptions about the basis of 'sameness' of citizenship that may not reflect the lived experience of citizens (and the needs they may have). A number of sources of difference can be briefly considered in relation to citizen status, which inform a further discussion in Chapter 4.

Before exploring this in more detail, we need to establish how the broader idea of sameness was generated. It originates with industrialisation, which facilitated the formation of the economy as a distinct sphere of social interaction (no longer integrated into the family and home). This ushered in a number of radical changes in terms of social organisation, and social relations has aligned the rise of social welfare with labour movement struggles. Thus, class becomes a central division demarking difference between citizens. Marxist class analysis distinguishes between the ruling class and the working class in society; the former is seen to be exploiting the labour power of the latter in order to create profit and maintain capitalist relations of power. The welfare state was a compromise between these classes to compensate for the tensions and damage caused by industrialisation. From this perspective, social rights do not seek to challenge inequality or the dominance of capital, because they are the basis of the compromise and therefore exploitation. Social rights ameliorate exploitation, but do not remove the roots of material inequality. Consequently, Offe (1984) suggests that the welfare state is ineffective and inefficient, as it acts to compensate certain people for the negative consequences of capitalism. However, this generated the view of a class distinction in society as the primary means of framing citizenship rights, duties and lived experience.

Yet, class as a central aspect of identity has come under increasing scrutiny. Stratification theory has grown to encompass a range of different sources of identity within the contemporary world (Anthias, 2001). This broadening of theory resulted from a rise of social movements, which highlighted new sources of (social) inequality and exclusion that cut across class divides. As Annetts et al. (2009) demonstrate, these social movements started to challenge universal notions of citizenship, which excluded the difference of wider social groups. These tended to form around a particular identity: gender, ethnicity, disability, sexuality and so on. These movements seek to secure recognition in not only legal frameworks but also broader social interactions. The latter is achieved through the promotion of a positive identity for the group that seeks to challenge stigma (and often through demanding affirmative action and positive discrimination to secure equal opportunities). It is through these activities that policies and practices change and the notion of citizenship becomes more nuanced.

Such developments facilitated critiques of the universal application of citizenship status. Lister (1997) suggests that the boundaries of citizenship are drawn around a narrative of citizen-the-earner (linked to work) but that there is a need to recognise the difference within citizenship itself, as well as the importance of other narratives such as citizen-the-carer, and that policy should be supportive of both. This appreciation of difference cuts across a range of narratives around citizenship, which includes gender, disability, 'race' and sexuality (to name some of the prominent sources of stratification). It is not the purpose here to explore social divisions in detail; rather, the intention is to highlight how diversity/ difference are essential for understanding the concept of citizenship (see Best,

2005; Payne, 2013), and how this can impact on the provision of welfare (see Chapters 4 and 5).

Summary

This section has sought to briefly outline key theoretical debates in relation to citizenship. At this point, it is important to reiterate the original contention of this chapter. Citizenship has often been presented with a universal discourse (universal human/social rights), which blurred the diversity of social life. On the one hand, this universalism was integral to suggesting a common, shared need for welfare (as indicated in this chapter). On the other, it was part of a nation-building project requiring the unification of all those living within certain territorial boundaries (as discussed in the next chapter). This developed in parallel with a consideration of duties and the protection of social rights alongside equal treatment (through the auspices of the market or intervention by the state). The challenge at this stage is how citizenship has been constructed, which has demonstrated a gender bias, not only in terms of how a citizen is defined but also in the form of duties the citizen must discharge. This is further problematised when white, able-bodied, heterosexual men are assumed to reflect the characteristics of a citizen. This not only ignores the diversity of 'types' of people in society but also informs a notion of social rights, needs and equality, which may also reflect a number of these biased assumptions. Citizenship, therefore, needs a much broader and critical framing than has historically been the case. As Chapter 4 will demonstrate, this is integral in terms of how welfare support is devised, because these debates inform both whose (and in what conditions) welfare is met and the well-intentioned aim of universal provision for welfare needs.

Chapter summary

We started this chapter with the idea of an entitlement triangle. Entitlement is about not only who has access to welfare support but also the type (and extent) of that support. Our review of the concept of needs started to unpick some of this discussion, identifying the items that underpin welfare and the thick/thin distinction between the levels of sufficiency to which these items are provided. Our review of equality and citizenship illustrated these needs in relation to conditions, opportunities and who has a claim to have their social rights protected. Universality has played an important role in these discussions; needs, equality and citizenship are applied to all citizens, often with scant attention to diversity, which may require differentiated treatment of certain groups. Figure 3.8 illustrates how the entitlement triangle frames our welfare debates.

I have framed Figure 3.8 to illustrate how we could draw some of the debates in this chapter together (there are, of course, others). If welfare support is provided to all citizens (the top of this particular hierarchy), it is underpinned by different notions of equality and need. On the one hand, we can assume some level of

Figure 3.8: Framing the debate: the constituent elements of social rights

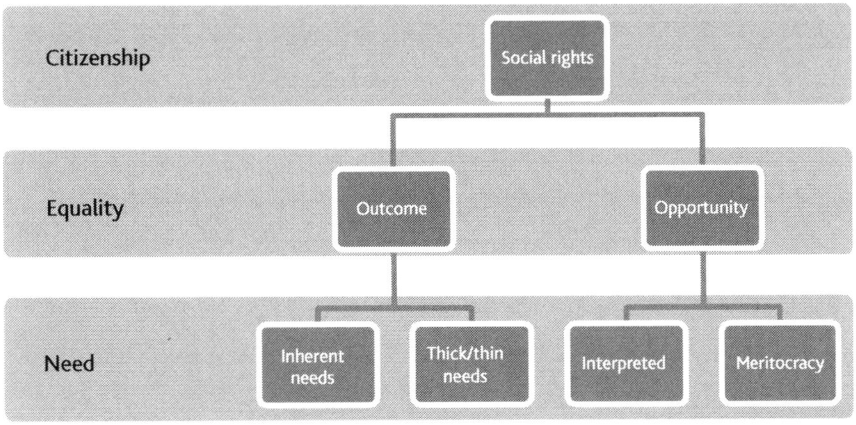

equality of outcome regarding certain inherent aspects of human need (healthcare, basic education and so on). We can argue about the extent to which these are provided (the thick/thin debate), but we can generally agree on their significance to the attainment of welfare. On the other hand, other aspects of welfare focus on the need to secure opportunities for citizens to attain their welfare where their own merit will carry them. I have placed this example alongside interpreted needs, because these often result from individual preferences (not everyone desires a university degree or the same career). As such, the opportunities available are likely to reflect different customs and cultures of particular societies.

While much of this chapter has suggested that definitions of these core concepts are either one set of ideas or another, in reality, welfare provision conflates various sets of ideas. It is not simply a matter of all needs being inherent, or equality referring only to opportunities. Theoretical boundaries often mean little in practice; but we need to recognise these boundaries so that our analysis of welfare provision can unpick the rationales of different interventions.

In the opening speech bubbles to this chapter, we noted that rights would be a fundamental aspect of the debate. For many, there can be no provision of social rights unless duties are discharged. This might be paying taxes so that the state has the resources to provide services, and/or it might require that certain behaviours or duties are discharged (we explore this argument a bit more in later chapters). As such, it would be possible to add the need to meet these duties to Figure 3.8. However, the second speech bubble suggested that social rights take priority. Early configurations of welfare entitlement predominantly fell in line with this argument, and this is what Figure 3.8 illustrates. Where social rights are identified as an integral part of your citizen status, there is a duty upon the state to ensure these are met. As we will see from Chapter 5 on, such views have been significantly reorientated in contemporary welfare debate.

Entitlement to welfare support is fraught with a range of challenges, both theoretical and practical. Combined, these challenges shape different arguments about who receives support, what form the support takes, and how this promotes greater freedom and equality within social life. However, such arguments are meaningless unless they receive some recognition by the state. Chapter 2 suggested that efforts to define welfare and promote state intervention into its pursuit generated a series of social rights. These rights are constructed in relation to need, equality and citizenship, which in turn determine who has access to these rights. Such articulations require confirmation by the state. Essentially, governments need to not only recognise certain rights, and the groups of people who have access to those rights, but also accept the need to offer support. Having outlined this broader debate, it is now possible to pay explicit attention to the provision of welfare, the focus of Chapter 4.

Critical thinking activity

With reference to the entitlement triangle, assess the relevance of social rights to the concept of welfare.

Further reading

Bradshaw, J. (2013) 'The Concept of Social Need'; in R. Cookson, R. Sainsbury and C. Glendinning (Eds.), *Jonathan Bradshaw on Social Policy: Selected Writings 1972-2011*. York: University of York pp1–12. Available at: https://www.york.ac.uk/inst/spru/pubs/pdf/JRB.pdf

Dean, H. (2015) *Social Rights and Human Welfare*. Oxon: Routledge.

Doyal, L. and Gough, I. (1984) A Theory of Human Needs. *Critical Social Policy* 4 pp6–38.

Don't forget to look at the companion website for more information.

4

Who should provide welfare support?

If you've got citizenship, your rights and entitlements are absolute.

The state's responsibility for welfare has to be adjustable according to need.

Key concepts in this chapter:
mixed economy of welfare • nation-building • universalism
• welfare regime

The previous chapter provided insight into how entitlement underpins the concept of welfare, and illustrated some of the links between the three concepts of need, equality and citizenship. Indicating the nature of welfare provision, this leads us to explore how that provision is to be designed and pursued. We have already reviewed some hints of this in terms of the debate between the state and market as providers of welfare. Starting with an account of nation state and **nation–building**, this chapter examines some of the key issues and tensions at the core of welfare support, which leads into a broader discussion of welfare systems: the means of providing welfare support through the mixed economy of welfare. Finally, the chapter examines the arguments in support of **universalism** in welfare provision. Accepting for the moment that the concepts of inherent need, social rights and citizenship outlined previously are accurate, these concepts lead to the development of welfare provision of secure universal services. This provides our first insight into how concepts can shape welfare provision, which we will question and challenge in the next chapters.

Building the nation, confirming citizen status

The discussion of social rights and human rights illustrated a clear division in which the latter was universal, shared by all humankind, but the former contained an explicit association of citizenship status. While citizenship has been presented as a universal and totalising concept (Dean and Melrose, 1999), this is not a shared universal set of characteristics of all humans; rather, it refers to the sameness of a certain group, implicitly with a shared culture, territory, norms and values. Canavan (1996:51) suggests that: 'Part of what is involved in belonging to a nation is some conception of citizenship, however attenuated: some notion that a nation is a *people* all members of which are politically connected with one another in a way that lords and subjects in pre-national societies were not' (emphasis in original). Recognition of social rights as a means of securing welfare is therefore associated with something other than entitlement; it requires a broader political entity, with the power and ability to enforce the conditions of entitlement. This entity is the nation state.

States, nations and imagined communities

The most commonly used definition of 'the state' suggests that it is a compulsory political organisation with a centralised government that maintains a monopoly of the legitimate use of force within a certain territory (Weber, 1946:76). General categories of state institutions include administrative bureaucracies (government, monarch/president, civil service), legal systems (the courts) and military or religious organisations. It is through the legitimised use of force that the state is able to collect taxes, which are used for public expenditure. This legitimate authority is underpinned in some countries (such as the UK) by democracy, wherein those in political office are granted power through collective will. This is similar to Tilly's (1975, cited in Bottomore, 1979) definition of a state: a well-defined, continuous territory, relatively centralised, clearly differentiated from other organisations and with the monopoly of the means of physical coercion within its territory. However, as Canavan (1996) notes, states are not always nations and nations are not always states. A number of nations have not been separate states; the UK consists of four nations under one state (although post-1997 devolution [the dispersal of governance powers and functions to regional levels] has altered this concept in various ways), and postcolonial states have engaged in nation-building activities since gaining independence.

Explanations of the formation of nations draw on a range of theories to elaborate the source of collective sentiments and experiences that create the political community and identity associated with the nation. Finlayson (2008) draws a number of these ideas together in his discussion of imagined communities. These imagined communities are built around people who draw on the same set of symbolic resources to articulate a sense of identity, usually within a specific geographical territory (although today, political communities need not be attached to geographical territories). Such communities are imagined to be natural and often form the basis of political organisation, ethical perceptions and ideological claims. This creates particular images of the community, establishing a number of boundaries (social and geographical) and informing the specific contexts that dictate action towards social justice and meeting people's welfare. Anderson (2016) suggested that such communities provide a source of identity to promote community, contingency and connections between people within the same time across space. In the UK, for example, this can be played out through national identities such as Scottish or English, but also the identity of British. The 1940s saw the development of a British welfare state, but post-devolution there is a question as to whether the welfare state is now fragmenting across the constituent nations.

Returning to the cultural explanations of nation formation, which developed alongside industrialisation in western societies, Anderson drew attention to the cultural changes that occurred through political and economic development (the move away from feudalism towards capitalism). A form of high culture was required, referring to literacy and numeracy, which underpin a range of occupational activities and foster a shared commonality. This culture reflects the declining importance of privileged access to particular languages (such as Latin) and a movement away from the divine right and hereditary of the monarchy. Taking up similar themes, Gellner (1983) argued that culture became the mechanism for social integration and managing greater fluidity in social life. This gives us a clear definition of *imagined* communities. They are imagined because they are social constructs. They act to unify people who will never meet or speak to each other, but who share a commonality. They provide a means by which we can define ourselves and a means through which we can be defined by others. Yet these social constructs have very real and tangible effects and consequences.

There is, therefore, a sense that nations are not simply constructed but also arise out of historical processes, particularly modernisation. Canavan (1996) sums up such theories, suggesting that an ersatz (meaning an artificial and inferior substitute) community arises to meet the needs of modern society. Nations provide social and political functions required for not only the modern economy and the emotional needs of the population (the sense of community and belonging as social, political, economic and cultural order changes) but also the tactical needs of politicians. Bottomore (1979) suggested that this development occurred in the late 19th and 20th centuries, and that two key conditions instigated the development of the nation state: first, the development of modern centralised government; and second, the rise of nationalism. The first is relevant to Social Policy because, without the establishment of centralised government the formation of the welfare state (discussed shortly) would not have been possible. The second, nationalism, refers not to the nationalism we see in political debates but to ideas of self-determination, changes in political power and the development of the imagined community.

Such developments occurred alongside industrialisation in western societies, giving rise to the suggestion that the nation state was found to be the most suitable form of government to assist the development of capitalism. This is because the nation state offered, as Bottomore (1979:112–13) explains, 'a stable, well organised political system, with a national and effectively administered body of law, especially in so far as it related to property and contracts'. Underpinning this development was a sense of national identity. The formation of the nation state required a sense of nationality: the creation of a fundamental social bond between the members of the territory. The development of the nation state consolidated this sense of national identity, although it may simultaneously cause tension and conflict at the international political level, as different identities emerge around various beliefs and values. Generally, this national identity fosters a sense of belonging attached to a particular territorial space, which can be used to galvanise support for the aims of the state.

Framing citizens and the nation

Nations thus formed through a socially constructed identity, which was reinforced through an emerging centralised state with a distinct territorial claim. This fostered a particular identity, which, as Lewis (2002:4) reiterated, facilitated the social construction of not only the nation but also the citizen:

> Who constitutes the nation; what the appropriate forms of behaviour were; how new authority codes between socially 'superior' and 'inferior' groups (both at home and in the colonies) were to be produced; and what form the relation between state, economy and the people was to take, were all pressing questions. It was in this crucible of transformation that new forms of social cohesions, stability and dominance were to be produced, and in this sense, too, the nation was being formed … The point is that 'nations' are always made and remade and that their boundaries, real and imagined, internal and external have provided the frame within which welfare regimes are constructed and practised.

Such constructs exist because they have come to be socially created, accepted and acknowledged. The nation is one such construct, forged through a series of social interactions that define and shape it. The development of the imagined community partially relied on a series of policies, which played an integral role in shaping the territory, scope and intention of activity; the beneficiaries; the role of citizens, state and other sectors; as well as who will be excluded from a policy. As such, we are able to draw out three key questions from the Lewis quote:

1. Who constitutes the nation?
2. What are appropriate forms of behaviour?
3. What relationship exists between state, economy and people?

Canavan (1996), in her review of the theories of nation, highlights the central role of ethnicity as an organisational feature of identity formation. Nation implied a homogeneous ethnic group with values, norms and culture transmitted via the family, resulting in a sense of identity based around birth and blood. While historically there were no truly homogeneous ethnicities (except, Canavan posits, perhaps Iceland), this sense of one ethnicity was influential in the formation of nation as an imagined community. Subsequently, policy is used to reinforce these common identities as part of the nation–building process. Policy both implicitly and explicitly integrates definitions of who counts as subjects (members of the nation) and is therefore supported by policy. This is influenced by a range of assumptions, particularly around gender and 'race'/ethnicity (Williams, 1989).

Williams's (1989:xiii) exploration of the UK is useful here. She suggests that family and nation have been central organising principles of the welfare state, because 'welfare policies have both appealed to and reinforced (and occasionally challenged) particular ideas of what constitutes family life, and what constitutes national unity and "British culture", although notions and reality of Family and Nation have themselves changed over time'. Focusing on these themes brings issues of gender and 'race' to the forefront of analysis, illustrating how the development of the British nation embodied imperialist and patriarchal social relations: for example, the assumption of men as breadwinners and women as dependent housewives. Understanding how the nation is *presented* and *recreated* through policy is therefore an important addition to the theories of imagined communities: it emphasises the socially constructed nature of this concept.

This is particularly important in relation to diverse citizens. Towards the end of the previous chapter, the discussion of citizenship highlighted the importance of recognising diversity. Nations, as imagined communities, contain assumptions around membership and how certain individuals are recognised (especially in relation to social rights) by political actors and within policy and practice. Implicit or explicit ethnic or gendered assumptions of the nation infiltrate into the concept of citizen; certain groups are recognised while others are not. Often, such distinctions are still found in relation to migrants, refugees and asylum seekers who do not have official citizen status.

A further illustration of this can be found in the reporting of Nong Pee, a child who shot to fame via YouTube for football skills. Interested parties looking to sign him up to their youth academies faced a challenge: Nong Pee was stateless (Sky News, 2017). His parents emigrated from Myanmar to Thailand, where Nong Pee was born. As such, while his parents have no legal recognition in Thailand, Nong Pee has no legal recognition in either country: he is stateless. Thailand is not a signatory to United Nations (UN) conventions on refugees or stateless people; consequently, Nong Pee has no automatic legal rights to education, healthcare or a passport. This illustration reflects the stateless position of at least 10 million people around the world, which the United Nations High Commissioner for Refugees seeks to address through its campaign to end statelessness. Being stateless results in having none of the protected rights or entitlements that come with citizenship status. It is also important to recognise a range of global processes (some explored in Chapter 7) that have moved traditionally nation-state practices into private and supranational institutions, generating a form of denationalised citizenship associated with globalisation and consequent changes in the role of the nation state due to privatisation, deregulation and increased human rights (see for example Sassen, 2000, 2002). These points seek to illustrate how the concept of the nation determines citizenship and, therefore, access to welfare services. However, the concept is challenged by social movements built around social divisions, as well as by changing global socioeconomic contexts.

Nation-building in a changing world

Nation-building refers to the use of policy and practice to create and reinforce notions of who is (and is not) a recognised citizen of a particular social and geographical group, and the support and distribution of social goods this engenders. As such, the development of welfare systems both reflects and creates national identities; but this is not static. Social, economic and global changes generate new forms of territorial politics, inequalities and entitlements, altering key concepts that shaped welfare provision for most of the 20th century. This occurs at the global, national and local scales; devolution and new global pressures create a new social topography that contributes to the emergence of a new discursive terrain. In part, such arguments suggest that decentralising and devolving tendencies can undermine social citizenship and a shared national sense of social justice and belonging. In relation to UK devolution, Davidson et al. (2010) explain that there was no ill feeling towards the entire political–economic system, but rather towards a particular form of governmental power assumed by the UK state. Devolution therefore starts to gain political credence, as national identities (Scottish, Welsh and so on) conflict across the nation state, generating a desire for greater local control over policy, politics and economics. This is the mechanism through which significant areas of policy are removed from the centre of the political apparatus and relocated to a regional or local level.

These new locations of governmental activity are not only involved in developing and promoting distinctive identities but may also act as policy 'laboratories', facilitating experimentation in addressing the same social problems. Thus, policy learning and transfer can now occur within a nation state as well as across national boundaries, illustrating the idea that policy is being decentred: the development and implementation of social policies is no longer a national state activity alone. Increasingly, globalisation, regionalisation and Europeanisation are generating new types of multilevel governance – and diverse forms of regionalism, decentralisation, federalism and devolution – disrupting the assumptions of a close fit between welfare and nation.

For Ferrera (2005), the changes happening at the regional and European levels relate to the voice/exit relationship. Voice refers to demands made by citizens for change to welfare provision, while exit refers to citizens opting to remove themselves from state provision and secure their needs through other means. Ferrera suggests the welfare state has traditionally served people within a specific territory, but these global and regional changes (especially the development of the European Union (EU), but also devolution and localisation; see Adams and Schmueker, 2005; Schmueker and Lodge, 2010) destabilise the policies based on territory and increase the potential for exit; that is, people moving to other nations/regions where they can access different welfare settlements.

As a contemporary illustration, devolution in the UK creates new means through which a national identity and citizenship characteristic can be developed: a distinctiveness from British to be Welsh or Scottish or Northern Irish instead. Béland and Lecours (2008) suggest that social policy stimulates nation-building as a collective frame for common sense-making across otherwise divided social groups. Consequently, social policy operates as a potent nation-building tool by shaping, regulating and directing the meaning and possibilities of collective existence, experienced in national terms. Devolution in the UK has provided space for new forms of nationalism to arise within policy making, which help shape new nation-building projects. Taking the example of Scotland, it is possible to see how policy documentation exhibits this nationalist identity; pronouncements such as a 'New Scotland' are routinely prefaced as providing 'Scottish solutions to Scottish problems' (Mooney and Scott, 2005). Thus, the Scottish parliament sought to offer a distinctive approach to addressing social problems, leading to policy divergence: the development of different solutions to the same problems compared to the rest of the UK. This has been described as welfare nationalism, which seeks to generate support for devolution based on the view that the Scottish state is smaller, more responsive and accountable, and can experiment with the various policy instruments under its control to reduce social inequalities. Subsequently, a shift is generated through policy and rhetoric, which reinforces a different concept of the nation – or, in other words, recreates a new imagined community (Paterson, 1994). Similar independence and nationalist narratives can be found in many nations (such as Catalonia and Taiwan).

Devolved governments thus become 'social policy'-focused organisations (Chaney and Drakeford, 2004), able to pursue distinct national projects that can generate different ideologies, senses of belonging and subsequently policies which reflect this devolved framing. These policies therefore can diverge from those of the national state. Devolution provides opportunities to use policy to redefine national identities within efforts to tackle social problems. But it also demonstrates how states seek to justify social interventions.

Clarke (2004:28) provides a useful way of summarising the foregoing argument in his analysis of the trinity of nation, state and welfare. He suggested that nations are a 'potent source of attachment', which have both material and symbolic resonance for the citizen. The development of devolution in the UK (and similar could be claimed of other devolved and federal systems) creates 'multiple contexts' within social policy making, altering the analysis of the nation as a concept in Social Policy. The devolved/federal territories become the frame of reference for a consideration or construction of 'social problems' in themselves, and act as primary sites for the contestation of social citizenship. Thus, policy acts as a project to promote re-nationalisation. This becomes an important consideration within the globalised context (examined in Chapter 7).

Citizenship as an identity is tied into these debates around the political community and national identity. These identities attached to particular nation states inform an understanding of not only the duties and expectations of citizens but also the protections afforded to them in terms of civil (legal), political and social rights. Coming out of this, therefore, is a wider debate as to how welfare provision is secured through the state.

Social justice and political communities

The idea of the imagined community was central to the preceding discussion for creating a unified (if problematic) sense of identity, alongside which citizenship and social rights can be constructed. This is important to consider for, as Canavan (1996) suggests, theories of social justice often assume the existence of a political community capable of pursuing justice – or, for our focus, citizen welfare. She suggests that social justice requires a political community for two reasons: first, to distribute social goods to achieve social justice aims (it is necessary to identify boundaries, both social and geographical, within which said distribution is to occur); second, to offer clear reasons as to why goods should be shared. Chapters 2 and 3 engage with the second point, but not the first. Any argument for helping people to secure their welfare requires the political power to create the forms of redistribution necessary to achieve welfare goals. Such power will rely on the achievement of a consensus in favour of feasible redistribution, which in turn requires a degree of communal solidarity. This solidarity is based on deciding who has membership of a political community and which associated rights and duties are to be shared between members. Such a distribution, however, presupposes a group of people committed to dividing, exchanging and sharing social goods. But these determinations can have bias and implicit assumptions that exclude some from full citizen status and recognition (as illustrated briefly earlier regarding gendered assumptions in social security).

Theories of social justice facilitate the development of state institutions to secure welfare. This in turn requires an explicit consideration of the political communities around which welfare institutions will be created. Such communities will rely on a sense of mutual trust and obligation to generate the required support and sharing. However, Canavan (1996) is critical of Rawls's work in relation to these debates. She suggests that Rawls's theory of justice implicitly assumes a community of obligation but gives no indication as to how this membership is constructed. In his later work, Rawls refers to a closed society in which people enter through birth and exit through death; as such, it is assumed that co-nationals (people within the nation) will have claims against each other, expressed through social rights. This does not reflect all humans (or issues around migration), only those identified as citizens of the nation in question.

This next bit gets a little theoretical and abstract, but keep with it as it will become clear. Recall the veil of ignorance suggested by Rawls in the last chapter. Pogge (1989; cited in Canavan, 1996) suggested that there is a need to take the veil of ignorance a step further. He suggested that national identity is a further bias, which the veil must remove if we are to truly pursue justice. This would result in a distribution of resources that does not reflect the co-nationals focus implicit in Rawls's work, and would challenge (as Canavan (1996) notes) his focus on how co-nationals have claims against each other. Rawls's failure was to broaden this debate over resources to consider interactions with members of a 'superior caste'. We can illustrate this through the debate between human and social rights. Focusing on national boundaries and closed communities, Rawls seems focused on relations within national borders – and, as such, *social* rights. But in a true veil of ignorance we would not be aware of our national identity; as such, we would broaden the notion of social rights to be universal across all humankind, and the unjust distribution of resources adopts a *human* rights perspective. To pursue intervention into and protection of people's welfare, there needs to be an explicit account of the political communities with the authority and capability to intervene in people's lives. Yet the socially constructed nature of such a body, which informs notions of citizenship and dictates who is (and is not) included in said intervention and protection, must be an explicit focus of analysis.

Essentially, the formation of nations rests on a socially constructed concept of citizenship (with a range of potential biases), and requires a political centre capable of facilitating and pursuing a sense of social justices. Taking this argument further, we can return to Titmuss's suggestion that social harm/diswelfare results from the same modernisation process that gave rise to the nation and industrialisation/capitalism. How social systems are designed can generate both economic and social inequality, which can have a range of consequences – from educational achievement to lifespan. As such, there is an argument that the pursuit of welfare requires the design of institutions to intervene and support citizens so they are not the victims of accidents of nature and social circumstances. Conceptual justification for state intervention into people's welfare rests on the claims co-nationals make against each other, seeking to ensure they share a common fate. Social systems are neither unchangeable nor beyond human control. The right arguments can convince others of intervention and change (recall the Beveridge Report in the UK during the Second World War, which gained popularity as a means of using collective effort to create a welfare system that would create significant change to social systems). But these need to be achieved through popular consent. Once welfare institutions are established, they require democratic support for their instigation, and their continued presence should not rely on coercion; they need to be seen as legitimate.

Legitimacy will be tied into a range of different debates. As noted in the previous chapter, debates around need and equality (for example) inform different perspectives on not only the level of need to be met but also the tensions between state intervention for the promotion or curtailment of freedom. The following chapters discuss some new trends in welfare debates that further question the legitimacy of welfare interventions, which in turn impact on how welfare support will be provided (we explore this in the next section). What is important for the debate here can be summed up as follows. Any theory for action into welfare provision presupposes the existence of a political body with the power to act to redistribute resources. Such a body is not natural, despite its presentation as such. Rather, it is a social construct, which gives rise to the imagined community, informs who is and is not included in the nation, influences the development of guidelines for how resources are distributed within specified social and geographical boundaries, and sets out the behaviours and duties expected of citizens.

Summary

This section has examined some fundamental, but complex, debates. It has highlighted the socially constructed nature of nations as imagined communities, and how this influences notions of citizenship. Policy helps to create and replicate many of these ideas as part of the nation-building project. Figure 4.1 illustrates how a number of different factors influence the formation of the nation, some of which (such as policy) operate as an expression of certain values but also a means by which they can be created and sustained – for example, early exclusion of minority ethnic people from housing access, or the assumptions in the Beveridge Report regarding women as housewives and carers, not employees.

Rather than accept the implicit assumption (embedded in a number of theories of justice) that such a political authority exists, this section demonstrates the

Figure 4.1: Factors influencing the formation of the nation

need to adopt a more critical stance towards how these imagined communities are constructed. A nuanced discussion underpins debates regarding welfare interventions and the requisite citizen characteristics for entitlement to support. This informs political authority and support for providing welfare services, and determines the nature of the distribution of social goods and resources against criteria established in terms of welfare, social rights, needs, equality and citizenship status.

Such debates rest at the core of the 'political community' – the series of institutions that exist to pursue a notion of social justice within a defined territory. On the one hand, the influences examined in Figure 4.1 are expressed through the establishment of welfare institutions and the access criteria associated with them. On the other hand, welfare institutions recreate those ideas that shape the nation, to ensure stability of both the nation itself and the concept of citizenship. Thus, in addition to market failure (discussed in Chapter 2), we can see an alternative explanation for justifying state intervention into welfare provision. We can now explore the role of the state, and other providers of welfare within the nation, more explicitly.

Providing for citizens: the mixed economy of welfare

The outcome of the aforementioned debates – how nations and citizens are constructed, how entitlement to support is determined and whether state intervention is supported or challenged – influences the development of the kind of welfare system each nation adopts to pursue its welfare goals. This section explores the construction of welfare systems and the different sectors involved in the delivery of welfare services.

Exploring welfare systems

'Welfare systems' refers to the variety of ways in which nations have influenced the provision of welfare. While the term 'welfare state' may be more commonly used, it refers to a specific configuration of the **mixed economy of welfare (MEW)** involved in the provision of welfare. This MEW typically consists of four sectors – the state, the market, the voluntary ('third') sector and the informal sector – although some have suggested inclusion of social enterprise and faith-based organisations. A welfare state refers to a configuration in which the state is the primary provider of welfare. Using the concept of the MEW in a descriptive way allows us to examine the balance between sectors, and thus to explore the different ways in which welfare is secured in different nations. However, it is also possible to use the MEW in a prescriptive way, whereby political actors articulate the need for a specific configuration of the different sectors to be pursued through policy. As such, a justification for welfare intervention could argue for increased use of state institutions to provide welfare services on the basis of need, equality and common citizenship (and as part of the nation-building project). Other ideological and philosophical standpoints would argue for different configurations, potentially advocating less state involvement and increased reliance on the market.

Variation in the MEW can be found in Esping-Anderson's (1990) investigation, which provided a three-part typology of the **welfare regimes** into which different western nations can be placed (Table 4.1). This discussion of regimes pays attention to how conceptual debates, such as decommodification of needs, have informed the design of welfare provision in different nations.

Table 4.1: Esping-Anderson's welfare regimes

Regime	Characteristics	Examples
Liberal	Means-tested assistance Modest income transfers Work ethic stigma Market efficiency and commodification	UK US
Corporatist–statist	Private insurance backed by the state Rights according to class and status Strengthens civil society (e.g. the Church) rather than the market	Austria France Germany
Social democratic	Equality and universalism State primary provider of support Welfare and work linked to full employment	Scandinavia

The centrality of decommodification in Esping-Andersen's work has been critiqued for its perceived methodological flaws and exclusion of gendered issues (O'Connor, 1993; Lewis, 1997). While developments in comparative and international Social Policy have sought to establish a clearer methodological account of welfare regimes, however, regime analysis remains an important approach in differentiating welfare provision across nations. Particularly relevant to our discussion here is how these different systems result from variations in conceptual justifications – 'rationales' (Levin, 1997) – for welfare provision.

Considering its prominence, the term 'welfare state' should therefore be seen as one welfare *system*, in which the state plays a central role in the provision of welfare. Titmuss (1967) suggests 'welfare state' implied that the nation state had to fulfil both moral and spiritual functions to promote human welfare. This resonated with the Second World War Allied Nations Atlantic Charter, mentioned earlier, with its four freedoms (of speech and religion; from want and fear). While there was growing international agreement about the need to address social problems, nationally this varied. In the UK, the term 'welfare state' shaped the programme of social reforms and post-war reconstruction. In the US, the term was seen as a label disguising the totalitarian state – a threat to the individual. Scholars tend to agree that there is no neat definition of the welfare state, but Briggs (1961:228) offers a generally accepted definition:

in which organised power is deliberately used (through politics and administration) in an effort to modify the play of market forces in at least three directions – first, by guaranteeing individuals and families a minimum income … second, by narrowing the extent of insecurity … third, by ensuring that all citizens without distinction of status and class are offered the best standards available in relation to an agreed range of social services.

Limitations can be highlighted in relation to how to define 'organised power', 'minimum income' and even 'citizens'. Yet Biggs's definition does differentiate between the social state (the state using communal resources to halt poverty and assist those in distress) and the welfare state (which is concerned with not only the abatement of class difference or the needs of different groups in society but also equality of treatment and aspiration of different citizens).

Titmuss (1967) discusses the definition offered by Swedish economist and political scientist, Gunnar Myrdal, who defines the welfare state as pursuing the following goals: 'Economic development, full employment, equality of opportunity for the young, social security, and protected minimum standards as regards not only income, but nutrition, housing, health, and education for people of all regions and social groups'. For Titmuss (1974), such definitions remain too broad, as there is a need to encompass three sources of welfare – fiscal, occupational and social (Table 4.2) – which opens up analysis beyond the direct activities of the state. The term 'welfare state' should therefore be applied where the state is involved in addressing *social* problems, reflecting the acceptance of collective responsibility to address those issues which cause diswelfare. Generally speaking, this was seen to only apply to the 'big five' – poverty, unemployment, ill health, housing problems and education – although the subject of Social Policy has since expanded.

Competing explanations also confound the origin of welfare provision. Typically, it has been seen as an achievement of the political Left; social democratic, socialist and labour movements or parties seeking to secure human welfare (such terms do not apply equally across nations; in the US, this would more accurately be labelled 'liberal', which has a different meaning in UK politics). Exploring the Norwegian context, Wahl (2011) suggests that there are efforts by the political Right to claim the welfare state as their own, relating to a view that the welfare state arises from compromise between different political factors. Wahl suggests

Table 4.2: Social divisions of welfare

Division	Description
Fiscal	Provision secured through the use of the tax system, such as tax incentives on pensions savings or tax credits
Occupational	Provision secured through your form of employment, such as an employee creche
Social	State-provided welfare support

this lack of clarity over ownership reflects a sense that welfare systems are formed through political debates and compromise, drawing attention to national political contexts and how these influence definitions, pursuit and concepts of welfare.

Rodger (2000) provided an interesting addition to this debate. He suggested that the modern welfare state placed family and community at the heart of activity. This relationship between the state, family and community was seen to be integral to determining the level of social provision to be provided – what needs were to be met – and by whom. It was modern because it drew on the scientific values of the **Enlightenment** to abolish human misery. This can be contrasted with the anti-modern welfare state, in which tradition, religion and conservative ideas suggest the family lost its function to the welfare state, and that this undermined the patriarchal national family and dissolved the nurturing environment in which children grow. Rodger's analysis illustrates how the notion of the welfare state is not specific, but generally applies to efforts to improve human welfare that involve the state in some form, as well as that the notion of the welfare state will change over time.

Underpinning Rodger's (2000) analysis was a focus on a theoretical debate between three competing schools of thought: modernism, anti-modernism and postmodernism. Modernist ideas aligned with the foundations of the welfare state: a pursuit of welfare through the redistribution of income and provision of welfare services to align with principles of equality and social justice (similar ideas were outlined in relation to Fives' (2007) suggestion of perfectionist accounts of welfare). Anti-modernist thinking was more critical (akin to non-perfectionist accounts), and suggested that the state undermines the market and the family. Diminished family and individual responsibility for welfare weakens the social fabric and results in disaster.

An alternative account originates within postmodernist ideas to argue for a decentralised social policy. Each citizen has their own individual ambitions and likes, which cannot be secured through collective welfare. Removing the centralised state and privatising services creates a space for needs to be met in line with these individual preferences. Notions of equality or social justice are nothing but grand narratives, which no longer fit the contemporary world. Rodger uses the term 'welfare society' to emphasise the conflict and change surrounding the welfare state, and suggests that the voluntary sector will dominate as the main source of welfare in the future. The term welfare society is important for Rodger (2000:9) because it summarises the 'undertheorised relationship between state-sponsored welfare programmes and their reception by and impact on society, both at the level of individual behaviour and of social and community relations'. Essentially, this term provides a broader framework to consider the efforts to secure human welfare, and the complex debates associated with it. Thus, it becomes necessary to explicitly consider the different components of the MEW.

The providers of welfare

Baldock (2012:) states that social policy deliberately seeks to intervene into social and personal lives through state activity in order to facilitate the redistribution of resources to achieve a welfare objective. This definition explicitly places the state as a provider of welfare services. But despite justification for the state to provide welfare services, it is not automatically the case that the state will do so; it may choose not to act, leaving provision to other sectors. Furthermore, even if the state decides there *is* a need to act, it need not be a direct provider; it may supply the finance for which others can bid so that they can provide the services. Consequently, Alcock and May (2014) suggested four general functions of the state:

- **Provision:** the state raises money through taxes to use in the provision of a range of social services designed to enhance citizen welfare. This can range from direct provision of income support to buildings, purchasing equipment and paying workers involved in the delivery of social services.
- **Subsidisation:** the use of public money to subsidise welfare services provided by private, voluntary or informal organisations. These can be direct subsidies (provision of money) or indirect (tax emption).
- **Regulation:** a role for the state in monitoring and developing legal regulation of the quality of services provided by commercial and voluntary organisations. This is perhaps the oldest aspect of the state's policy intervention.
- **Employment:** essentially, the state is an employer, and in providing occupations is the source of income and employment conditions for a large number of citizens.

In relation to direct provision, this effort draws attention back to universal citizenship and social rights debates. Through provision, the state can foster a web of mutual connections to generate support and obligations within a nation to hold diverse groups together. As such, state provision is reliant upon policies with a shared understanding of citizenship, resting (as noted) on a national identity and culture. But this is also informed by different philosophical or ideological viewpoints regarding the role of the state and the various other sectors, throwing open questions of what balance between providers should be struck. Should there even be a balance, or should all provision be through one provider? And what role should each provider play? (See Table 3.5.)

Additionally, determining the state's role within any welfare systems depends on the strategy a state adopts towards securing welfare. Spicker (2008) suggests the existence of six different strategies of state activity:

1. A status quo approach: the state may not do something, thus requiring that citizens use their own resources to make their own provision.

2. A market approach: the best method for arranging production and distribution of resources. This utilises the price mechanism as a means of using demand for a good or service to reduce the overall price so that more people are able to access it.

3. A residual approach, which assumes that most people can organise their welfare; the state only provides a 'safety net' for those unable to fend for themselves.

4. A selective approach, which develops criteria to judge, can add conditionality on top of criteria requiring citizens to discharge certain responsibilities in order to receive support.

5. A social protection strategy offers protection against changes in circumstances and undesirable effects of different life-course changes; it is not necessarily just about responding to individual need.

6. A universal strategy seeks to ensure that welfare services are available to all, often by a predefined category, such as universal education being available to all children and young people up to a certain age, or universal healthcare for all citizens.

Despite the predominant view that universal needs establish a set of social rights that apply to all citizens, which in turn justifies state provision, there are some claimed weaknesses of state provision (see Table 4.3). The central argument here is found in the work of Hayek, among others, and suggests that the market – or, perhaps more accurately, the commercial sector – is better suited to satisfying welfare (returning to the debate of preference satisfaction through the free market, discussed in Chapter 2). The term 'commercial sector' encapsulates organisations working on a for-profit motivation: private businesses, which may have to comply with some forms of state regulation, but are not subject to the whim of governmental aims and goals. As such, unlike state-provided services, the commercial sector's involvement in welfare will largely be determined by the pursuit of profit – and the business case for providing welfare.

Table 4.3: State failure in welfare provision

State failure	Description
Self-interested voters	Voters are motivated by not altruism but self-interest; they vote for what best helps them, not their neighbour. Additionally, in relation to need, new demands are made, which politicians seek to secure in order to gain electoral support.
Self-interested bureaucrats	Those who oversee the delivery of welfare provision are more interested in their own departments and budgets and seeking to expand these.
x-efficiency	State provision is a monopoly, creating an inefficient non-competitive model of provision and poor working practices.

Consequently, welfare goods and services are treated like any other commodity in the marketplace. Holden (2003) suggests two reasons why this should not be the case: first, certain goods are considered important to secure welfare (as defined by human needs and arguments for decommodification); second, the market cannot efficiently provide these goods. This debate between the state and commercial sectors has underpinned the debate about crisis, as suggested earlier. As noted in Table 3.5, we can divide some goods across different providers and recognise that the commercial sector may be inappropriate.

Efforts to navigate the tensions between the state and commercial sectors have led some to focus on the role of the voluntary (or third) sector. How this sector is defined is less clear; indeed, it has been described as a 'loose, baggy monster' (Kendall and Knapp, 1994). Alcock (2008:153) divides welfare provision by three intersections: public/private, profit/non-profit and formal/informal. The state occupies the space created by the public, non-profit and formal divisions. The commercial sector occupies the private, profit and formal space. The voluntary sector however resides within the private, non-profit and formal space. It does not pursue profit, nor is it within the public space; such organisations tend to have Trustees or others who have shaped their mission and aims. As with the state and commercial sectors, however, it still relies on a formal organisational structure, and efforts have been made to match this to those found in commercial organisations. Essentially, however, the voluntary sector provides a form of support to those who fall through (or are ignored by) the welfare state. Often, this is because such organisations can access stigmatised groups, which the state cannot (or will not). However, it is important to appreciate that much voluntary sector provision of welfare pre-existed the welfare state. The move towards central state provision often sidelined these organisations (in the UK), while other nations integrated some of them (such as trade unions) into parts of their welfare systems, and others continued to rely predominantly on them as providers of welfare. However, commercial and voluntary organisations are potentially selective in who they serve. The commercial sector is accessible only to those with the financial capabilities to access services. The voluntary sector targets resources at particular groups of people. State provision sought to challenge this through universal equality and citizenship arguments, which sought to ensure that, no matter where you lived, who you were or what you could afford, your social rights were protected.

The final sector occupies the space created by Alcock's (2008) informal, non-profit and private intersections. This is the space of the informal sector: family members, friends and neighbours who provide support. This could be through the caring responsibilities of parents for their children, or children for their elderly parents. As increasing attention is paid to this sector, it is becoming increasingly apparent that young children are taking on care responsibilities for their parents and siblings (Becker et al., 2000). Additionally, the informal sector weaves throughout the others. Families may pool incomes to purchase food or pay health insurance. When in hospital being cared for by the state, family members will take on duties around washing, providing fresh clothing and supplying additional food or other goods. Children in school rely on not only teachers for their education but also reading or working on their homework with parental supervision. Indeed, it could be argued that the informal sector is the primary provider of welfare – not simply in terms of goods and services necessary for survival, but also emotional wellbeing, forms of social support and so on. There is often a debate (as we shall explore in relation to the family) about whether state support helps to secure and strengthen this provision, or weaken and undermine it. How policy makers view the roles of these different sectors will shape and inform the system of welfare it pursues.

Summary

The section has sought to draw out the four components of welfare referred to as the MEW (Figure 4.2). Essentially, welfare systems will be constructed in different ways depending on the various articulations of welfare, social rights, needs, equality, social justice, citizenship and so on. The outcome of these philosophical and political debates informs the extent of welfare support to be provided. Subsequently, debate turns to consider how support should be provided. This encompasses a debate about the social divisions of welfare as well as the roles of different sectors within the MEW. How welfare is provided and secured across nations will vary depending on the various debates and outcomes of those interactions. Esping-Anderson (1990) offers one way of starting to map out differences across nations globally, despite some limitations. The essential point here is that different welfare systems will result from conceptual debates around welfare and welfare provision.

Welfare support has often been associated with the promotion of universal services based on not only accepted universal needs but also universal social rights of citizens. As such, the state as a provider of welfare has received significant attention as the means by which this 'gold standard' of provision can be met. Discussion now turns to the argument for universalism, which is critiqued in the next chapter.

Figure 4.2: The mixed economy of welfare (MEW)

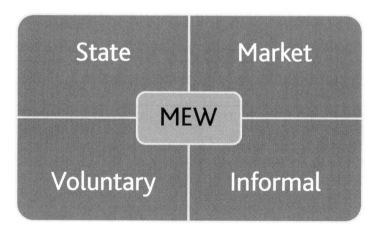

The case for and against universalism

Universal notions of social rights and the citizen have underpinned welfare interventions and social policy designs. Exactly how these policies have been designed can be reflected in the idea of universalism. Often, this requires the state to act as a provider of welfare. As noted earlier in this chapter, state action – while often assumed within arguments for social justice – relies on acceptance of the parameters against which social goods are to be distributed and political support for the institutions that provide services. Universal provision has long been viewed as a means for achieving both of these.

Altruistic intent

For Titmuss (in Titmuss et al., 1997), altruism was a central aspect of Social Policy, as it facilitated gift-giving across a social group without an expectation of a return for the gift. Similarly, Heywood (2007:55) suggested the term refers to a 'concern for the interests and welfare of others, based either upon enlightened self-interest or a belief in a common humanity'. Broadly speaking, discussions of citizenship (as with need and equality) are built around a view of a 'common humanity', which facilitated state provision to citizens. Yet, Land (2012:48) suggests 'the collective obligations which underpin social policy are based on a mixture of altruism and self-interest'. Consequently, welfare gifts are not entirely selfless; rather, there will likely be some benefit, even if this is the psychological reward of having provided a gift. For Page (1996), altruistic acts contain three elements: giving (or at least the desire to give), empathy and no motives for reward from the object of altruistic behaviour. Acts of giving are treated as ends in themselves and are given voluntarily, and – perhaps most importantly – the act is an effort to 'do good' rather than to harm or incur costs out of proportion to the act. He starts to suggest, however, that an altruistic act need not be one without some level of self-satisfaction, and that there is a distinction to be drawn between self-interest and self-satisfaction.

Titmuss et al. (1997) sought to illustrate much of this argument through the analysis of blood donations, illustrating how payments for donations in the US resulted in supply from the unhealthiest blood, rather than (as was the case in the UK) out of a sense of helping fellow citizens, which yielded better-quality donations. Although seeking to distinguish between social and economic policy, there have been a number of critiques, in terms of methodology, analysis (do we need to separate out donor and market systems? Why not use both?) and how altruism itself is defined (Rapport and Maggs, 2002).

Ideas of altruism have also been used to explain popular support for welfare intervention, especially in relation to welfare states. Yet, as Page (1996) notes, despite increasing altruistic sentiments there were also negative, stigmatising assessments regarding the character of the working class. Despite this, altruistic sentiments fostered a desire for an integrated, mutually supportive and equitable society, based on a sense of common citizenship. Through welfare institutions, citizens would have access to services as a right; they would be universal in nature and not discriminate. Thus, as Titmuss (1971:114) states:

> How to include poor people, and especially poor coloured [sic] people, in our societies, and at the same time to channel proportionately more resources in their favour without inducing shame or stigma remains one of the greatest challenges for Social Policy in Britain and the USA. The answer will not be found by creating separate, apartheid-like structures and 'public burden' services for poor people.

Citizens have universal social rights, even if we recognise difference (see Chapter 7) and all share in collectivist and altruistic sentiments towards the security of these for themselves and members of their wider society.

Universally provided

These collectivist and altruistic sentiments are expressed through universalism, as a means through which welfare services are provided. The intention is to provide free-at-the-point-of-use services – such as education or health – to all citizens, while ensuring that similar principles are drawn on to encompass systems of support that are triggered during times of need (such as social security provision for the unemployed). Universal provision is based on social rights rather than needs per se, and as such is presented as less stigmatising. Consequently, this not only provides accessible services but also results in welfare provision that is not humiliating, degrading or shaming. To reiterate, welfare support should not result in a loss of status, dignity or self-respect. Additionally, universal services may only apply to certain groups. For example, child benefit in the UK was historically provided to all families with children, recognising the costs of childcare. Healthcare services are not provided to the healthy; just because someone wants an X–ray does not mean they will receive one. Services can be provided for all as a right, but only when there is a specific need to be met. The important aspect is that access is not through an assessment of need.

One challenge for universal approaches, however, is cost. Providing services to all, even if they are able to purchase services elsewhere, is costly and may result in diluting services provided due to limited public resources. The above suggests that this cost is perhaps acceptable in light of the alternative, whereby the costs associated with means testing (see Chapter 5) result in residual welfare provision, which lowers the quality of service or support offered to those facing destitution or hardship. Universal provision with a progressive tax system would, however, ensure that while everyone is entitled due to their citizen status, tax ensures those who are able to pay more to finance services. Additionally, access depends on how citizen status is defined. Increasingly, debates around migrants and their entitlement to welfare provision illustrate how there might be caveats around who has entitlement to, for example, social security support – or even healthcare. Citizenship remains integral to who is included, and under what conditions individuals are given access to social rights.

A claimed benefit of universalism is the notion of shared entitlement, as has been noted. One potential challenge here is the need to accept that some level of dependency, or reliance, on the state is acceptable. This posits the idea of respectable dependency: a form of entitlement that contains the elements of deservingness and access to welfare provision, which would go against the current grain of ideological convictions about welfare provision in a number of countries, such as the UK and US. For example, the early development of social housing (homes provided by the state and rented by individuals/families) was initially targeted at '"respectable" working-class families ... tenants [who] were skilled manual workers, foremen, some managerial grades and a few other white-collar workers including salesmen and teachers. There was also a small number of unskilled workers' (Robertson and Smyth, 2009:94). Since the 1980s, however, there have been significant contextual changes (economic, social and political), resulting in 'a more socially polarised society, council housing has become the only tenure now open to the marginalised. Council housing has replaced the slums, but at the same time has been abandoned by "respectable" working-class families who no longer view it as a socially acceptable commodity' (Robertson and Smyth, 2009:104–5). Notions of respectability have changed. Once, access to welfare, which was largely secured through taxation and contributions, was seen as a collective effort to protect all citizens and secure social rights. The influence of different political discourses, as well as concepts such as globalisation and risk, have redirected policy focus towards the provision of residual and conditional services to those incapable of looking after themselves. This has little to do with respectability or deservingness, and it is unclear if such a notion could be easily re-established. Such an effort would require promoting the notion of altruism to strengthen the discourse around institutional welfare, which Titmuss associated with universal provision: the efforts of state institutions to promote integrated, mutually supportive and equitable societies.

Regardless, universalism brings together specific narratives around citizenship and social rights, need and equality, to create a narrative – threaded together with the idea of altruism – that provides a clear framework for welfare entitlement. Combined with the justification for welfare intervention, the drive towards improving the welfare of individuals and society takes on a convincing tone. There are cracks in this account, generated in part by crises narratives, but also by some of the assumptions around the centrality of altruism and universal provision.

Challenging the altruistic and universalist assumption

One of the wider justifications for universal state provision of welfare relates to claims of market failure and negative externalities. Additionally, there was the suggestion that social rights provided a new and different set of rights associated with citizens that facilitated claims against the state. Notions of need and equality (often drawn together within wider debates of social justice) provided another justification for the state to intervene and seek to correct for the effects of the free market. This suggests that market-like transactions fail to secure essential components of welfare – hence the need for alternative sources of provision, and for altruism within welfare provision.

Pinker (1971), however, has been more sceptical, and suggests that the most authentic rights we experience as we grow up relate to buying and selling in the market place. We do not need to be persuaded of our rights to buy as we please. The implicit suggestion is that this is not the same for social rights, and there is an effort to convince the public of the need to support social rights. This is exacerbated by debates over whether these rights are 'deserved' by some but not others, as well as debates over the level of provision and the potentially stigmatising effects of assessing such rights (we explore stigma in Chapter 6). Such complexity and uncertainty does not exist with market-based rights. A potential counterargument could be that, through payment of taxation, we generate authentic citizen claims; but it could also be suggested that certain people are labelled 'undeserving' because they (supposedly) have not 'contributed' in this way.

To this, Pinker (2006:16) suggests that Titmuss sought to promote institutional arrangements that facilitated citizens to act in altruistic and moral ways, which implied that those working within welfare institutions also exhibit altruistic values. However, Le Grand (1997:154) argues that 'the assumptions concerning motivation and behaviour are explicit; more often they are implicit, reflecting the unconscious values or beliefs of the policy makers concerned'. He introduced three positions: knaves (people motivated by self-interest), knights (altruistic providers) and pawns (people who are passive or unresponsive). He later added queens (active consumers). Policy makers adopt a position whereby they view human behaviour through one of these four positions; but these are assumptions, not necessarily reality, and the interaction between assumptions and people's behaviour is crucial to the success of policy. Le Grand seeks to reconceptualise the claims of altruism associated with welfare provision. For example, the post-war expansion of welfare could easily be presented as middle-class self-interest, rather than altruistic gestures of the better off. Politicians seeking to secure electoral victory promise more to the middle classes because of the 'swing-seat' phenomena of a small number of (often middle-class) constituencies, which, if won, can provide an overall majority.

Expanding his argument, Le Grand (1997) introduces a fourth social division of welfare: legal/regulation (the other three are listed in Table 4.2). This refers to government use of regulation and legislation to intervene in social matters. He draws on examples such as the UK's Child Support Agency (CSA), a legal intervention to ensure estranged parents continue to support their dependants, as examples of legal interventions. Such interventions become necessary when human behaviour is perceived as being predominantly knavish and policy makers wish to ensure individuals do not shirk their responsibilities. Consequently, in the example of the CSA, legal means are utilised to ensure a transfer of income to maintain dependants after marital breakdown. An alternative, such as the introduction of quasi-market mechanisms (the use of market-like practices within the state when outright market exchange is not possible or desirable), also draws on a knavish view of human nature. Such designs rely on self-interest to improve the responsiveness of the welfare system; like a market, it is said to respond to the desires of citizens in ways that are more efficient and less wasteful of scarce resources.

Summary

Universalism as a means for justifying and providing welfare support seeks to secure a unifying narrative for a number of different debates. It incorporates the justification for welfare interventions explored in Chapter 2 and the basis of entitlement examined in Chapter 3, and can help form the imagined community upon which nations are constructed. Theories of universalism highlight the role of altruism in supporting the development and expansion of welfare services. But, as this chapter notes, this could also be presumptive: there may be other explanations of human behaviour informing the design of welfare services and practices. In practice, it is also important to note that, while universalism has been pursued as the 'gold standard' for many advocates of welfare states, other forms of provision have developed and (it could be argued) dominated welfare provision. These are explored in the next chapter.

Chapter summary

Mouffe (1992:225) suggests that the way we 'define citizenship is intimately linked to the kind of social and political community we want'. The chapter has illustrated that the same can be said of the nation itself, which affirms citizen status. This is an important debate to consider, for how the nation is constructed is reinforced through policy. While the narrative around citizens can often overlook diversity and difference of people within a given territory, these dynamics interact with the conceptual debates outlined in Chapters 2 and 3 to inform who receives welfare support – and, ultimately, who is a member of the nation. Global and local trends further challenge the concept of nation, as policy is increasingly decentred from the central state. Yet, the state plays an integral part in welfare provision, as outlined in relation to the MEW.

Many of the debates supporting welfare have culminated in an argument in favour of universal provision. This recognises the equal needs, social rights and citizen status of certain members. However, as with all welfare provision, it relies on a specific political entity with the authority to redistribute resources towards a notion of social justice. The outcome of conceptual debate will alter how nation states pursue welfare systems; as such, different welfare regimes exist globally.

These rest on different articulations of concepts that lend support in different configurations of the MEW in efforts to provide for welfare needs.

Figure 4.3: Nation-building and access to welfare support

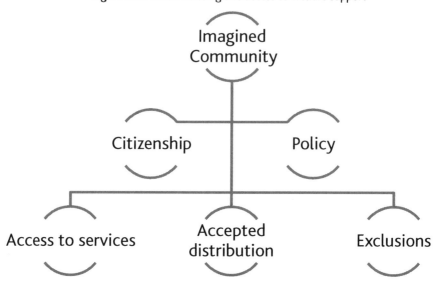

The first speech bubble at the opening of this chapter presented the idea that all citizens have the same rights, provided by the nation. Consequently, universal provision – which recognises this common, universal status – has been put forward. The second speech bubble offers two different elements. In relation to Figure 4.3, it illustrates how the imagined community of the nation is formed and reinforced through the concept of citizenship and the policy designed and enacted to support citizens. This determines who is accepted as a member of the nation and therefore has access to services, and who is not a member and therefore excluded (leaving aside, for now, exclusion within co-nationals), as well as the accepted distribution of social and material goods within a society. Here, in particular, notions of equality of opportunity and outcome will have an influence, as will concepts of need and social rights. This pathway assumes a particular notion of universal provision between co-nationals, and does not fully accept the universalism required to accept all humans as being in need of support, which would erode territorial boundaries and operate at a global scale in the way the UNDHR seeks to achieve. Thus, social rights are contained, constructed and produced within specific nations, with their social and geographical boundaries. This can be referred to as a 'rights–based approach'. However, need still triggers welfare support. Critiques of universalism, and suggestions of alternative forms of selective provision of welfare services, are explored in the next chapter.

Critical thinking activity

Identify key arguments about the nature of nation-building, and assess how this creates a notion of citizenship that reflects the type of political and social community desired by powerful groups in society.

Further reading

Pinker, R. (2006) From Gift Relationships to Quasi-Markets: An Odyssey along the Policy Paths of Altruism and Egoism. *Social Policy and Administration* 40 pp10–25.

Powell, M. (2007) *Understanding the Mixed Economy of Welfare*. Bristol: Policy Press.

Titmuss, R.M., Ashton, J. and Oakley, A. (1997) *The Gift Relationship: From Human Blood to Social Policy*. New York: New Press.

Don't forget to look at the companion website for more information.

5

Is universal provision sustainable?

> Welfare support should be provided on certain conditions. One of those is that people accept responsibility for themselves.

> Welfare needs are the same for everyone, but people experience different barriers to satisfying them.

Key concepts in this chapter:
deserving/undeserving • selectivism • underclass

The argument so far suggests that welfare is achieved through the determination of a number of key components:

• entitlement to support;
• how support is to be provided;
• a move towards universal provision as the 'gold standard' of rights-based support;
• the nation state as the primary provider of universal welfare needs.

This requires a commonality shared between those with access to welfare support, which can exclude others. Despite this exclusion, social policy has sought to provide welfare support that often presents universalism as the primary approach to welfare provision. As this chapter will demonstrate, there are some potential problems with this.

Starting with an analysis of the challenges to universal provision, the chapter moves on to explore **selectivity** and the various alternatives this suggests in relation to welfare service design. The final section returns us to a consideration of diversity within citizens as a further critique of universal provision, but also seeks to find ways of recognising diversity while not losing some of the beneficial aspects of universal provision, which generally seeks to be inclusive and avoid stigmatising treatment of citizens. This prepares the discussion for the following chapter, which considers how narratives around welfare provision shape the experience of citizens in terms of support, paying particular attention to the family.

Challenges to universal provision

Despite a generic view that social rights entitle citizens to welfare services, access to services is shaped through a wider set of debates. As noted in the final part of the previous chapter, universal provision was seen as the 'gold standard'. Reflecting the altruism of citizens, it aligned with the idea of social rights: that all in need had equal access to support in attaining particular needs to secure welfare. The rights component is essential; there was no impediment to access support – as a citizen, it was an entitlement. However, there are some limitations here. Historically, there has been a debate as to the character of claimants, fostering a distinction between **deserving** and **undeserving**. This in turn generates demands for welfare support that can require certain demonstrations of need, or a willingness to complete certain activities or tasks to receive support. Alternatively, debate around social divisions and diverse citizens has generated criticisms of universal approaches for failing to recognise the distinct needs of certain groups. Resulting in revisions of welfare support that reflect diverse rather than universal citizen needs have therefore grown in importance. Consequently, a number of debates in favour of non-universal approach can be put forth: some that abandon the idea, and others that seek to support the diversity of citizens within a universal framework. Our analysis of the alternatives to universalism begins with recognition that an element of selective provision has also been present in welfare services. This highlights a number of discourses, in particular a moralistic one about who is deserving (and therefore who is undeserving) of welfare support.

Consequently, welfare provision is challenged on the basis of rights and needs assessment (similar to the end of our discussion of needs in Chapter 3), and conditions for receipt of support come to dominate welfare provision. This section starts by exploring the debate between deserving and undeserving.

Initial divisions of welfare recipients

Since the early Poor Law reforms of the 1800s, consideration has been given to deservingness of welfare support. Generally, such narratives are based on a moral prescription of who is worthy of support. This creates a different dynamic to policy debates, altering how policy responses pursue welfare goals. Thus, for example, when someone becomes unemployed, the provision of income support is reframed through the question of their deservingness rather than universal rights-based support; such deservingness may be determined by having paid regular National Insurance contributions to fund your claim for income support. However, a distinction can be drawn between individual faults and societal faults (Titmuss, 1967). It is possible to suggest that wider socioeconomic factors cause social problems, such as poverty, and so individuals cannot be held responsible; thus, all unemployed people are deserving of support. This is the basis of universal provision. Alternatively, the cause of unemployment can be located with the individual, resulting in the suggestion that policy needs to encourage the adoption of certain behaviours (to encourage the individual to return to employment). These tensions are played out through political debate about the causes of various social problems and the required responses, via debates around policy formulation, the level of discretion given to frontline welfare services, and wider factors such as media reporting and public attitudes. A complex web of factors is therefore drawn into the debates around deservingness.

In particular, the political debate – as with public attitudes – can be influenced by the media. Media outlets can often replicate such narratives but also generate a public perception that, for example, fault *does* lie with the individual. Usually, a role is played here by 'moral panics' (Cohen, 2002; Goode and Ben-Yehuda, 2010), whereby concerns over a (perceived) troublesome group are expressed through the media feeding into public anxiety and the demand for the state to respond. Stigma (see Chapter 6) plays a significant role in the formation of this, in terms of labelling certain groups of people and judging not only their access to welfare but also their worth to wider society. These pressures inform a notion of undeservingness, which has more recently been illustrated with the notion of an **underclass**.

The underclass

In his discussion about the underclass in the UK, Murray (1996) suggested the concept refers to a *degree* of poverty but to a *type* of poverty linked to perceived personal characteristics: 'Other popular labels were "undeserving", "unrespectable", "depraved", "debased", "disreputable" or "feckless" poor' (Murray, 1996:24). Pilkington (1992) suggested that the term gained popularity as a result of economic polarisation resulting from economic changes in the 1970s and recognised disadvantages of minority ethnic groups and women. Specifically, however, the work of Murray (and others following in his footsteps) suggests that some people exhibit behavioural and cultural differences that single them out from the respectable working class, and that they therefore do not respond to their circumstances in a 'normal' way. Thus, Gilder (1981:122) states that this term refers to: 'a constant, seductive, erosive pressure on the marriage and work habits of the poor, and over the years in communities it fosters a durable "welfare culture"'.

At the core of the underclass concept is the view that welfare creates dependency, which erodes personal responsibility and self-help. Welfare support from the state does not encourage acceptable behaviours; rather, it removes the fear of poverty and insecurity necessary to ensure good behaviour and acceptance of responsibility (Murray, 1996). Welfare systems that rely on the state to provide support are the culprit. This provision is based on rights discourses, and sends a message that paying taxes is the only responsibility one has. Commitments to family and the wider community are obligations that are lost through the dependency fostered by state support. In essence, it creates a claiming class.

The culture of poverty argument started to gain credence as a result of Murray's arguments, especially in the US and the UK during the 1980s. Lewis (1966) argued that deprivation resulted from low material and social aspirations, which generate a new cultural norm within the community. Perpetuated through parenting practices, this gives rise to new generations of citizens who have grown up accepting these impoverished cultural values. For politicians across the western world in the 1980s, this cultural dynamic of poverty was presented as the cause of the problem, which is counter to Lewis's argument; he did not specifically link causation of poverty with culture. However, such pathological explanations were drawn into arguments around the underclass, drawing policy attention to individual characteristics and marginalising the impact of socioeconomic forces in the creation of poverty and other social problems. This is problematic, as Field (1989) and Rex and Moore (1979) have used the concept of the underclass to draw attention to these wider structural factors. Field suggests that individual behaviours have little to do with the cause of poverty; rather, the poor (and often minority ethnic groups) live in a state of deprivation because they have limited access to secure, well-paid jobs. Furthermore, changes in economic policy pursued by government, as well as reforms to welfare provision, reduce the support provided. Rex and Moore offer a similar argument, referring explicitly to the discrimination experienced by minority ethnic groups in trying to access housing and other services, resulting in impoverishment. Regardless of this, state provision of welfare support has often been associated with the dependency messages suggested by Murray (1996), which has consequently moved policy practice away from universal provision to consider means testing and conditionality, explored shortly.

The label of 'welfare queens' in the US (not in the way Le Grand uses the term 'queens' to review motivations) and the more recent idea of troubled families in the UK have sought to capture many of these dependency arguments. This focus on individual behaviours has continued to gain support, despite the fact that:

> [t]hese ideas are unsupported by any substantial body of evidence. Despite almost 150 years of scientific investigation, often by extremely partisan investigators, not a single study has ever found any large group of people/households with any behaviours that could be ascribed to a culture or genetics of poverty ... any policy based on the idea that there are a group of 'Problem Families' who 'transmit' their 'poverty/ deprivation' to their children will inevitably fail, as this idea is a prejudice, unsupported by scientific evidence. (Gordon, 2011:5–6)

Despite evidence to the contrary, the language and perceptions persist. This has been attached to a focus on one of the central distinctions between deservingness and undeservingness: the relationship between the citizen and work.

Work and welfare provision

This debate regarding the underclass links into the earlier discussion of how imagined communities require a political authority able to distribute social goods on agreed, and popular, principles. The political authority seeks to reflect how certain characteristics and behaviours reflect a commonly accepted moral standard to be shared by citizens. But it does so without a critical evaluation of some of the underpinning assumptions. These narratives have proven to be popular ways of contesting the provision of welfare as a social right, suggesting that duties have been marginalised through the expansion of state welfare provision. A consideration of duties, in turn, drew out the relevance of work (as examined in relation to citizenship in Chapter 3) as the primary duty to be discharged by a citizen.

The principle of duty is placed over the idea of rights in the social sphere, thus ensuring that notions of desert or merit are promoted to protect a particular moral order – which, as we saw, had a number of gendered assumptions and biases. Yet, the centrality of work as a duty of the citizen forms part of a wider concern with work, and its connection to social policies, in relation to four dynamics:

1. Economic resources are required by the state to provide welfare services (this is based on growth through production, which relies on labour);
2. Decommodification reduces the need of citizens to rely on the sale of their labour to secure their welfare, and that of their family;
3. It can be established as a prerequisite for entitlement to some welfare services; and
4. It is a duty of all citizens.

It has long been recognised that work is a central feature of social policy: idleness was Beveridge's 'evil giant' of unemployment, and welfare systems are dependent on tax revenue largely generated through employment activities. While research has indicated that 'good-quality' work is linked to lifelong health and wellbeing (Waddell and Burton, 2006), historically there has been a more mechanical link between work and social policy. It also features in Marshall's (1992) discussion of citizenship: workers should put their best effort into *good-quality*, *worthwhile* work. Finally, such views have not only persisted over time but also morphed. One illustration of this is embedded within the SID of Third Way advocates, such as the UK Labour Party and the US Democrats during the 1990s (Levitas, 1998). Here, social inclusion was presented as dependent on employment for providing the resources required to participate as a full citizen. This instigated a number of welfare reforms, especially in relation to welfare-to-work initiatives, to facilitate a move from unemployment to employment.

Yet, such analysis often overlooks how work itself is defined. This is fundamental, because work is often presented as the *opposite* to welfare: if one is not in work, then one is 'on welfare'. The wider sociology of work has relevance to these debates; it cannot be fully surveyed here, but as an introduction, Grint and

Nixon (2015:6) suggest that: 'Work tends to be an activity that transforms nature and is usually undertaken in social situations, but exactly what counts as work is dependent on the specific social circumstances under which such activity is undertaken and, crucially, how these circumstances and activities are interpreted by those involved'.

As always, language is important here; how work is depicted in discourse and policy documentation, or in our day-to-day lives, indicates what is glorified and what is despised. As noted later in relation to the family, this can have gendered assumptions as to what roles individuals will have: work often linked to employed activity, but rarely domestic work, clearly demarks the former as glorified and the latter as despised. In relation to the state and social policy, this is, in part, a distinction between the economically active and inactive. It emphasises formal employment because this is what not only pays the taxes and National Insurance contributions that underpin public expenditure but also reflects the dominant economic ideology (we will explore this in Chapter 7). What is important at this point is how work is given a prominent role in the construction of both citizenship status and the welfare system. This reminds us of the integral relationship between full employment and welfare provision (as argued by both Keynes and Beveridge; see Chapter 2). As such, while significant work in Sociology and beyond questions this definition of work in relation to paid employment and its supremacy in contemporary societies (see, for example Frayne, 2015), welfare debates (rightly or wrongly) retain employment as a central component for the attainment of welfare outcomes.

Thus, deservingness of support is tied, in some way, to a history of employment and contributions through the tax system. If the duty of each citizen is to be in gainful employment, taking greater responsibility for the welfare of themselves and their families (see Chapter 7), then universal services responding to specific social problems (such as unemployment) become inefficient and ineffective. They fail to appreciate the nuance of behaviours that result in lack of employment because they tend to respond to wider socioeconomic contexts and pay little attention to what individuals must do for themselves. Such analysis builds on ideas we have already explored: Hayek's critique of the state and the concept of social justice to promote the free market, and Novak's concept of freedom suited to the operation of the free market.

Summary

The foregoing suggests that, despite the general argumentative turn towards universalism, historically there have been critiques of this. On the one hand, the duty to work remains the primary focus behind policy. As such, efforts to tackle dependency on welfare need to reinstate a work ethic; certain cultures develop, which are enhanced by welfare provision, which fosters dependency. On the other hand, this created political space for *pathological* explanations of *social* problems: individuals' behaviours are at fault and need correcting. This is illustrated in Figure 5.1 as the three pressures that have generated interest in more selective, as opposed to universal, services. As we will see, however, while these three debates have dominated recent arguments for selective services as opposed to universalism, there is a needs-based argument for the use of selectivism as a means of targeting resources with greater effect. We will review these various arguments throughout this (and the next) chapter.

Figure 5.1: Pressures towards selective service provision

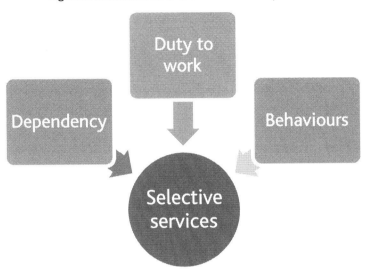

Selectivity: an alternative approach?

The centrality of work and the perceived existence of a dependent, undeserving underclass have informed the design of welfare provision. There are two prevailing trends relevant here. First, some inequalities do exist in society that require a state response: some form of social policy intervention to address inequalities where they are not the result of behaviours and lifestyle choices. Second, that work is a core duty of the citizen; as such, welfare provision should in some way support the unemployed. For those who have demonstrated a history of work, there is entitlement to welfare support; for those with a history of unemployment, support is either stigmatising or seeks to encourage behaviour change. In practice, however, policy rarely distinguishes between the two groups, as we will discuss shortly. In both instances, universal services may be inappropriate. Rather, targeting support at specific geographies or categories of people, or even establishing conditions to secure entitlement to support, may offer more suitable alternatives for achieving policy aims.

Selectivity and citizen support

A key aspect of policy making is the allocation of scarce resources. Often, demand (or need) exceeds the supply of welfare provision. The drivers of demand are varied; for some, this relates to socioeconomic changes, a context beyond the individual's or group's control, which creates new possibilities as well as problems to which policy seeks to respond and alleviate. Others argue that the rise of the welfare state reflects political parties responding to untameable public demand and capitulating to these requests to secure political success. Here, our concern is not the drivers but the consequences. Scrivens (1980) suggests that there are two responses. First, restrict provision – by denying it, limiting access, establishing eligibility criteria and so on. Such an approach underpins the development of selective provision and means testing: seeking to focus limited resources where the need is greatest. This could rely on rationing, whereby demand exceeds supply, and attempts to balance supply and demand at the point of delivery (Spicker, 2008). Charges, waiting lists and eligibility criteria are some ways in which services have been rationed (for example, see Klein and Maybin, 2012). Second, according to Scrivens, it is possible to dilute provision; this is simply a reduction in the service, offering less, so that resources are used to provide *some* level of support.

Thus, rather than promoting universal services, there has been a push for selectivism. Selectivity is a term used interchangeably with targeting. The former means, quite literally, that provision is intentionally for specific (select) groups and is not universal; it implies that there is a distinction between groups, which is reflected in the services provided. Thus, some particular needs that only certain groups experience may require intervention. Such support could be provided as a right (for example, the recognition of the additional cost of children triggering a child benefit to all households with children) or through a needs test: an assessment of income, for example, to determine eligibility for support.

Targeting is slightly different, as it can refer to goals or objectives to which efforts are directed; for example, more resources for a particular health condition, or the creation of services in particular geographical locations where there are greater health inequalities. In the first example, any citizens who currently or might experience the health condition will benefit from additional support; in the second, everyone resident in the identified geographical areas will benefit. Therefore, targeted services can be 'universal', in that all who meet the parameters of support gain access without a need for a further needs test. Selectivism, however, requires some form of assessment to recognise the needs exhibited.

Selective services are efforts by government to focus provision to meet the specific needs of individuals or groups. Often, these are aimed at people in lower socioeconomic groups to help them meet exceptional needs. But such provision can also recognise benefits to be provided to specific groups, such as disabled people, widows/widowers, pensioners and so on. By its nature, however, the provision of selective services requires a complex layer of administration.

Essentially, the cost resides in the need to employ assessors to carry out assessments of claimants and determine the legitimacy of their claims. This requires not only the employees to conduct assessments but also the wider bureaucratic mechanisms and organisations within which such assessments take place.

Service provision is dependent on two primary activities: the willingness of the citizen to identify themselves as being in need, and a means test. The means test is the method through which the need of a citizen is measured and determined to ascertain whether they meet certain (predefined) thresholds, which enable support to be provided. Such testing can be utilised in a number of settings, such as adult social care, income maintenance provision or financial support to attend university. However, efforts to target resources at select groups are often open to critique because of the two debates – the issue of deservingness and the practice of means testing – which we will explore in turn.

Deservingness

The deserving poor tend to be classified as 'those in social groups who were not felt to be able to do much to help themselves ... For them poverty was an unfortunate event and would justify state help to alleviate their plight' (Alcock, 2006:9), Children, the elderly and disabled people often fall into this category. The undeserving poor, however, are the working-age population (traditionally men) who can, and are expected to be, in employment to support themselves and their dependants. If in poverty, this is seen to be the result of idleness, and potentially criminal or other morally repugnant habits, which can be changed to encourage employment and self-sufficiency. The undeserving poor therefore have a number of labels attached to them, such as scroungers or skivers (people who actively avoid work), and are contrasted with strivers (people who want to achieve). Such views not only inform political debates and influence public attitudes and understanding of social problems but can also be found in explanations of problems and proposed solutions.

The underclass theory presented by Murray (1996:24) draws out similar ideas in relation to the US:

> In the small Iowa town where I lived, I was taught by my middle-class parents that there were two kinds of poor people. One class of poor people was never even called 'poor'. I came to understand that they simply lived with low incomes, as my own parents had done when they were young. Then there was another set of poor people, just a handful of them. These poor people didn't lack just money. They were defined by their behaviour. Their homes were littered and unkempt. The men in the family were unable to hold a job for more than a few weeks at a time. Drunkenness was common. The children grew up ill-schooled and ill-behaved and contributed a disproportionate share of the local juvenile delinquents.

Murray argues that the welfare state acts in ways that makes acceptable short-term behaviours that are damaging in the long-term. Policies encourage bad behaviour, as they erode responsibility, self-help and individuality. Policies also remove the fear of poverty and insecurity necessary to ensure good behaviour and acceptance of responsibility.

Murray suggests abolishing the welfare state and replacing this with a small grant, which citizens use to make their own welfare decisions. Should they spend it too soon or unwisely, that is their fault; there will be no additional state support. Other arguments, however, have put forward a move towards residual welfare services, providing the bare minimum required for survival and changing how some policies, particularly social security, work to promote responsibility (the introduction of conditionality, considered below).

Means testing

A means test is, essentially, an assessment carried out of a citizen's circumstances (usually financial) to determine if they lack sufficient resources to support themselves. According to Titmuss (1971:116), the design of means-testing mechanisms must reflect a number of key tensions/debates regarding how to:

- define people outside of employment, and the level of income they should receive as a minimum;
- determine charges or rents for services, and who should and should not pay those charges;
- determine who should receive free services while the rest of the population buys the same service on the market, or payment for public provision and who is entitled to a reduction in a universal change; for example, the UK has council tax (a property tax that, in certain circumstances, can be reduced) and entitlement to free prescriptions for some in England, whereas in Wales and Scotland they are universally free for everyone.

Titmuss considers these factors because they relate to the minimum cost of living in society; lack of income determines the ability to secure these goods and therefore maintain our welfare.

A number of additional complex considerations feed into the design of selective services, which require consideration by policy makers. Depending on the intent of policy, these considerations can include a range of issues, such as the need to:

- deter people from using or abusing a service;
- induce a sense of inferiority (discussed shortly in relation to stigma);
- develop different standards of service;
- raise revenue;
- help students from poor families to access university;
- ration resources.

This list is by no means exhaustive; the point is that the means test will always vary in design and application. Inevitably, this leads to greater complexity and increasing costs to design and administer in comparison to universal services.

Further illustrating this complexity, Titmuss (1971:116–7) explains how:

> Not only must means-tests differ in content, scope, characteristics and frequency according to their particular functions but, more complex still, they must differ in all these factors according to (a) the kind of service or benefit provided and, to some extent, the causes of need; (b) the actualities of need; immediate and temporary, weekly, monthly, yearly etc.; (c) the characteristics of the consumer (age, sex, marital and household status, dependants, etc.); and (d) the extent to which a variety of economic, social and psychological incentives and disincentives have to be taken into account in the structure and operation of the test.

This complexity is exacerbated by the need to draw a line – to determine who will or will not be included within the parameters of provision. This consequently results in some individuals narrowly missing out on provision because they have, for example, an income slightly higher than the means-test threshold, or because they have a 'spare room' in their house and therefore have their housing benefit reduced (commonly referred to in the UK as the 'bedroom tax'). As illustrated in Chapter 3, need is neither easy to define nor grasp. A means test must seek to operationalise theoretical debates into a measure against which citizens' incomes can be considered (although it is important to note that a means test need not only be applied to income).

Additional challenges to the use of means testing include the risks associated with indicating you are a 'needy case'. First, there is the potential for being refused support; just because you feel (and express) you have a need does not mean the need will be met. It depends on another's opinion as to whether you meet the set entitlements – or, in some cases, their own discretionary judgement. Second, the process of signalling your need requires a willingness to disclose your health status, relationship status, inability to cope or poverty. Securing assistance through means testing can be a shameful and stigmatising experience (we explore this in detail in the next chapter). These feelings can generate isolation and withdrawal and/or a breakdown in social cohesion, potentially threatening efforts to create a common citizenship status integral to nation-building projects. For Titmuss, among others, this is the primary weakness of selective provision compared to universal provision. Spicker (1988) notes that the approach to means testing is intrusive, and starts from a position of assuming that claimants will be dishonest. This, in turn, is likely to enhance feelings of stigma and shame.

The implementation of policies based on means testing may therefore have a number of limitations, which have potential consequences for achieving broader policy aims. For example, policy makers and advocates seeking to promote egalitarian ideas may argue that selective services instinctively treat citizens differently; difference, rather than social rights, becomes the basis of welfare support. A consequence of this is to divide people in to haves and have-nots, which undermines efforts to achieve equality and justice. However, as Fitzpatrick (2001a) notes, it would be possible to argue in favour of means testing from the same egalitarian position. Accepting that citizens all have different starting points in life, we could target services at certain groups, using progressive taxation to redistribute resources vertically from the better-off to the disadvantaged. From this position, it would be possible to claim that universal benefits actually limit egalitarian aims. In providing a benefit to all, some well-off individuals will receive a benefit they do not need, limiting the potential redistribution of resources to lower socioeconomic groups: the danger of dilution. Rather, effective equal opportunities policies require targeting, but this would require a different justification than that currently found within means-testing arguments.

A further limitation of selective benefits relates to the claim that services for the poor lead to poor services. The argument here is that targeting resources at select groups sends the message that only certain types of people receive welfare. These people are often labelled scroungers, skivers and other terms seeking to reinforce the undeserving label. When services are presented in this way, a process of residualisation occurs. Means testing is a move towards a residual welfare state – the provision of services at the barest minimum, so that those unable to take responsibility for themselves and secure their own welfare have their minimal needs met. This residual provision, as Spicker (1988) notes, is a move towards control of the individual with the aim to develop them as a person. We saw this in the discussion of conditionality of citizenship, and will see it again in the next chapter. Pinker (2006) reflects on a number of these themes in the context of the UK in the 1980s, the rise of neoliberal economic and political theory across most of the western world. The rise of selectivism alongside a number of changes within broader conceptual debates fosters a residual welfare state, attached to a thin notion of welfare. Such an approach does not accept or promote the broader notion of flourishing.

As such, selective provision becomes important in relation to certain people with additional needs. For example, universal education is provided to children and young people up to a certain age, but additional provision is offered for children with special educational needs. The intent here is to note that certain groups have additional needs to be addressed. A different example will help here. All citizens have access to healthcare, but we know there are geographical differences in how long people live. This can result in area-based initiatives: selectively securing additional resources for particular locations to address the multiple causes of differences in life expectancy. Thus, we do not remove the universal healthcare provision from those with good life expectancy to compensate others; we retain universalism, and blend it with some level of selectivity. We will explore another way of framing this in relation to diverse citizens shortly. First, we must explore one recent consequence of mean–tested/selective approaches, which relates to the challenges posed to universalism above: the issue of conditionality.

Conditionality

Returning the notion of deservingness to the forefront of debate, conditionality recognises that there are certain duties to be discharged if citizens are to gain access to benefits, and extends this idea to establishing conditions for the receipt of support. The debate around conditionality is linked to the wider discussion of anti–universalist policy approaches. As Chapters 7 and 8 will illustrate, there have been significant changes in the wider political and policy context, generating a shift in language and resulting in significant reform of welfare provision. Such reform promotes a new contract, which seeks to rebuild the work ethic, create behavioural changes and promote a notion of citizenship steeped in individual and mutual responsibilities, not individual rights. This is the basis of conditionality. Support is no longer provided as a right, but by meeting certain requirements to gain support. The implicit assumption is that claimants are undeserving for not clearly demonstrating how they meet their duties. To respond to the morality concerns noted earlier, conditionality can be summarised as a set of expectations written into policy that claimants must discharge in order to receive the associated benefit. It is best illustrated in the following:

> Welfare conditionality is about linking welfare rights to 'responsible' behaviour. A principle of conditionality holds that that access to certain basic, publicly provided, welfare benefits and services should be dependent on an individual first agreeing to meet particular obligations or patterns of behaviour. Those in favour of welfare conditionality believe that individuals who refuse to behave in a responsible manner (for example engage in job search activities, ensure their children attend school), or who continue to behave irresponsibly (for example engage in anti-social behaviour, refuse to accept help in tackling the problems they may face) should have their rights to support reduced or removed. (www.welfareconditionality.ac.uk)

The key issue here is that the social right to a 'benefit' is altered – you are no longer entitled to provision; you must demonstrate your deservingness. This approach has gained prominence alongside the rise of active citizenship.

The notion of active citizenship seeks to promote voluntary and charitable work, defining the active citizen as someone who is individually and socially responsible, while simultaneously meeting the welfare needs of the less fortunate. This latter part is unclear. Is this through taxation, or through efforts to reduce central state provision of welfare in favour of local community provision, as overtly pursued in the UK in the post-2010 period under the guise of the 'Big Society' (see Ellison, 2011; Lister, 2011)? Policy efforts are essentially renegotiating citizenship in a way that reduces state provision of services in favour of other forms of non-state provision (this links to the important debate about welfare delivery; see Alcock, 2016). Related to this, Coffey (2004) suggests that the concept of an **active citizen** has continued to be the focus of policy, particularly in relation to young people and education. It was introduced into the UK national curriculum, seeking to promote certain moral values and the learning of practical competencies, and fostering a willingness to contribute at the community level. This illustrates that citizenship is not simply something young people are educated about; it is something they are educated *for*. Thus, as with the debates explored earlier, not only does how citizenship is conceived shape policy formulation but also the implementation of policy reinforces these interpretations.

There is a correlation between obligations and duties and the rise of conditionality. Access to social rights becomes dependent on fulfilling certain obligations as a prerequisite of support. Dwyer (2004:44) explains: 'Social rights are universal rights in the sense that once certain criteria of individual need, contingency or past contribution are met, access to the entitlements specific to that provision becomes available as a right'. Initially, such contributions are met through National Insurance (or similar) contributions to the 'welfare pot', securing access to benefits (such as social security or healthcare) in relation to a particular need (such as unemployment or illness). The work ethic is deeply rooted here: contributions are discharged via taxation on earnings and as such unpaid care and formative years spent in education were not recognised as contributions, resulting (in particular) in the initial exclusion of women from social welfare provision. While this has slowly (if incompletely) been rectified for women, young citizens have seen their entitlements renegotiated; age-graded benefits or the outright removal of provision have been advocated due to lack of employment and therefore contribution. Such changes overlook how education can be conceived as a contribution: gaining qualifications that will benefit or support wider society in the future (as with the debate about care, contribution through employment need not be the only contribution a citizen can make).

Regardless of such critiques the promotion of conditionality has resulted in a rise in welfare-to-work schemes, based on the arguments of Mead (mentioned briefly in relation to deserving/undeserving narratives). Originating in the US, this practice has gradually been drawn into other nations as part of their 'welfare reforms' (Peck, 2004). Entitlement to social security is now secured through meeting certain conditions (attending work interviews, training, appointments with advisors and so on), and failure to comply results in sanctions (usually various levels of reduction in social security income).

But this conditionality need not only apply to discussions of work training. Moral behaviour is also promoted through these policy changes. For example, in the UK, not only have there been suggestions that social housing tenants sign contracts that include the provision to seek employment (Wintour, 2008b) but also changes were actually introduced, and enhanced post-2010, to link behaviour and employment into tenure renewal (Fitzpatrick et al., 2014). Preceding this, there were efforts to use policy to promote 'respect' from citizens, especially young people. In the late 2000s, the UK Respect agenda sought to bear down uncompromisingly on anti-social behaviour (especially among young people) and to tackle its perceived causes. This was built on the notions of conditionality and active citizenship, and intentionally sought to bring together a range of government departments (from schools to policing) to intervene and promote acceptable behaviour, primarily from young people. Although the initiative was closed down in 2007, the lead figurehead post-2010 was placed in charge of a new intervention: the Troubled Families programme, which adopted many of the same themes. The key point here is how policy interventions have been established to influence and control the behaviour of citizens to conform to an established standard. Conditionality and active citizenship have been key ways of achieving this, shifting welfare away from the language of social rights. Presented as alternatives to universal services, conditional provision seeks to correct the behaviours, dependency and lack of work ethic claimed to be exhibited by citizens reliant on welfare support. This alters social rights and notions of citizenship.

Summary

There are arguments for a more select design to welfare than universal approaches. While this can be used to target scarce resources towards particular social problems or the needs of certain groups (such ideas overlap with debates around targeting), a parallel development has been pathological explanations of welfare needs in terms of undeservingness: the result of inappropriate behaviours and personal failures. These are often aligned to criticisms of state provision of welfare services: the suggestion that dependency results in a corrosion of character which needs to be rectified. Figure 5.2 demonstrates the four consequences of selective approaches to welfare design explored thus far. These suggest that on the one hand, resources are scarce and need to be targeted, either based on need or after an assessment of means; and on the other, the behaviours of certain citizens need to be changed – hence the implementation of conditionality. Blended together, variations of these different accounts support the development of alternative forms of support that do not fit the universal aim. While such approaches have gained popularity, they have limitations and critiques:

• additional costs and administration;
• stigmatising practices;
• erosion of rights-based narratives for welfare support.

Citizen welfare in a diverse society

As noted in Chapter 3, citizenship is often presented in a universal, totalising concept that prevents recognition of greater diversity in citizens. This diversity

Figure 5.2: Forms of selective welfare designs

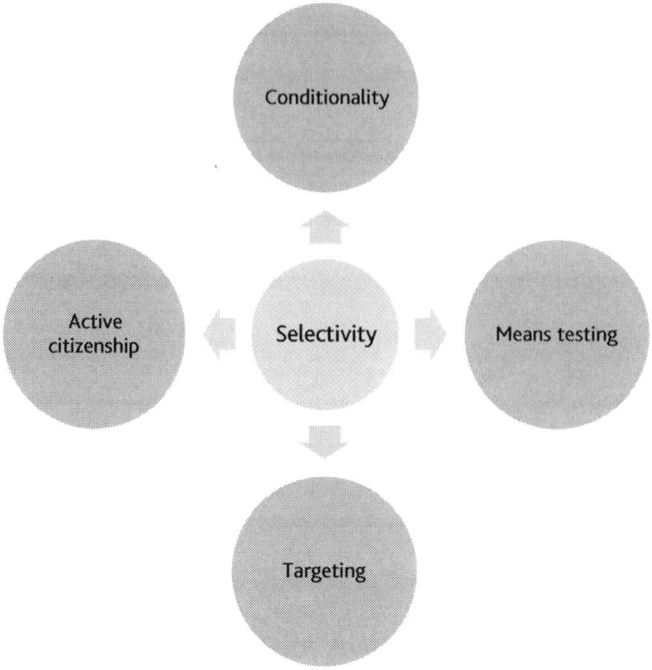

has often been drawn on to highlight the specific needs of citizens other than the male, white, able–bodied and heterosexual citizen.

Diversity challenges for citizenship and social rights

Some of the debates around different social divisions will be briefly reviewed here to facilitate a discussion of universalism and selectivism. Within anti–racist theories, attention has been given to the ways in which policy has sought to cast those from minority ethnic groups as 'other'. First, in relation to the concept of citizenship, early debates around definitions of minority ethnic groups focused on the concept of 'race' – the implication being that certain characteristics exhibited by some constituted a separate 'race' (skin colour being a predominant distinction here, but other attributes could include religion and culture). Such narratives were used to construct policies that had an implicit ethnic bias.

Contemporary analysis reiterates the socially constructed nature of 'race'. Such analysis drew out the term ethnicity as a 'self–conscious and claimed identity that is shared with others on the basis of belief in common descent, and may be linked to country of origin, language, religion or customs' (Platt, 2013:227). In part, this categorisation is necessary within Social Policy, for it facilitates research into inequalities experienced by different groups of people in their efforts to secure their welfare – demonstrating that access to services based on a common citizenship is not shared by all. It was not until various anti–discrimination laws came into force in the 1960s and 1970s that equal treatment was a feature of UK law. However, concern with institutional racism remains a prominent feature in analysis. This refers to how the design of welfare institutions continues to discriminate, leading to unequal treatment and outcomes by ethnic group, including the failure of an organisation to provide an appropriate and professional service to people because of their colour, culture or ethnic origin (Macpherson, 1999:6.34).

Black and minority ethnic group social movements have played a key role in campaigning for equal treatment and the protection of their human rights. This has required changing citizenship narratives to accommodate the 'other' rather than drawing a distinction from it. While efforts to tackle institutional racism can form part of a broader equality strategy, policy has also sought to promote integration and cohesion between different ethnic groups. However migration has generated new racial tensions within nations, often leading some to support an alternative policy approach based upon efforts to promote multiculturalism (Modood, 2007). This draws attention to the different lived experiences of minority groups, which opens up challenges to the all-embracing notion of citizenship that has driven much welfare reform. There is also a growing awareness (similar to that offered by feminist critiques) that the construction of welfare disadvantages minority ethnic groups because it does not sufficiently prioritise their particular needs. Here, the concept of social rights is insufficiently broad to encapsulate the diversity of life within a specific national territory (Rose, 1996).

In a similar way, Annetts et al. (2009) demonstrate how the lesbian, gay, bisexual and transgender (LGBT) movement has pursued efforts to not only promote equal status within the law but has also challenged stigma. The use of policy to prevent the teaching of same-sex relationships in school, efforts to prevent lesbian couples using IVF treatment to have children and the campaigns for equal marriage are just a few examples of these efforts to promote diversity in social life, which totalising narratives of citizenship, based on **heteronormative** assumptions of personal lives, ignore. Consequently, as with gender and 'race', the impact of social policy on LGBT people is an area of growing investigation within Social Policy, casting a light of inequitable treatment (McGhee, 2003; Carabine, 2009; Mitchell et al., 2013).

This brief account of different social divisions illustrates the need to consider difference within citizenship, which may challenge universal approaches. In the first instance, social movements can be effective in generating legal changes that recognise unequal treatment of certain groups of citizens. As Priestly (2016) shows in relation to disability, success in legal changes may create equality within the existing system, but this should not be assumed to be the same as social change per se; wider social structures and social relations may still be discriminating and exclusionary. For Priestly, this was why the social model of disability was an important element attached to the legal rights approach. The social model sought to fundamentally question and challenge social structures beyond legal changes within existing social systems: a critique of oppression, generated by social relations, to which legal change is just one part of the solution. Such social relations include welfare provision, where the concept of citizenship recognises diversity of citizens' lives and uses wider social change through welfare institutions to achieve:

- non-discriminatory welfare provision;
- redress for inequalities generated by diversity which have disadvantaged certain citizens;
- recognition of any additional needs related to diversity.

Inequality and the challenge to universalism

Such broader debates draw attention to inequality as well as the challenges of welfare provision that recognise diversity: there is no universal citizen, so debates around need, equality and social justice need to be rethought in relation to diversity. Thus, it is essential to explore inequality per se as a prelude to a wider consideration of the applicability of universal terms to welfare provision. It is not the intention here to explore specific challenges of inequality; insights into how specific groups of citizens experience inequitable treatment can be found elsewhere (for example, Hills et al., 2009). What is important here is to set out how, despite claims to universal needs and citizenship status, it is possible to identify specific groups as disadvantaged and discriminated against in contemporary society.

Welfare provision has a firm root in class and income inequality – a response to changing industrial conditions. However, the broadening of Social Policy investigations away from its class-based analysis to incorporate the wider range of social divisions and marginalised identities within society has significantly enhanced an understanding of not only the nature of people's lives but also the injustices they experience. This offers a series of alternative lenses through which we can interpret welfare and develop policies which recognise diversity.

Inequality is a pertinent issue in Social Policy not only because of its historic link with poverty and material resources but also because it can be used as a proxy for identifying where needs are not being met. Where inequalities exist in physical security or health outcomes, for example, it is clear that something is lacking: that a need is going unsatisfied. Understanding this is quite complex, and there are significant debates around the nature and construction of social problems that inform analysis of such matters (Connor, 2013). Put simply, the historic link between class and inequality informed Marshall's (1992) theory of citizenship and the development of the concept of social rights. However, as Dean (2012) explains, sociological analysis has also drawn attention to the interaction between socioeconomics and sociocultural differences in society: identities are as important as living standards. While occupational status may be a source of prestige and standing, a means by which social value is determined, this may not be the only factor to consider in relation to meeting needs. Rather, one's identity characteristics may influence the type of provision one is able to secure; for example, one's ethnicity, gender or disability may lead to inferior and stigmatised forms of support. As material security improved, as for example in the UK following development of the welfare state (George and Wilding, 1984), attention to social divisions grew – partially from an increased focus on the individual and personal identity, and partially from the rise of various social movements. These movements have fostered more diverse forms of solidarity than the class divides which informed early welfare provision. Research into welfare provision has since been able to draw this into an analysis of diverse citizens' lives, providing a new critical lens for our understanding of welfare provision.

It would be more appropriate to use the term social inequality to distinguish the potential range of inequalities that come under the consideration of Social Policy. This refers to a range of different groups (or divisions) in society: for example, gender, age, ethnicity, religion, disability, sexuality, and gender identity – as well as occupational social class, social background, housing tenure, nation and region, and area deprivation (Hills et al., 2010). Tackling social inequality has been an essential part of anti-poverty policies, often seen as the foundation upon which welfare is secured. The pursuit of welfare requires that attention is given to the full range of sources of inequality – but with a note of caution. As Dean (2012) noted, it is possible to see the development of the concept of wellbeing as a means of displacing the focus on income and wealth to consider other sources of exclusion (see Chapter 2). A similar comment could be made here: that a focus on the wider social divisions, while rectifying earlier ignorance, distracts from other fundamental causes of inequality such as material inequality.

The challenges for policy noted by Hills et al. (2010) included public ignorance over the extent of inequality. Despite progress, difference in economic outcomes remains, as unequal treatment and constrained opportunities persist in people's daily lives. Bagilhole (2010) offers an interesting introduction to equality policies from a Social Policy perspective, providing insight into this debate. Additionally, there is a life-cycle effect of social inequalities; that is, circumstances of birth impact on life chances across different life stages. Such accounts consider access to income and opportunities, but inequalities in access to welfare services have also been noted historically across a range of social policy domains (Rex and Moore, 1979; Mitchell et al., 2013; Bennett and Daly, 2014). On the one hand, universal services may facilitate equal treatment of citizens; on the other, they are limited when they are constructed around the 'sameness' of citizens and aligned to a particular concept of who and what a citizen is. Essentially, Social Policy focuses began by focusing on class and income inequality, and now integrates diverse social lives into this analysis. This complexity results in a significant flaw in early welfare interventions, which treated citizens as being the same. While securing universal welfare provision and recognising equality for all citizens are fundamental, there is a need for greater nuance in the analysis.

Diversity and postmodernity

The foregoing illustrates how diverse citizens' lives can be. This is a challenge for social policies to reflect on while trying to secure overarching policy aims (for example, securing a minimum subsistence, or a notion of justice). This generates debate around the role of social policy in relation to social divisions (Saggar, 1993; Drake, 2001; Carabine, 2001, 2009; Pascall, 2012) and locates social divisions at the centre of citizen debates, leading Ginsburg (1992:2) to note that:

> supporters and detractors of the welfare state would agree that one of its purposes is to heal fundamental social divisions or at least to mitigate social inequalities … There is considerable evidence that, in fact, the welfare state institutionalizes class, gender and racial divisions and inequalities. Yet it is also true that without the welfare state, the extent of class, race and gender inequalities and divisions would in most instances be even more substantial.

This analysis demonstrates that, while critical Social Policy has drawn attention to these divisions, they still occupy an ambivalent position in terms of how welfare policies respond to these citizens; such policies both address and reinforce the structural conditions that create divisions. However, an alternative analysis suggests that such divisions illustrate the limited explanatory power of grand narratives: theories that seek to explain all social relations.

Wider debates in Social Theory suggest that society had significantly changed from the industrial capitalist order of the early to mid-1900s; modernity was over, and society was moving into something new: postmodernity. As Chapter 8 will demonstrate, there are alternative accounts in relation to late modernity and risk society, but of relevance here is the suggested abandonment of universal aspirations (often found in key concepts of Social Policy), acceptance of local narratives and celebration of relativism. Thus, diversity is different from selectivity or targeting. The former refers to subcultures and self-determination, offering a means through which need as a concept can be articulated, which in turn generated new demands and expressions of citizens.

However, Social Policy at its core is about universality: of rights, need, citizenship and so on. There have been suggestions that efforts to promote the postmodern are fraught with problems. Hewitt (1994) highlights the impact of cultural diversity on definitions of and provision for need, and the abandonment of universal reasoning (the ideas embedded in grand narratives) presents difficulties in conceptualising structural inequalities and forms of deprivation central to Social Policy research and thinking. Taylor-Gooby (1994:388–9) has been openly critical of postmodernism, suggesting it obscures focus away from the wider structural relations of global society. Hillyard and Watson (1996:323) are critical of Taylor-Gooby, suggesting this new theoretical framework draws attention to 'a differentiated and fragmented impact of these trends globally'. The traditional approach in Social Policy is centred on the idea of 'the expert' and the building up a body of knowledge to provide solutions to a range of social problems, generating improved welfare for all. As such, Social Policy has a universal focus which prevents localised and differentiated narratives. Postmodernism challenges this by providing new forms of representation to reproduce expert knowledge. While this brief sketch of the debate is relevant, it serves to underline Carter's (1998) suggestion that postmodernism brings cultural and discursive practices to the centre stage of welfare studies, allowing welfare academics to embrace fluidity and difference. The result of this is to make universality redundant in light of particularistic terms.

Engaging with in this debate, Williams (1992) argues that Social Policy has always privileged certain groups' views and interpretations of social order, ignoring the interpretations and experiences of others. Within society, there are a number of social divisions that influence how we experience our lived reality; difference and diversity are at the core of social life. Williams suggests the development of postmodern thinking need not divorce itself from universalism (as do Thompson and Hoggett, 1996, in their discussion of particularism); rather, we should seek to find ways of developing a universal approach that recognises shifting multifaceted realities. Alongside this is a political dimension, which requires a consideration of how 'to articulate and identify common demands which unite those who are concerned with the pursuit of specific welfare needs' (Williams, 1992:216). Essentially, universal aspects of citizens' lives exist alongside diversity; we need an approach which recognises both.

Diverse demands are encased within narratives of human welfare, which provides a starting point for moving forward. Williams (1992:209) is clear that 'social policy is about collective ways of meeting social need. It has to deal with things central as well as local, things public as well as private, with the totality as well as the fragment, with the universal as well as the diverse.' The concept of citizenship must encompass a means through which basic entitlements can be secured through the collective articulation of need, with diversity generating specific or niche needs for certain groups. This does not mean such needs cannot be met – but neither does it require abandoning a narrative of universalism, as postmodernist thinking suggests.

The alternative approach is to reshape universalism to embrace diversity. Williams (1992) builds this around three key issues (see Chapter 9 for a discussion of some of these):

1. Articulating and identifying common demands that unite those with specific welfare needs;
2. Addressing fragmented, competing and conflicting demands; and
3. Generating greater empowerment and representation of citizens, and accountability of services, in a shift towards greater citizen–centred approaches.

Citizenship is therefore the vehicle through which creative and imaginative ways of developing services, and reinforcing the notion of entitlement through social rights, are possible. This can be done in a way which embraces and utilises the diversity of citizens within a narrative of collective provision. Initial responses to diversity have been to increase individualistic and market-based responses to welfare, representing the citizen as a consumer of welfare as if they are engaged in commercial exchange (Clarke et al., 2007).

Drawing on the last section, targeting is not problematic in and of itself; rather, it is the reliance on selective (means-tested/conditional) provision alone that should be avoided. Titmuss (1971) accepted that some social problems have 'deep roots' (which might relate to gender, ethnicity or any other social division). The question remains whether means testing is a practical possibility for welfare provision. With regards to difference, there is potential scope for developing a blended universal and selective approach to service design, found within the idea of progressive universalism.

Progressive universalism

The foregoing suggested that an element of selective/targeted services can focus scarce public resources where they are most needed. Universal provision, however, is better equipped to emphasise notions of citizenship and social rights to foster social cohesion and avoid any stigmatising consequences from receipt of welfare provision. Providing a starting point for navigating the two different sets of ideas is the suggestion of progressive universalism. The following discussion explores this idea through an examination of policies developed to promote this approach to service delivery.

In UK policy, the term was first used in the 2002 *Pre-Budget Report*, which argued for a 'new welfare system [that] puts into practice the principles of progressive universalism, with support for all, and most support for those who need it most' (HM Treasury, 2002:86). **Progressive universalism**, Wilby (2007) suggests, endorses the universal approach to state services, regardless of means: this is the *universal* aspect. The *progressive* element relates to the provision of extra resources to the most disadvantaged. The aim is to ensure that all citizens gain access to the services they require to gain assistance suited to their particular circumstances. Drakeford (2007:5) suggests that such services retain the essential element of universal provision, as they 'provide the glue which binds together a complex modern society and gives everybody a stake'.

What do such services look like? There are a number of ways they can be achieved. Gwatkin (in Starr, 2014) suggests that countries seeking to roll out universal healthcare can recognise that some geographical areas will have greater need for universal provision than others; this would result in early healthcare systems being established in these areas first, before expanding provision across the nation. A further example can be found in New Zealand, where the Well Child/ Tamariki Ora programme is a universal service provided to all babies and young children from birth to five years old. However, assessments are made during regular check-ups, allowing support workers to determine if families have additional needs; if found, they are referred to the Family Start programme, thus providing additional support without a stigmatising self-declaration of need. Additionally, in the UK the now-defunct Child Trust Fund (CTF) was designed to help all children from birth to develop a pot of savings they could use in adulthood. This provided a starting deposit for all newborn children, with additional support to those identified as being from the lowest-income households: providing support to all, but additional support to those with greatest need (Gregory, 2010). Similarly, experimental policies such as SEED OK in the US, while not yet universal in coverage, have similar features to progressive universalism. SEED OK provides US$1,000 to open accounts, but provides a match-saving incentive for young people that differs by household income. For incomes below US$29,000 per annum, the match rate is US$1:US$1 for yearly deposits between US$25 and US$250, resulting in a matched saving between US$25 to US$250 per year. For households with incomes between US$29,000 and US$42,449, this match rate is halved; so, yearly matching will be between US$12.50 and US$125. For households with incomes over US$43,500, there are no matched savings.

While these policy examples are useful, it is not so much their detail but what they are illustrating which has significance here. As Drakeford (2007:6) claims: 'Universal services, with a progressive twist, combine the advantages of the classic welfare state with some of the benefits which can be claimed for targeting'. The intention is to work beyond the universalism/selectivism divide in an explicit way. As Gwatkin and Ergo (2010:2161) remind us:

> Of course, to show that progressive universalism is feasible is not to argue that implementation will be easy. But consider the alternative: in the absence of a determination to include people who are poor from the beginning, drives for universal coverage are very likely, perhaps almost certain, to leave them behind.

This chapter has highlighted how certain debates around the work ethic, the underclass and deservingness have sought to isolate certain groups from public support, and therefore welfare support. Progressive universalism is an attempt to counter these charges while accepting some of the weaknesses levelled at universal provision. Although there has yet to be significant theoretical reflection on this term, its presence in policy objectives can be noted within a number of policy domains and across different nations. It is possible, therefore, to draw some tentative conclusions.

In terms of costs, there should be potential savings due to variation in levels of provision. Those with greater need receive more, while ensuring that all receive support; this avoids, to an extent, the limitations of both universalism and selectivism. Administrative practices in relation to cost may depend upon the policy design. The concern that means-testing provision can increase the overall cost can be addressed if other mechanisms are used as a trigger for additional support (such as claiming child tax credit, in relation to the CTF example, using existing administrative data to inform the delivery of additional support). Thus, existing practices can be used to keep the administrative burden low. Along similar lines, key characteristics or situations can be identified as requiring an additional form of support, and can be integrated into automatic triggers to receive the benefit without requiring claimants to go through the 'confessional' process of an application/means test to demonstrate not only deservingness but also need.

Yet, progressive universalism may be subject to some of the same limitations as those approaches it seeks to unite. Retaining the universal aspect will require a unified narrative of citizenship; this may require overlooking some key divisions between categories of people to ensure that the unified concept retains some meaning. It still provides some level of provision to all, and is consequently open to arguments about inefficiency over the use of resources: could we not give more to those in need by reallocating the little offered to those who do not need the support? The answer will depend on whether welfare interventions are simply about individual need or foster a sense of collective purpose and endeavour across a society. Additionally, the fiscal considerations and constraints of many governments are not neutered by the progressive universal framework; rather, this is part of a wider attempt to justify state spending, which seeks to challenge rather than satisfy financial constraint arguments. Government only has so much money to spend, and often in a context of tight finances. Finally, some specific needs may not easily integrate into a progressive universal service: homelessness and truancy, for example. Can these be addressed in a progressive universal framework, or do they rely on targeted intervention? What can be suggested here, as was suggested in relation to universal provision per se, is that some citizens suffering particular social problems will require specific targeted intervention operating alongside (not instead of) a progressive universal model of welfare.

Summary

The debate around diverse citizens has not only drawn out tensions in relation to social divisions but also broadened this consideration to an account of postmodern theory and the need for diversity to be at the core of social policy. This particular approach was critiqued briefly to suggest that we cannot abandon universalism outright, for it fosters close ties between citizens and is integral to justifying welfare provision. Rather, it is possible to integrate the key aspects of diversity into a universal framework seeking to promote the similarity that has been the basis of social rights, as well as to shape welfare responses to address particular needs of a diverse citizen body.

Chapter summary

This chapter has reviewed a number of complex debates that relate to the design of welfare services. Figure 5.3 starts to depict the decision pathways that follow various arguments in this chapter to inform the design of welfare interventions. The first pathway suggests three arguments dominate debate:

1. Needs do not exist, they are essentially false demands driving political promises which expand state provision and intrude on people's lives;
2. Equality of opportunity is facilitated through the free market; and
3. There is a duty to work in order to not only meet your wants but also ensure individual freedom from the state.

The first two points relate to a conception of welfare found within neoliberal theory (discussed in the previous chapters). This leads to the third argument about duties, which we have explored in this chapter. Combined arguments about dependency on the state and the need to revitalise the work ethic foster the development of welfare services based on conditionality.

This differs from the second branch in Figure 5.3. Here, welfare is shaped in the same way by three aspects:

1. A recognition of needs as social rights to be satisfied if we are to secure our welfare;
2. The state must intervene in the market (and wider social context) to address social inequalities through legal changes and redistribution; and
3. Despite a common humanity, there is variation in citizens' lives: a level of diversity which must be recognised in welfare provision.

Figure 5.3: Welfare design

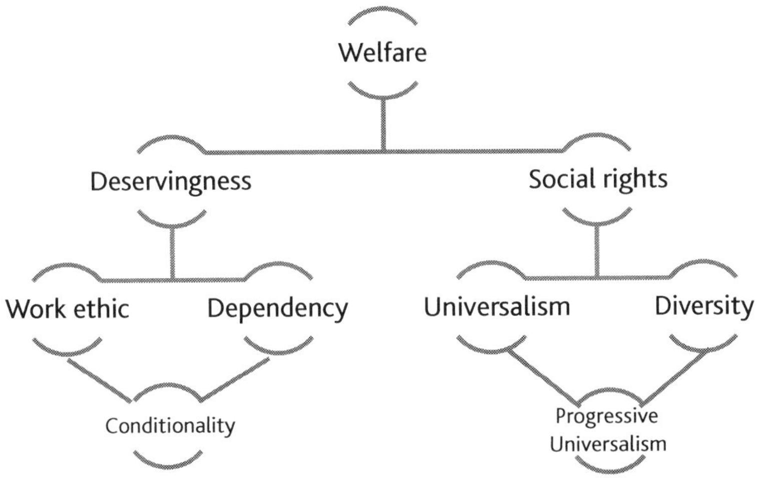

Thus, it is possible to accept both universalism and selectivism in a rights-based discourse, which would foster progressive universal welfare systems. There can be debate here. We can accept, for example, the two basic rights suggested by Doyal and Gough (1984) (personal autonomy and physical health) but recognise that the intermediate needs to secure these will vary across different social divisions. Thus, welfare can retain a universal framing and diversity in practice. However, welfare reforms have tended to go down the 'deservingness' path; this forms the focus on the following series of chapters. It is time to explore how welfare debates have significantly changed since the 1980s.

Critical thinking activity

Evaluate the suggestion that universalism is the most suitable means by which to secure social rights.

Further reading

Drakeford, M. (2007) Social Justice in a Devolved Wales. *Benefits* 15 (2) pp171–178.

Dwyer, P. (2002) Making Sense of Social Citizenship. *Critical Social Policy* 22 pp273–299.

Nelson, J.M. (1996) Promoting Policy Reforms: The Twilight of Conditionality? *World Development* 24 pp1551–1559.

Welfare Conditionality project. Available at: www.welfareconditionality.ac.uk/.

Don't forget to look at the companion website for more information.

6

How does policy shape the experience of welfare support?

Providing more and more welfare services will do nothing to tackle dysfunctional family lives.

Welfare is needed to protect families from the strains of contemporary society.

Key concepts in this chapter:
family • familisation • shame • stigma

The previous chapter demonstrated how criticisms of universal welfare provision rest, in part, on commentaries about the character and behaviour of recipients of support. Additionally, a critique of means testing highlighted the potentially stigmatising consequences of the design of services, which can act as a deterrent to take-up of a benefit or service. Exploring the concept of **stigma**, this chapter examines how policy narratives can be generated to produce stories of citizens and their needs. This is illustrated through a discussion of the **family**. The family is not only a focus point for a number of narratives around deserving and undeserving citizens but also a key provider of welfare: part of the informal sector mentioned in Chapter 4. Analysis of such narratives suggests that they seek to create popular support for welfare provision designed to intervene in certain people's personal lives and correct perceived defects. This is important to begin to understand, because it underpins some of the contextual changes we will see in the following chapters. For example, Fraser (2003), suggests that the new globalised era rejects the universalist thrust of its initial policies in favour of a new policy approach that creates responsible, self-disciplined citizens (see Chapters 7 and 8). For others, this is simply a continuation of policies that seek to engender social control (see Chapter 9). What is important here, however, is that the construction of the label 'troubled families' implies a moral failure of some kind.

Policy narratives: telling welfare stories

The idea of policy narratives is used to highlight how concepts can be drawn into wider political debate. These inform views on how a social problem (such as poverty) has been caused, the potential solutions to be pursued and the design of services to achieve this. Figures at the end of each chapter have sought to illustrate how certain conceptual arguments lead to particular approaches to welfare provision (for example, Figure 5.3 in the last chapter). One dominant perspective in current western policy, especially in the UK and US, presents pathological explanations of problems (individual fault/failure, not social/economic structures); these are associated with minimalist definitions of need, with welfare services designed along the lines of conditionality and means testing to correct behaviours and check claimants. Such policy designs are often analysed by researchers and academics in relation to the stigmatising treatment of claimants they generate.

Stigma

The discussions of deserving/undeserving and the underclass in the previous chapter highlighted how these distinctions have rested in the centre of welfare debates, which focus on 'dangerous classes' (Morris, 1994). A recent variation of this theme is found in the 'troubled families' debates in the UK. The suggestion here is that certain families reflect a '*Shameless* culture' (Cameron, 2011), referring to a TV comedy programme highlighting the chaotic and dysfunctional lives of an unemployed father and his family, and exhibit a range of inappropriate behaviours that need to be addressed: drinking, smoking, bad parenting, worklessness and so on. This is part of a longer historic concern with a perceived small group of 'troublemakers' or 'neighbours from hell' (Welshman, 2013), who exhibit characteristics of chaotic or dysfunctional lives.

The language used in reference to such people is our initial focus. We use terms such as stigmatising because it generates a derogatory image of those in receipt of (certain) forms of welfare support. It could also be argued that this is an intentional effort to influence public support for welfare provision and facilitate a move towards residual forms of welfare provision (with significantly less state involvement). Consequently, stigma has long been an essential concept for understanding not only policy narratives that generate change but also the consequence of accessing and using welfare services. As such, we need to explore what this concept means. Stigma can be defined as a visible or invisible stain that generates emotive feelings, both in the person carrying the stigma and in others towards that person. Typically presented as 'inferior' forms of physical appearance, conduct or ethnicity, we can reflect on two aspects of a stigma.

First, it presents the question of what is classified as social normality. Such ideas can be found implicitly, or explicitly, within concepts we have explored. For example, in relation to nation-building, we noted that ethnicity is a theme around which a common identity can be created in the formation of a nation.

We can see how stigma has previously played, and continues to play, a role here. Thus, **eugenics** arguments suggesting the inferiority of races can be seen as one driving force behind the development of the British Empire. The politics and subsequent policies found in Nazi Germany in the 1930s and 1940s, and the sterilisation practices of the Indian Health Service in the US during the 1960s and 1970s (Lawrence, 2000), are more contemporary examples. But these were rather explicit accounts of a perceived notion of normality. Less extreme examples can refer to the preference for the nuclear family, thus stigmatising other forms – particularly lone parents, but also families with same-sex parents. In a range of ways, dominant ideas inform narratives around a perceived social normality, which may result in exclusion, criminalisation and degradation of those who do not fit that image.

Second, as Baumberg et al. (2012) demonstrate, there are three forms of stigma relevant to social policy and welfare provision (Table 6.1).

Table 6.1: Forms of stigma

Stigma	Description
Personal	Felt stigma from receiving benefits, generated by perceptions of receiving a gift but not being able to give back
Social	Attitudes, thoughts and actions of the majority, and the perception and response to these attitudes by the stigmatised
Institutional	The framing structures of policy and its delivery

Such stigmas as outlined in Table 6.1 are generated by different social processes. According to Goffman (1963), there are three sources of stigma: physical, which relates to a visible or invisible disability or physical impairment that is negatively perceived by society; conduct, referring to attitudes, actions and behaviours disapproved by society; and negative perceptions of different ethnicities or religious affiliations (for example), which are considered to be tribal in their source. Page (1984) highlights how stigma can provide a 'master status trait', which overwrites all other characteristics and traits of an individual, fostering the assumption that their character is shaped and dominated by this one aspect; for example, being a lone parent, being LGBT, drug addiction or criminality. This is often reinforced by the visibility of the stigma.

When a stigmatic characteristic is visible, it can be attached to the category of discredited; here, the stigma is known about or obvious, and consequently intrudes into social interaction. As Page (1984:5) illustrates with the examples of a wheelchair user (physical), a well-known criminal (conduct) or a Black person (tribal), these are stigmas that cannot be concealed, and as such elicit stigmatic assumptions and attitudes within interaction. Other sources of stigma, however, are discreditable. Essentially, these are sources of stigma that can be concealed from others, and so do not disrupt social interaction. However, if discovered, they would be as disruptive as visible stigmas. Page (1984) again illustrates this with the examples of a woman who has had a mastectomy (physical), a gay person who hides their sexuality (conduct) or a Jew (tribal).

The disruption to social interaction caused by stigma results from this source of stigma becoming the focus of attention. As such, it can generate significant emotional responses within individuals, which can lead people to feel that their whole identity is tarnished. It is an intense feeling that can result in a range of different effects. Individuals may accept their stigma as evidence of inferiority, thus internalising the negative and destructive elements as part of their identity. Others, however, may challenge the source of stigma and take up 'stigma advocacy' (Goffman, 1963). Such individuals speak in front of both the unstigmatised and others similarly stigmatised, seeking to challenge the stigmatising views and narratives and illustrate the deservingness of the stigmatised. Consider, for example Martin Luther King or Nelson Mandela and their efforts to tackle stigma and discrimination based on skin colour. Alternatively, politicians such as the UK's David Blunkett, a blind former Member of Parliament, demonstrates the ability of blind people to engage in political occupations and reach high-level cabinet positions. Through such actions, whether intended or not, stigmas can be re-written – although this is a long and (potentially) incomplete process.

Where acceptance and advocacy are not pursued, people may try to avoid being stigmatised so as to facilitate undisturbed interactions, rather than embracing it and changing its meaning. Goffman (1963) discusses 'passing' and 'covering':

- *passing*: the ability to hide your stigma, this is usually easier for discreditable, conduct stigmas such as homosexuality;
- *covering*: where it is not possible to engage in passing due to the nature of the stigma, and so the inferior label is accepted, resulting in efforts to hide or obscure the stigma so it does not intrude into social interaction (here Goffman provided the example of US President Roosevelt, a wheelchair user who would place himself behind his desk before advisors came in for meetings to obscure the visibility of the wheelchair).

Both, however, preclude effective challenges to existing social values. Unlike the stigma advocates, therefore, such actions reinforce rather than challenge stigma. Additionally, such actions – especially passing – can be adopted by others with a courtesy stigma; that is, a stigma attached to someone via association with a stigmatised person, such as the parent of a gay child. For both stigmatised and the courtesy stigmatised, passing may be carried out in some situations to maintain 'face' and limit reputational damage.

Shame

Despite Goffman intentionally exploring the concept of stigma in relation to the reputational damage it generates, it has been suggested that the focus is really on **shame** (Walker, 2014). Shame entails a negative assessment of the core self, reflecting the perceived expectations of others and notions of powerlessness and inadequacy. This can lead to a number of associated psychological symptoms, including low self-esteem, depression, anxiety, suicidal thoughts and eating disorders. As a response to transgressions, shame not only engenders the disapproval of others but also relates to attributes, characteristics and circumstances that cannot be easily changed. However, the process of shaming is designed to bring about positive change in that individual's behaviours or attitudes. This differs from stigmatisation, which is unconscious, divisive and, at worst, malevolent. A shamed person feels they are not what they want to be, and aspire to change. The stigmatised person is not the same; they only feel shame if they are not proud of the stigma. Consider, for example, the difference between someone who accepts they are gay and someone who does not; the latter may seek to 'pass' in society, but may also seek to change their behaviours – and even their thoughts – in order to be different. Consequently, shame and stigma are intertwined.

However, while it is possible to adopt the stigmatised label and turn this 'on its head' to challenge the source of stigma, this is not so easily achieved in relation to shame. As Walker (2014:83) argues:

> Shame leads to social withdrawal, concealment, and fantasy; it saps morale and can precipitate loss of control resulting in mixes of anger, depression and despair. Only occasionally is personal good magicked out of the shaming process as when people strive to keep up appearances despite the risks entailed, and feel a sense of achievement in doing so.

While shame can be a source of motivation to fuel protest, Walker suggests that people in poverty and experiencing shame will likely lack the resources (economic and political) to change their circumstances. Additionally, while the family can be a source of support in addressing shame, it can also be a source of shame (in the poverty example, this may relate to the inability to provide for dependants or participate in reciprocal financial exchange). Subsequently, while some seek to challenge the blemish and remove the negativity attached to stigma/shame, for others this is not possible; the latter internalise the negative and acute awareness of their lack of capability to change how they live, thus generating a sense of shame.

Furthermore, Walker (2014) suggests that social stigma is used to justify patterns of inequality that help maintain the status quo, rather than pursue wider social change. As already noted, attitudes can be influenced to foster support for residual welfare services. In relation to shame, we have the same argument: the promotion of shaming narratives to help weaken the moral imperative to offer support to others. Only the individual can overcome the shame of poverty; they must improve themselves. Such narratives align with debates regarding the concept of risk, which we will explore in Chapter 8, and contribute to the re-articulation of entitlement concepts, which we started to suggest in earlier chapters. We now need to explore the relationship of stigma and shame to social policy.

How do stigma and shame relate to social policy?

Consider the following quote from Bosanquet (1902, cited in Squires, 1990:93), a social theorist and social reformist in the late 1800s to early 1900s:

> By the end of the 1860s the theory of the survival of the fittest has become a doctrine which many enthusiasts applied to human economy as well as the biologic world ... translated into a method of dealing with poverty, this meant the less relief the better. To be destitute to the point of having to ask for relief was to be guilty of a defect in character – in short, to be in need of reform.

Here, we can see reference to the provision of support only where citizens reach a point of destitution, which requires that through their guilt (and shame) they accept a defect in character and seek change. This not only assumes that destitution is the fault of the individual and their character but also shows how shame is presumed to be a useful tool in social reform. Such views are laden with potentially stigmatising attitudes and beliefs, and have formed the foundation of much social policy, through the distinction between deserving and undeserving citizens explored in the previous chapter.

To briefly recap, the deserving are seen to be those whose poverty is through no fault of their own, whereas the undeserving are seen to have caused their own impoverishment. This latter group has been referred to as an 'underclass' in more contemporary analysis offered by Murray (1996). Although there have been a number of criticisms of his work, the undeserving and underclass arguments are important in the analysis of stigma, because they offer stigmatising (or, perhaps more appropriately, shaming) narratives that seek to generate a change in the behaviours and characteristics of these identified groups. Thus, those who agree with Murray often suggest that stigma/shame can be a good thing, because the experience of stigma will ensure that children grow up realising that charity (especially from the state) is a disgrace and a personal flaw. Others suggest that such stigma and the context of impoverishment severely disadvantages those children in their physical, educational and personal development, and contravenes their human/social rights. Nevertheless, stigma has been presented as a means to tackle the suggested dependency culture, idleness, worklessness, addictive behaviours (be they gambling, drugs or alcohol) and promiscuous lifestyles that characterise the underclass; the argument here is that it can encourage people to want to escape their circumstances through self-help (a concept we explore in Chapter 8) and to develop self-sufficiency. For Murray, then, some non-negotiable messages are embedded in stigma narratives: notions of what is right and wrong behaviour, that it is better to be independent than dependent and that receipt of charity is a disgrace.

But this returns our attention to Walker's discussion of the relevance of shame to social policy. Shame can be used as a sanction for the transgression of failing to be self-sufficient and the inability to provide for your family. You are failing in your duties as both a citizen – to be in gainful employment and contributing to society (ignoring, as previously noted, other potentially important duties and their centrality to citizenship status) – and a parent. Shame, however, can result in depression or low self-esteem, creating significant barriers to the sort of change Murray (1996) advocates. There has been a range of critiques of Murray's work (see the commentaries in Murray, 1996), which focus on methodological problems and Murray's own ideological bias. Broadly, a number of challenges highlight the scant attention Murray gives to the employment and economic context. Changes in the types of work available (zero-hours contracts and underemployment linked to precariousness) have little to do with individuals' characteristics or behaviours (Shildrick and MacDonald, 2013).

One final consideration at this stage is the source of determinations of acceptable behaviours and characteristics. A certain power differential allows those in more privileged social class positions to influence and shape this debate, placing some forms of activity as inferior and as examples of the stigmatising/shameful behaviour to be corrected. While drug addiction or alcoholism are not behaviours to be endorsed, other cultural, community or class values that do not align with those of the ruling elite are not automatically inferior. Some practices can be valuable aspects of identity and local community respect, and as such have real value for individuals in their day-to-day lives (Mckenzie, 2015). Thus, our analysis of welfare requires that we not only broaden our view to recognise that other practices may be important to the attainment of welfare by some groups in society but also question the assumptions and consequences of the dominance of certain values over others, and avoid assuming that somehow 'superior' and 'correct' behaviours and values should be imposed unilaterally across all citizens.

What are the potential consequences?

Goffman (1963) suggests that stigma interacts with an essential part of our personal identity. Identities are constructed around various interactions and artefacts, which can range from official documents to symbols of prestige and stigma. Combined, these can have significant impacts on our self-perception, which brings us into a discussion of status. Goffman (1963:59) explains that 'the social interaction conveyed by any particular symbol may neatly confirm what other signals tell us about the individual, filling out our image of him in a residual and unproblematic way'. As such, status or prestige symbols reflect a well-organised social position and convey information about a special claim to prestige, honour or other discernible position. This contrasts with stigma symbols, which draw attention to a debasing identity and break the coherent overall picture of the individual, resulting in a reduction in our valuation of them. In some circumstances, discredifiers can break the coherent picture in a positive way, such as a migrant with impeccable English. However, for our discussion, we focus on the negative consequences to status and the implications of these in welfare debates.

As suggested previously, welfare policy is shaped by particular discourses and ideas, presented through different ideologies, which facilitate the explanation of social problems and proposed solutions. These discourses, however, place certain values and ideas as preeminent in society and somehow right. Atkinson et al. (2012) suggest that those with the most resources and power impose their own way of life to determine what activities, behaviours and values are legitimate, worthy and 'right'. Those who lack the material conditions for achieving and maintaining these are 'denigrated'. They draw on the concept of symbolic violence to suggest that gentle, imperceptible, invisible messages are communicated to individuals and groups to reinforce feelings of unworthiness through the promotion of acquisitiveness and claimed virtues of self-sufficiency and resilience. Stigma and shame, therefore, are labels attached to those who fail to establish and demonstrate the presence of such symbols. Similarly, Sennett and Cobb (1993) suggest class is about not only wealth or power but also meanings attached to different symbols associated with class. They suggest that there are 'hidden signals of class', through which one's worth as a person is judged against the lives, occupations and items that society holds up as symbols of esteem. Such symbols are used to establish a hierarchical respect within society.

Thus, while social policies are designed to promote welfare, they are shaped by concepts including stigma and shame; they can generate symbolic violence. Presenting people as lacking in work ethic, respectability and sobriety generates feelings of shame. The idea of an underclass implies that you exist below the hierarchy in society. Related to this is the idea of status anxiety, whereby the cumulative effect of these subtle attacks on one's status increase incidence of depression, anxiety and a range of other negative health consequences. Marmot's (2005) study of status syndrome suggests that it is inequality in the social system that creates this situation, but our explanations focus on characteristics and behaviours and thus reinforce and perpetuate systems of disadvantage and harm (see, for example, discussions of social harm in Pemberton, 2015). Welfare systems were designed, on the whole, to tackle the social inequalities that cause these harms. However, post–1980s changes could be seen to reinforce status anxiety; interventions initially designed to help you achieve your welfare as a right of citizenship have moved towards conditional, residual forms of provision, which affirm your identity as being inferior to a 'normal' citizen. Such welfare systems result in people lacking autonomy, and while notions of need are clearly important here, they are now attached to the requirement to demonstrate your deservingness by accepting the conditions of welfare support that simultaneously confirm your stigmatised characteristics and your personal shame.

The overarching problem is that stigma/shame not only have these consequences for individuals but also damage society. As Walker (2014) argues, shame results in defensiveness, interpersonal separation and distancing. It generates an inward focus on one's own hurt and limits empathy with other citizens, which can lead (rightly or wrongly) to blaming them for the shame you experience. Walker cites Scheff to suggest that this situation generates hostility within the shamed, which can underpin perceived anti-social behaviour that fractures social relationships, erodes mutual respect and solidarity. This in turn generates less forgiving attitudes in the wider community and reinforces the move towards more punitive welfare interventions. Consequently, welfare policy increasingly and overtly seeks to control behaviours in order to intervene in people's lives to manage their risk factors (as we will see in Chapters 8 and 9).

Such narratives seek to influence public perceptions of and attitudes towards welfare support. While this is a complex area of research and debate, the general argument is that arguments drawing on stigmatised views of citizens intentionally seek to promote residual, limited-state welfare systems. Seeking to show claimants rather than social systems as defective serves only to promote the political ideas associated with academics such as Hayek, Freedman and Murray and politicians such as Reagan, Thatcher and their contemporaries of similar political persuasion. Overlapping with the conceptual arguments explored in the following chapters, this creates a powerful framework for reshaping welfare systems, and challenges the claimed altruism that underpinned earlier development of welfare provision. Taylor-Gooby (1985) illustrated how public attitudes have also supported the distinction between deserving and undeserving. Combined, such views generate support for conditionality in welfare provision. This not only questions the idea of equality of treatment but also has implications for the concepts of citizenship and need. Needs do not change if we accept that there are some universal requirements to be met in order to secure our individual (and societal) welfare. Is there not therefore a moral duty to ensure people fully survive and engage in society, rather than perpetuate the idea that some are worthier than others? Baumberg et al. (2012) suggest that the changes in attitudes indicate a lack of feelings of reciprocity, reducing willingness to access services (see also Jensen and Tyler, 2015); consequently, recognising the importance of altruism and reciprocity in welfare provision.

Summary

The previous section illustrated a number of ways in which stigma influences welfare debates. It is essential for understanding not only the experiences of those who claim welfare support but also the design of welfare support and institutions. This is a useful reminder that the concepts examined can be used to underpin policy design as well as to provide analytical lenses through which policies can be assessed. As such, Figure 6.1 illustrates how several overlapping arguments and ideas converge into an argument in favour of residual welfare support; that is, providing a bare minimum for survival because support is considered to generate dependency, while also suggesting that social problems result from individual faults and failures and so are not the state's responsibility – except, perhaps, to correct.

This adopts a restricted definition of welfare with survival rather than flourishing at its core. As illustrated in earlier chapters, there are broader definitions. While there has been a gradual movement towards residual welfare (and growing support for the various arguments that underpin this) it is not inevitable. We will soon investigate some of the broader contextual concepts and narratives that are helping to facilitate this shift, which link to stigma and shame. The final chapter also provides some insight into how to challenge some of these developments. But before we can go any further, we need to consider how narratives interact with wider social changes, and how policy can support – or seek to resist – change. The family provides an example of this.

The family as an example: definitions and debates

Social policy has had a long preoccupation with the family. In the UK, the idea of the underclass has paid particular attention to single parents, and the contemporary focus on troubled families continues this 'concern'. Other debates have considered both the centrality of the family as a provider of welfare and the support required to ease the burden and familial conflict that care responsibilities may engender. Yet,

as with the notion of citizenship, the definition of 'the family' was initially rigid and presented in a universal language, which did not necessarily reflect social developments. Welfare policies, however, sought to support more traditional family forms, which have now come under increasing scrutiny. This section continues to explore policy narratives through the dominance of a particular concept, shifting now from stigma/shame to the family; we will also note overlaps between the two.

Figure 6.1: Narratives supporting residual welfare provision

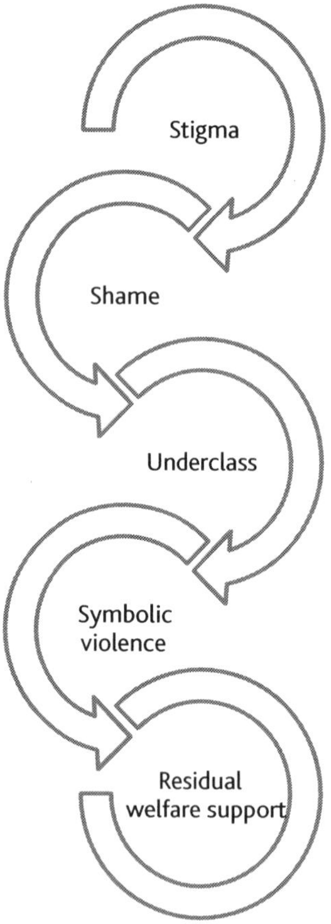

Stigma

Shame

Underclass

Symbolic violence

Residual welfare support

The universal family

The family is considered to be an important institution within, and a building block of, society; it offers a sense of identity and belonging to its members, and failure within families is seen as an indicator of broader societal failure. Murdock (1949) defined the family as a social group characterised by a common residence, economic co-operation and reproduction, adults of both sexes (at least two of whom maintain a socially approved sexual relationship) and one or more children (own or adopted). This definition has quite specific characteristics, creating potential problems: other forms of relationship structure (such as polygyny, polyandry, extended families, the kibbutz and family formations in non-western tribal societies) all illustrate how Murdock's definition may not quite fit with family forms globally, and in western societies, same-sex families, lone parents and cohabiting partners are further variations that contradict the notion of a nuclear family. Responding to such claims, Murdock insists that the nuclear family is universal; it is the building block of these various forms and contains particular functions necessary for the survival of any society:

- facilitating biological reproduction;
- arranging the provision and consumption of basics (food and shelter);
- socialising young children into cultural patterns and approved behaviours;
- inducting individuals into established positions within the social structure.

Nevertheless, Muncie et al. (1995) note it is impossible to find a model of the family that will be universally accepted. Rather, the family is socially constructed. Hall (2002) suggests that, in the 18th century, there was no word for 'family'; rather, the term 'kin' was applied to reflect the wider household under the control of *paterfamilias* (father of the family who is father, husband, master and representative). From the late 18th to early 19th centuries, family become associated with blood ties of two generations, with co-residence and a male breadwinner. Alongside this, language started to associate men with the public sphere and women with the private home sphere, associating family outside of the public (that is, the state's) attention. This brief history starts to illustrate how the family can be seen as a social construction, created by lived social reality through the dominance and enforcement of certain values and norms. Such constructions continued into the 19th century, as middle-class values – particularly around gender roles – generated social reform that sought to take women out of the workplace. Thus, new gendered narratives informed the construction of the family during the early stages of industrialisation, which in turn start to be reinforced through policy.

Reflecting on policy towards the family, Muncie et al. (1995:1) state: 'ideas about the family generated in the political sphere may be partial or rhetorical, but also powerfully influence the ways in which we experience family life'. As such, political debate will generate various ideals, norms and stereotypes of the family, which in turn influence policy making. Policy designed to promote welfare will then reinforce these dominant norms, ideals and stereotypes (Muncie and Wetherell, 1995). Similarly to stigma/shame, we can see how policy can play a vital role in maintaining or changing these assumptions. A classic critique of social security provision illustrates this; think of the idea of a male breadwinner model, within a society that prioritises men in employment, and the assumption that women will remain within the home to provide care to husbands and children. Unemployment protection through social security provision is designed around these assumptions: protection for men as employees, and for women as dependents on a husband (care work is offered limited, if any, support through welfare provision). Such assumptions rested at the core of the Beveridge 'blueprint' for the welfare state. Efforts to question and challenge this model are about not only equality, equal care and equal employment between the genders but also redressing the power imbalance based on the social construction of gender roles. This is why feminist critique has emphasised the need to make the personal (or the private) political. Placing the family within the private sphere leaves it immune to critique of the 'dark side' of family life: exploitation (by men and/or the capitalist system), abusive relationships (emotional and physical) and the power imbalance, which establishes men as decision makers while relegating women to unwaged domestic workers catering for the needs of their husband (emotional, sexual and physical) and child rearing.

Diversity of family and relationships

Flawed assumptions about gendered roles underpinned a number of early attempts to create welfare systems. These efforts also made a number of assumptions about the type of families that existed, and assumed this would be static; essentially, that the nuclear family would remain the only form of family formation. Using the UK as an example, we can illustrate how families were not static in society – and nor will they ever be. The Office of National Statistics (2016) indicates that there are 18.9 million families in the UK, of which 12.7 million are married or civil-partner families: the most common type of family. Cohabiting couple families were the fastest-growing over a ten-year period: from 1.5 million to 3.3 million between 1996 and 2006. During this same period, there was also an increase in the number of young people (aged 20–34) still living with their parents. There have also been changes in terms of the numbers of single people living alone, as well as 'concealed families' (in which elderly relatives and adult children share a household).

Some sociological analysis has taken this further, suggesting there have been significant changes in society more broadly in terms of love and intimacy (Giddens, 1992; Beck and Beck-Gernsheim, 2002). This suggests changing patterns of family formation and development resulting from a wider reconfiguration in society, partly due to changes in employment, welfare, education and law (for example) creating new and inescapable pressures on the family, generating needs and pressures on individuals that create change. In part, Beck and Beck-Gernsheim suggest that the desire to have children remains, but the wider social support for doing so has fundamentally changed. As part of this analysis, Giddens puts forth the idea of a 'pure relationship', referring to social relationships entered into by individuals for their own sake – the relationship offers something to each individual that sustains the relationship, which not only starts to emphasise personal autonomy and choice but also draws attention away from the family towards other networks and friendships. Smart (2007) suggests this forms part of the wider focus on personal lives developing within sociological thought. Here, attention is given to bonds beyond kin and marital ties to encompass a wider range of relationships that citizens can have.

Roseneil (2004) draws attention to how such a conceptualisation of relationships also breaks down heteronormative frameworks, highlighting how networks of friends and ex-lovers are important elements of gay and lesbian lives – a reflection of the diversity of citizens' lives previously discussed. Generally, this has facilitated a focus on relationships with social significance, not just family ties. As such, policy should focus on not only family formations but also our wider social networks and personal relationships, as part of our concept of welfare. Kneale et al. (2014) argue for a relationship perspective to be adopted in policy making in response to the global financial crisis of 2008 . Similarly to the family perspective (Lewis, 2002), this seeks to support social relationships that weather the storm of economic recession. Although at present there seems to be limited engagement with this idea in wider policy debate and discussion, it is an interesting conceptual development. Such analysis may start to decentre the family as the central means through which policy intervenes into our welfare. It may also generate a debate about what relationships are appropriate – just as certain family forms have been promoted through policy as appropriate.

Muir and Cooke (2012) do suggest a need to rethink the purpose and intent of the state, and that questioning the goals and practices of government uncovers a need to find a new approach to governing. The collection of essays they edit proposes such a new model within the idea of the relational state. Embedded in their analysis is the idea that welfare reforms may have improved responses to social problems, but have also created new challenges resulting from uniform or mechanistic responses. There is growing recognition that many social problems, from obesity to climate change, require investment in human relationships – and that this human relationship element has been neglected. As Muir and Cooke (2012:7) state: 'Targeting only the outcome forgets that the way people are treated matters too – it underplays the role of relationships in improving people's lives. A purely outcomes-focused mode also involves certain people – invariably elites of various forms – deciding for others what they should choose to value.'

Consequently, it is suggested that human relationships should be placed at the centre of reform of welfare services and provision (Mulgan, 2012; Stears, 2012). For Mulgan, the intent behind a relational approach is to deepen the relationships citizens have with each other. Improving education standards (for example) is insufficient by itself because the state must engage in new ways of supporting the subjective/relational aspects of life – not just the material and objective. Thus, within concepts of welfare there is a need for a broader view, which seeks to include measures of happiness (one of the debates we started to explore in the opening of this book). This differs from Stears, who suggests that relationships are not simply another 'outcome' to be pursued, and that transforming welfare into a measurable number removes the distinctive human quality of the experience of relationships. Noting that relationships have increasingly become a key part of sociological understandings of the world, similar ideas have started to migrate into Social Policy debates. What remains unclear, though (as noted), is what sort of relationships policy might seek to foster as part of the promotion of welfare – and how policy narratives may promote some relationship forms over others.

These theoretical debates are important to recognise in our discussion of the family, but there are also other reasons to be aware of these demographic changes. It can be noted that there is some movement towards diversity of family formations, potentially illustrating a move towards post-traditional families (see Giddens, 1998). However, it is clear that married families remain the primary family form, despite political concerns to the contrary (as suggested by Murray, 1996) in relation to the underclass and a number of stigmatising narratives about the family. We need to recognise the diversity of family forms without necessarily passing judgement or making moralistic claims about the consequences of these shifts. For Giddens, recognising such diversity expresses the flexibility and rapid change that characterises contemporary society. Such views foster an approach in which governments should value (rather than judge) diversity in family type. Here, two policy approaches can be adopted: one seeks to support and stabilise diverse family forms, while the other promotes one particular type over the other (as we will see in the next section). We noted in previous chapters that the lived diversity of citizens' lives contradicts the assumptions of universalism within welfare debates, and the need to revisit universal arguments that allow for diversity, as opposed to the rigid imposition of one dominant perception of the 'correct' form of life people should live.

Efforts have therefore been made to recognise diverse forms through a range of welfare interventions. However, such policy often retains a focus on traditional forms of family. As Driver and Martell (2002) discuss, the New Labour government of 1997–2010 attempted to recognise diversity of family form and provide appropriate welfare support; however, within their policy documents and rhetoric, policy makers adopted a more moralistic position that promoted the nuclear family. This was presented using the phrase 'hard-working families' (especially post-2007), which lacked a definition and did not specify the family type under discussion, but highlighted the primary duty of parents to be in employment (returning to some of the debates around citizenship). A hard-working family could be a same-sex couple, lone parent or a nuclear family. Later developments in the policy narrative around the family can be found with the Conservative-led coalition government (2010–15), which drew attention to the previously mentioned notion of troubled families.

Such terminology is important because of the impact it can have on those listening – and this returns us to the policy narrative of stigma and shame. Lacking a clear definition, those hearing (for example) the term 'hard-working family' will seek to position themselves within this category. Implicitly, it assumes there is an 'other', a group of people who are not hard-working, without ever specifying who this group is – or even showing that they exist; the *implication* that they do is sufficiently powerful. Consequently, policy seeks to penalise this 'other' through a series of welfare reforms that promote the means testing and conditionality explored in the previous chapter. As such, and without clear evidence, the policy narrative has positioned welfare policy within the 'deservingness' pathway outlined in Figure 5.3.

Thus, family formation is used to imply a stigmatised existence, which citizens would not associate themselves with but assume that others – predominantly those in receipt of certain benefits – reflect. This happens despite evidence showing the short-term nature of much unemployment support (because those receiving it are moving quickly in and out of employment), and despite those who found themselves in need of support due to the financial crash of 2007 finding only limited, conditional support (even though they had 'paid in' to the system). The key point here is that policy narratives around the family create an implied social norm, which can be used to further facilitate welfare reforms based around 'deservingness'. What is often overlooked, however, is that welfare reforms rarely create distinct policies for 'deserving' and 'undeserving'. Generally speaking, there will only be one form of income maintenance to support the unemployed, which will treat anyone in receipt of it in the same way. Means testing and conditionality will be applied to all equally, regardless of any perceived distinction of deservingness. If you are not in employment, you are no longer in a hard-working family. The false assumption generated by policy narratives is that welfare systems will treat deserving and undeserving differently, but the reforms to welfare systems generated by such narratives have made this highly unlikely. Variations of this debate can be found in the following discussion of the family and social policies.

Summary

While the nuclear family has been presented as the primary form of family life, lived experience indicates that this may not be the case. Rather, there is greater diversity in the form of family life, and a focus on relationships can be broadened outside of immediate family. This is important because the dominance of the nuclear family perspective has filtered into a range of policy debates; it has become a particular policy narrative around which significant welfare provision has been organised and provided. Figure 6.2 starts to illustrate some of this debate. From this, it is possible to consider how the family (and relationships) is drawn into policy debates and (as the discussion of stigma started to illustrate) forms particular policy narratives around:

- the sort of lives policy makers find acceptable;
- how policy can be used to create/reinforce these narratives;
- the consequences for citizens' welfare, in terms of the family formations they live in.

Figure 6.2: Forms of family life

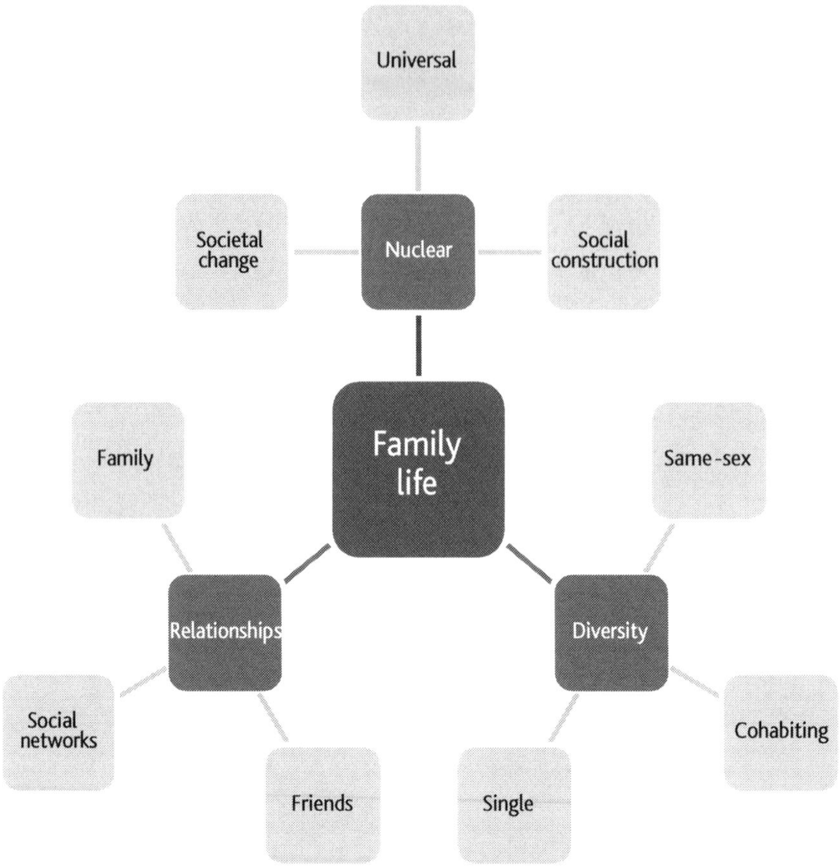

The family as an example: changes in welfare provision

As noted, family patterns shift and change as a result of a number of social changes, often instigated by the state. Changes in marriage/divorce laws, provision of welfare support, education and so on all generate changes in social life, cultural norms and practices over time. On the one hand, intervention into welfare will result in a shifting context in which families are formed; on the other, welfare systems rely on the family (as the central part of the informal sector) to provide welfare support. As such, it is possible for families to be supported by welfare but also relied on when the state (or other sectors) refuses to provide welfare support. Thus, the relationship between family and policy is not simply a socially constructed narrative; it is also a lived experience that can radically impact on people's lives (for example, see Calder's (2016) discussion of the family and social mobility).

Policy and the family

The foregoing has highlighted how policy narratives around stigma/shame and the family influence the design of interventions to influence welfare provision. Some hints of this, especially in relation to upcoming chapters, have been suggested. Here, we will make the discussion a bit more explicit and subsequently more policy-focused rather than purely theoretical, in a similar way to our discussion of progressive universalism. In Chapter 4, the discussion of the mixed economy of welfare (MEW) highlighted how state promotion of welfare starts from a decision to intervene – or not. As such, it is possible for nation states to limit their own welfare provision and allow the family to provide the bulk of social services and support. This **familisation** refers to the promotion of the family as a traditional institution in society and a provider of welfare. As Davies (1993:7) suggests:

> our free and reasonably successful society will be able to remain free and stable only when each generation moves into maturity and its civic responsibilities when it has effectively internalised those values which makes for freedom and stability. The only institution which can provide the time, attention, the love and the care for doing that is not just 'the family', but a stable, two-parent mutually complementary nuclear family. The fewer of such families that we have, the less we will have of either freedom and [sic] stability.

The Beveridge Report (which, as noted, highly influenced welfare provision) contained a number of gendered assumptions about welfare. It paid little attention to changes in employment patterns, abortion and divorce law and equal pay, which started to give greater legal rights to women to make decisions about their own lives. Thus, state support for the family retained gendered assumptions and arranged social support to favour men, assuming married women would be dependent on a male breadwinner. This reflects the concept of familism.

Familism (or familialism) has been defined as the means by 'which the interests and needs of individuals – men, women and children – are subsumed within the family as a whole' and consequently reinforced by welfare provision (Alcock et al., 2002:84). Explicitly recognising that the family is invested with greater importance than its individual members, family needs gain priority. Within the western world, as noted, the nuclear family has been presented as the principal unit for human ordering and functioning. Within Social Policy debates, particular attention has been given to this idea with the framework of **defamilisation**: 'the degree to which individual adults can uphold a socially acceptable standard of living, independently of family relationships, either through paid work or through social security provisions' (Lister, 1997:173).

Similarly to decommodification, this idea recognises that women have an equivalent to market dependency in terms of their dependency on the family to secure their welfare. The rise of the welfare state in many western nations, however, precipitated a process of defamilisation: the reduction of family provision, which the state interceded to replace with public services and in–kind and in–cash benefits (primarily to individuals but also to families). As Bambra (2007:326) states, '[d]efamilisation can therefore be utilised as a way of testing the extent to which welfare states, and welfare state regimes, facilitate female autonomy and economic independence from the family'. Subsequently, two debates can be drawn out. The first refers to the extent to which the state offers support to the family; the second refers to the extent to which individuals, especially women, can meet their needs independently of the family. Which route a nation takes will depend on its own history and tradition; hence, there are noticeable differences between (for example) Japanese and UK welfare provision (Leitner, 2003).

Supporting the (nuclear) family

Whether the state should provide support for the family or not has been a source of debate. Arguments that the state should *not* support the family stipulate that the family is a private matter for individuals to enter and negotiate themselves. Efforts by the state will gradually erode responsibility and commitment, and end up weakening the family. Arguments that the state *should* support the family stipulate that doing so ensures that families remain strong within difficult circumstances. The state can relieve care burdens, prevent abuse and exploitation and help nurture loving and caring relationships (the counterclaim, of course, is that such support will replace the personal ties necessary for those relationships to form).

Despite its gendered assumptions (or perhaps as a result of them), the Beveridge Report did suggest the development of family allowances, recognising the additional cost of raising children and providing some form of state support. While historically this has been a universal benefit – the additional costs of children are experienced by all families with children– this has now shifted towards a means-tested benefit targeted at certain families. It is perhaps interesting to note the differences between support through social security and family allowances. The latter can be tied into a wider nation-building narrative. Post-Second World War, there was a need to promote repopulation as a result of the loss of life during the war. Thus, policy that sought to encourage family growth ran parallel to policy narratives focused on re-building the nation, in both subtle and explicit ways. The aim was to encourage more births, which in turn facilitated women's subordination, despite their fundamental position in ensuring members of society exist. Women's role in reproduction required that they were protected as a vital source of the nation's future survival. Although in this instance such arguments reinforced the subjugation of women into the nuclear family, the same arguments could be drawn out to support the distinctive needs of women and to illustrate diversity of citizens, which requires we rethink gendered assumptions.

Furthermore, as Fox Harding (1996) notes, policies may be directly targeted at the family, such as the provision of childcare services or the use of child tax credits. Additionally, there may be indirect consequences; for example, an increase in personal tax allowance will increase the amount of money a working parent takes home, but a decrease in housing benefit will reduce what money a parent has to cover their daily living costs. Policy (and, we could argue, most welfare narratives) tends to focus on the individual claiming benefit, despite the influence of familism on welfare systems. Subsequently, there has been analysis advocating a more explicit focus on the family unit per se.

Despite the influence of local, national and global trends and developments, generally speaking, Western nations have followed similar patterns and debates in relation to the family and social policy. Within this trend, however, there is diversity in how policy has developed, as family formation constitutes part of dominant nation-building narratives: part of the common identity sought to establish shared national characteristics. Between the 1940s and 1980s, many nations developed their policies in line with the perceived tradition of nuclear families. In the 1980s, this started to change, as the battle between feminist critiques and moralistic efforts to 'save the nuclear family' played out in the political sphere. Post-2008, there was increased focus on these moralistic concerns within a context of restricted public spending and removal of welfare services, which has predominantly disadvantaged women in comparison to men (Dermott and Pantazis, 2014). Thus, while family policy has shifted, it is often mapped against some of the aforementioned changing demographic and theoretical explanations.

Meil's (2006) discussion of Spanish family policy, for example, charts its rise and fall as an overt policy within the wider political landscape, noting that the term was used under the dictatorships from the 1930s but retained a patriarchal bias; this only gradually changed as the country adapted to the demands of capitalist markets and started to transition to democracy, reflecting a move towards promoting equal treatment of family members, especially in relation to equal employment opportunities. In contrast, Norway maintains a simplistic divide in its policy on the surface; men can claim benefits as earners, and women can claim benefits as carers. But, as Ellingsæter (2003) suggests, this overlooks the complexity beneath the surface; parental support for fathers has also improved, alongside childcare provision (which typically gives women greater employment opportunities). In Germany, this division between care and work remains quite explicit; the introduction of *betreuungsgeld* (childcare subsidy) ensures that parents (particularly women) are paid to remain at home and raise their children, rather than placing them in childcare to allow the parent to work. In Japan, the dominance of the nuclear family waned in the 1980s, as the country adapted to the new economic conditions instigated by the oil crisis. Parallel to this was the increased activism of the women's liberation movement and its challenge to traditional family values. Thus, there was a shift to encourage more women into the market via employment to allow them to be competent economic subjects (Hiroko, 2008). Equality was linked to employment activities; similar patterns can be found in other nations, such as the UK and US. This, as illustrated by the experience of Taiwan, was accompanied by changing attitudes towards marriage, children and care for older generations. Chen et al. (2010) state that this resulted in a move towards increased defamilisation.

Bould's (2006) analysis of international policies and families suggests that childcare has been ignored by gender mainstreaming, as the focus of policy change has been to empower women for employment, not to consider the wider roles of care. Citizen–as–worker (rather than citizen–as–carer) has come to dominate in policy discourse. The discussion of the family has therefore remained within the realms of patriarchy; women are still primary carers, but they must now juggle this alongside work commitments, at a time when employment – particularly for men – has become increasingly unstable and insecure. We need not accept such analysis and narratives as found in these dominant policy positions. Rather, they can be challenged by questioning the dominance of employment as the primary duty of a citizen, and the policy designed to support this (see, for example, Bryson, 2007; Gregory 2015). We cannot fully explore this here, but general comments on challenging and changing narratives and the conceptual arguments that underpin them will be explored in the final chapter.

Reflecting on these debates about supporting the family through welfare policies leads to two considerations. First, there is an argument in favour of specific **family policy**: the development of policy explicitly designed to support/intervene into family life (as witnessed in the Third Reich in 1930s Germany, the one-child policy of the Chinese government and the Soviet Union). Lewis (2002), however, suggests a second approach based on a family perspective. This would require that policy makers pay attention to changing patterns in family type and adjust all policy accordingly. Additionally, it would require a more explicit consideration of family roles and functions, not merely renegotiating the care activities of families more equally within policy. Finally, the **family perspective** needs to evaluate the effects of policy in relation to the welfare of families, which requires cross-departmental consideration (all government departments – education, health, social security, environment and so on – working together rather than in isolation). The family perspective promotes consideration of the impact of *any* policy on the family, and its ability to survive and thrive in a changing social and economic context, rather than just promoting specific policy designed to support families. Both approaches have benefits, but the latter allows for a broader questioning of the ideological assumptions underpinning policy aims.

Family stories

Debate regarding the support of the family is explicitly attached to narratives about the family, which inform the policy goals pursued. This relates to the type of family to be supported. The nuclear family has dominated policy debates and been the focus of intervention and support, despite the continuation of diverse family forms. Yet, perpetual fears that the welfare system somehow erodes this 'traditional' family continue unabated, generating demand for policy to intervene to protect and maintain the nuclear family. This reflects the conclusions that can be drawn from the previous section regarding how we define the family and how it has changed over time. Political and policy debates in the UK since the turn of the millennium have illustrated various ways in which the family, and citizens more broadly, can be depicted: 'hard-working families', 'ordinary working class', 'strivers and skivers', 'shirkers and workers'. This language often presents polar opposites, one of which is favourable and approved of and the other negative (or unsaid).

Such language, as discussed throughout this chapter, seeks to promote particular perceptions of different families (and citizens) and emphasise the pathological failures of some, which need 'corrective' intervention – returning us to the idea of shame. In their discussion of narratives around welfare provision and stigmatised groups, Jensen and Tyler (2015:478–9) introduce the idea of benefit brood:

> 'Benefit brood' is a cultural figuration of disgust aimed at families that are deemed to have become 'excessively' large as a result of over-generous welfare entitlements; 'benefit brood' parents are regarded as almost pathologically fertile in their desire to secure greater amounts of welfare payments by having more and more children. 'Benefit brood' narratives form a staple of disgust across news media, lifestyle and 'real life' magazines, and pseudo-documentary (reality) television such as the genre of 'poverty porn'.

This indicates how stigmatised/shaming narratives are used to portray a particular view of some groups, which enables more punitive reforms to social welfare provision and, in turn, allows for greater control over behaviours perceived as inappropriate for citizens. The following quote from David Cameron (2011), when he was UK prime minister, illustrates this point:

> Drug addiction. Alcohol abuse. Crime. A culture of disruption and irresponsibility that cascades through generations.
> We've always known that these families cost an extraordinary amount of money … but now we've come up [with] the actual figures.
> Last year the state spent an estimated £9 billion on just 120,000 families … that is around £75,000 per family.
> Now there are some who say, 'Yes, this is terrible, but this "shameless" culture is now a fact of modern British life, and there's nothing we can do.'

On the basis of this argument, the 'Troubled Families' initiative was launched. According to Casey (2012), these families are characterised by intergenerational transmission of the cultures and behaviours outlined by Cameron – essentially, a view that troubled families beget future troubled families – a modern retelling of the culture of poverty argument. This implies that such families are characterised by a large number of children; shifting family make-up (separated or multiple parents); dysfunctional relationships; unhelpful family and friends; abuse; institutional care; teenage mothers; early signs of poor behaviour; troubles at school; anti-social behaviour; mental illness; and drug and alcohol use. The accuracy of such descriptions is open to debate, but they have been fundamental for generating 'appropriate' policy responses, which explicitly adopt a 'less understanding approach' and embrace stigmatising narratives to reinforce the inappropriateness of these behaviours (Chorley, 2012).

The intention here is not to engage in the policy detail or critiques of these claims, but to provide a contemporary illustration of how stigmatising discourses are drawn out in policy debates, and to consider their impact on interventions designed to secure welfare. It is particularly interesting how politicians were arguing for a 'less understanding' approach, the implication being not only that welfare support has historically been 'soft' on certain groups (as Chapter 9 briefly demonstrates, this is not the case) but also that stigma is no bad thing. This echoes Murray's (1996) argument that those growing up in such families must learn the shame of their situation so that they desire to escape it. However, such narratives fail to go deeper into the analysis of these circumstances to explore *causes* beyond claimed individual failings. Rather, as Jensen and Tyler (2015) suggest, this effort is pursued to identify particular family types that do not neatly fit into the preferred family form of those in power. Thus, narratives are developed that facilitate punitive interventions into the daily lives of this particular group of citizens in order to correct their behaviour and bring them into line with the 'accepted' moral norm.

The consequence of policy narratives

Throughout this and the previous chapter, we have started to tease out a distinction between needs-based and rights-based welfare discourse. We can now draw this out a bit more explicitly to draw this chapter to an end. Table 6.2 offers a brief summary of some core debates. First, we need to separate out an earlier argument. It was previously suggested that social rights were constructed through an account of need: the identification of certain goods/services essential to welfare. Framed in the language of rights, this ensured states provided support for securing these needs. However, as suggested in Chapter 5, it is possible for a demonstration of need to be required in order to access services, with potentially stigmatising consequences. It is this latter view of need that we are drawing out here; not needs as the content of social rights, but the requirement to complete an invasive needs assessment in order to access welfare provision.

As we have just seen in relation to stigma, shame and the family, a number of powerful discourses shape broader welfare debates. We cannot rely on the entitlement triangle as the sole means of evaluating access to welfare support. Rather, we must be aware of broader policy narratives that reshape the debate and influence the design and implementation of welfare policies. We can associate this with a distinction between needs-based assessments and social rights. The former facilitate access to welfare based on potential recipients declaring a need, which is then reviewed by a welfare professional to determine if support will be provided, and to what level. It is possible, therefore, for the determination of no support to be offered. This differs from a rights–based approach, where an identification of a need triggers an automatic provision of welfare support.

Table 6.2: Rights and needs-assessment access to welfare services

Welfare provision through social rights	Welfare provision through needs test
Universal provision to all citizens	Selective support, provided that applicants meet predefined requirements (either through an assessment of needs or means, i.e. current income)
Potential use of targeting or progressive universalism to facilitate welfare support	Potential use of targeting to reduce universal provision and foster residual welfare to those unable to meet their own needs in the market
Non-stigmatising treatment: welfare support available to all	Stigmatising treatment: Murray's argument that fear motivates
Welfare support is liberating and facilitates citizens in attaining their full potential and welfare	Welfare support is conditional and is designed to remove perceived dependency on welfare provision

The importance of this distinction is relevant here if we recall how needs can be interpreted. Bradshaw (2013) drew attention to how different actors are involved in the process of defining needs (politicians; civil servants; academics; journalists; lawyers; medical practitioners; and social workers). To various extents, these groups will have different interactions with people in deprivation, and varying understanding of their lived experience. But these actors all operate within a context whereby various policy narratives are drawn on to explain the need for welfare. Policy makers, adopting particular narratives (as outlined in this chapter), will require that assessments take a particular form. Thus, in practice settings, service providers will be involved in a range of decisions regarding what services best satisfy clients' needs. Essentially, these individuals act as 'gatekeepers' to services, and determine citizen access.

Consequently, any effort to support welfare begins with some form of needs assessment. The aim is to identify needs, determine which services are appropriate and create a suitable support package, before eventually reviewing that package to see if the client's needs have changed and whether an adjustment to the care package is required. Parry-Jones and Soulsby (2001) suggested it is possible to appreciate that there is no consensus on how to define need. Operationalising abstract theories of need into practical concepts for policy making and practice is difficult; this lack of specificity overspills into the assessment process. Needs assessments seek to secure objectivity to determine what someone lacks, but will be influenced by the broader policy narratives we have just reviewed, which seek to foster particular forms of moral behaviours and social order. As such, efforts to establish an objective measure in practice will be open to political and ideological influences regarding the wider rationale of welfare support. Consequently, needs assessments may adopt a privileged position of service providers over service users, and still do not address potential ambiguity in how we operationalise certain items. It is through such practice that the stigmatising/shaming impacts of welfare provision may be borne out, because the definition of need has resulted from a series of social interactions that privilege the accounts of some actors over others.

Of course, we can apply this more broadly. Dominant notions of citizenship initially fostered a totalising, masculine narrative based on a number of gendered and ethnic assumptions. As such, the concept of social rights was based around a notion of universalism and inherent needs for all humans, which some later argued ignored diversity. Yet, here is the key difference to the needs–based assessment: social rights are constructed around a notion of universalism, giving us a sense of common treatment of all humans. Needs–based assessments do not offer this universalism; rather, they specifically set out to identify where certain deficiencies exist, and to determine the appropriate response to addressing them. When embedded within the policy narratives explored in the previous two chapters, welfare provision becomes increasingly means tested and conditional. Rights–based discourses do not, because they are based on the assumption that citizens have discharged their duties, and (as part of their humanity) require that certain needs be met to secure welfare. While this chapter has focused on policy narratives, it has facilitated a discussion whereby a shift in welfare provision can be traced. This shift is a move away from the rights–based discourse of welfare services towards one attached to needs assessments, which contains limited objectivity, as political narratives influence the nature of assessments and the subsequent design of policy. In the following chapters, we will explore some of the broader shifts that have facilitated this change.

Summary

This section has sought to draw out some of the particular examples of how welfare provision has changed in response to developing narratives. While the chapter has sought to draw this out in relation to stigma and the family, the implications are clear. Policy makers often create particular morality tales about certain groups of citizens who, for some reason, are identified as troublesome and a threat to social order. This depiction generates public support to intervene in the lives of these groups through a series of punitive policy interventions (a theme explored again in Chapter 9). Essentially, however, it has been noted that attempts to create these narratives take on a particular ideological bias, and often fail to look at broader evidence and insight into the lives of these groups.

Chapter summary

At the core of this chapter has been the suggestion that policy narratives are developed that seek to portray citizens, and in particular families, in a certain way so as to elicit certain public perceptions and support for policy interventions. Often, this draws on stigmatising narratives or policy designs, which can generate stigma labels for claimants. As part of a general shift in policy debate and wider concerns with welfare, this forms part of a move away from universalism and social rights towards conditionality, punitive means testing and the development of residual welfare systems. Broadly, this is an abandonment of the flourishing idea of welfare achieved through state support against the uncertainties, strains and harms of the socioeconomic world. In its place, individuals and families are left to pursue their welfare objectives and preferred end states for their lives through other means – typically the market. The role of the state is to provide the bare minimum support through residual welfare provision and greater familisation and commodification: the family and the market are placed at the forefront of need satisfaction to achieve welfare.

This brings with it a whole series of concerns around equality and rights; one's ability to pursue welfare objectives is tied to the accident of birth of which family you happen to be born into, and the resources and support they may or may not be able to provide. This is especially important when the family itself is often considered to be above direct policy interventions (see Calder, 2016). Furthermore, the affordability of objectives comes to the forefront, as some will not have the resources (material or social) to pursue objectives that others do. The role of the state in 'levelling this playing field' is largely eroded. Supporting these trends have been wider theoretical changes and developments, explored in the next two chapters. Thus the shape of the entitlement triangle starts to change to fit these different narratives.

In relation to the family, this chapter has demonstrated not only the centrality of the nuclear family as a concept but also its embeddedness within social policy. Wider social changes facilitating growth in alternative family forms have sparked fears for some about the future of the nuclear family, calling attention to alleged moral and social decline regarding these wider changes. Others, however, suggest that this is a broader reflection of change in society, which starts to highlight the importance of a range of personal relationships to our welfare. Thus, rather than supporting one type of family, policy should support diverse forms of relationships – from different family forms to community and personal acquaintances – that fill our day-to-day lives. Family/relationship perspectives seek to support rather than intervene into these relationships. It is not for the state to determine the type and content of these relationships – although significant amounts of policy, especially tied to nation-building, have done exactly that. The discussion illustrated how narratives around families, stigma and shame have consequential impacts on welfare objectives through policy. Often, this is presented as an attempt to correct perceived personal failings, rather than create a supportive context in which people can pursue the personal relationships they desire as part of their personal welfare preferences.

Figure 6.3 illustrates the flow of argument pursued by the two opening quotes of this chapter. The first of these quotes provides a view that state welfare provision supports dysfunctional family lives, and consequently that such support should be reimagined. No longer provided through entitlements to social rights, this support is conditional and targeted at perceived problematic families. While conditionality was explored in the previous chapter, this chapter has focused on the identification of certain types of lives and behaviours that are considered to be problematic. As such, certain groups are identified and exposed to stigmatising labels. This forms part of a longer tradition of promoting and supporting the nuclear family as not only the primary family form but also the only accepted one. In part, this relates to nation–building efforts, wherein national and citizen identities were built around particular norms and expected behaviours. Wider socioeconomic transformations have generated change, which has implications for family life but has also been the focus of vocal critique. Interestingly, these same changes (outlined in the next chapters) are also drawn on by many of the same critics to facilitate the move towards residual forms of welfare provision.

Figure 6.3: Framing welfare provision

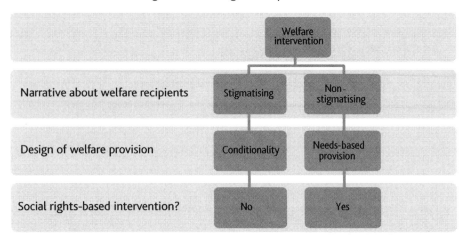

Contrasting with this, the second opening quote encourages welfare support for the family that does not pay attention to behaviours per se but instead seeks to recognise the challenges of contemporary life for maintaining and sustaining a family. One the one hand, this can still adopt the nuclear family as the acceptable family form to support. On the other, it can also accept greater diversity of family forms. Support for the family can therefore produce many forms of support across a range of different policy narratives. It can support specific family policies that seek to correct behaviours, or it can pursue specific policies that recognise challenges for families in the contemporary economy – such as childcare support when a household needs two incomes to survive. Alternatively, support for the family could suggest that welfare provision removes family functions and therefore weakens the nuclear family, consequently requiring a reduction of invasive welfare, which creates dependency and inappropriate behaviours. For some, however, a family perspective pays greater attention to how all policies impact on the daily lives of families, and seeks to ensure that policy does not hinder but assists families in securing their welfare.

Different policy narratives inevitably exist, and some have come to dominate, as this chapter has suggested. The early development of welfare systems supported freedom from dependence on circumstance of birth and affordability of goods and services in the market; so, the state stepped in to provide welfare support. The debate across this (and the previous) chapter illustrates the reversal of this position: a trend that is reinforced through the concepts of globalisation and risk.

Critical thinking activity

Evaluate the significance of stigma and shame for the pursuit of welfare, drawing on debates regarding the family to illustrate your answer.

Further reading

Calder, G. (2016) *How Inequality Runs in Families: Unfair Advantage and the Limits of Social Mobility*. Bristol: Policy Press.

Fox Harding, L. (1996) *Family, State and Social Policy*. Hampshire: Macmillan.

Page, R. (1984) *Stigma*. London: Routledge and Kegan Paul.

Don't forget to look at the companion website for more information.

7

Is the welfare state always in crisis?

> There are economic constraints to welfare support and social rights. We can't provide more than we can afford.

> In our globalised world, nation states have less freedom to design their own welfare systems.

Key concepts in this chapter:
crisis • globalisation • neoliberalism

The previous chapters introduced you to a number of concepts. But the intention has also been to show their entwined nature, and the contradictions and tensions that ensue (as the book cover illustrates!). Furthermore, the discussion has sought to demonstrate how welfare provision is both justified and criticised – without going into too much policy detail, as these debates can be found within all nations where welfare systems have developed. Much of this debate has been theoretical, but we must also add an economic dynamic to this. Economic change has underpinned a number of reforms, as new socioeconomic conditions develop out of industrialisation, modernisation and (arguably) postmodernity. But this is not an economistic approach to welfare. Rather, economic debates exist within the conceptual and theoretical debate of welfare (we cannot divorce the economic from the political and social, as many would assume/desire). Thus, as we have explored, economic narratives around the state–market relationship and definitions of needs, equality and citizenship have persisted and influenced a range of welfare debates.

Many of these economic criticisms draw attention to **crisis narratives**, which is the next part of our journey exploring welfare debates through the conceptual lens. Essentially, these are a set of arguments regarding limitations resulting from state welfare provision, questioning some of the intent and purpose. Consequently, the chapter starts with a discussion of how a crisis is defined and used to promote welfare reform. It will be shown that crisis not only serves as another policy narrative (as we explored in the previous chapter) but is also drawn into a more explicit ideological debate around welfare, which is informed by neoliberal economic theories. Subsequently, the second section examines **neoliberalism** as an economic framework, setting out its dominant influence in policy debates. Reinforcing this dominance has been the rise of **globalisation**. This is a key concept in Social Policy for two reasons: first, it offers an explanation of change in society, which requires a rethinking of how welfare systems operate; second, it is a narrative through which welfare reform is pursued. This discussion enables an account of globalisation, specifically focusing on how it is drawn into policy debate to promote neoliberal economic ideas and practices, establishing a dominant ideological framework at a global level and influencing welfare debates.

The crises of welfare

From the late 1940s onwards, there was a general acceptance of the state's intervention, in some capacity, in the welfare of its citizens. This gradually changed due to a rise in critical accounts of welfare provision from a range of political perspectives from the late 1960s/early 1970s. This presented various crisis narratives, introducing another means by which broader 'stories' of the socioeconomic context inform welfare debates.

Reflecting on the term itself, a **crisis** can have a number of definitions. It can refer to a time of intense difficulty or danger, a time when important or difficult decisions are to be made or, in medical language, a turning point in a disease when a change occurs that will result in either recovery or death. Such definitions capture the essence of how the crisis of welfare is often presented. The challenge, however, is that different crisis narratives exist, each emanating from different ideological positions.

Donati (1987) and Mishra (1984) separately demonstrate the first challenge when discussing the crises of welfare: there are many types of crisis. For Donati, there are 'crisis paradigms', which converge around the incompatibility of the welfare state with economic growth. It is not a coincidence that the welfare state developed and expanded when it did. Enlightenment thinking and industrialisation resulted in growing ideological pressures for state intervention (see Chapter 2; George and Wilding, 1976). Thus, as the economy developed into a separate sphere of social activity (no longer a part of existing family structures) it provided new sources of income and wealth, creating a new pool of taxable money. This, in turn, could be used to fund state interventions to tackle social problems generated by social change. Consequently, welfare provision has always been attached to economic fortunes: economic growth facilitates welfare provision. Such links establish two particular crisis narratives, one linked to the New Right and the other to Marxism. The former has had a significant impact on state welfare, and so is given primary consideration in this section.

Economic crisis narratives

Much of this New Right critique illustrates an emotive, ideological criticism linked to a revised classical liberal economic theory referred to as neoliberalism (see below). The suggestion that this is emotive is not a criticism (political debate often strikes a chord with the deep beliefs of advocates, to which they have a personal attachment), but it is a comment that such work should not be simply read as a dispassionate economic analysis. For example, Hayek's (1944) claim that centralised governments result in totalitarianism is based on concerns regarding the Second World War and the rise of the Third Reich and Stalinist regimes. Historical development of welfare systems since the 1940s would throw considerable doubt on the idea that this 'road to serfdom' results from welfare provision. Yet, economic critics have continued to be persuasive.

Writing during the revival of economic critiques of state provision, Marsland (1996:xi) makes a number of accusations. The welfare state was said to be damaging democracy because of 'its commitment to a specious form of equality and to institutional envy', based on an intellectual bias towards welfare provision and generating a 'magic spell to thrall' citizens. Such analysis seeks to suggest that the notion of welfare (central to state intervention) is preventing people from having free choice over the use of their resources, for they are collected centrally and managed by state bureaucrats. As such, it is the promotion of the negative conception of freedom, a preference for want satisfaction via the market and equality of the kind found within market transactions and participation. Broader political conceptions of need and equality, and the concept of positive freedom, are misplaced. Pursuing welfare objectives based on these assumptions results in the curtailment of 'real freedom' based on individual choice, initiative, effort and self-reliance. We have already seen how such views overlook the potential limitations on choice and freedom where circumstances of birth and free-market practices limit your access to the resources required to secure your welfare needs or personal ambitions. Although Marsland (1996) develops his arguments around the need to develop a 'real' notion of welfare (without specifically defining what this is), Hayek, as we have already explored, was less keen to adopt political concepts such as justice. Despite differing starting points, both agree that reduced – or the complete removal of – state activity is the only viable option for freeing the market to deliver people's welfare needs. Such arguments are linked to the idea of state failure (see Table 4.3), facilitating a rethinking of key concepts of welfare, as traced in earlier chapters.

Economic critiques draw particular attention to the x-efficiency critique. This suggests that state provision limits competition between providers of welfare and, as such, there can be no real pursuit of innovation and development to find cost-effective means of delivering welfare. The term efficiency, however, has a broader significance than is usually suggested in these narratives (see, for example, Le Grand et al., 1992; Barr, 2012). Essentially, market theory assumes that the satisfaction of wants is achieved through the consumption of goods/

services available through the market, and that the price mechanism can ensure efficient allocation through its internal workings. This is not possible through the state, which cannot systematically accumulate and assess all the information involved in people's preference satisfaction. Knowing what people are willing to pay for (and how much) facilitates the market to respond to this information in ways the state cannot.

Additionally, the market is seen to be superior to the state because competition ensures innovation in goods and services, driving up the quality of welfare provision. Improvement in the quality of goods will therefore enhance the benefit enjoyed from their consumption. But improvements depend on the availability of resources, and some resources – such as land, labour and capital – are not available in an inexhaustible supply (for example, there is only so much land to be used in house building). Consequently, it may not be possible produce a sufficient quantity of goods to satisfy all of our wants. Because of resource scarcity, production of one good will have costs in the form of other goods that could have been produced: opportunity costs. Again, the price mechanism is seen to be a suitable tool for addressing this situation. The price attached to the use of resources will reflect its opportunity cost. Thus, within market calculations, there is a need to reflect on how the benefits and costs vary across different levels of output: seeking to achieve benefits while reducing undesirable costs. Advocates of the market suggest that the price mechanism is the natural way of securing equilibrium across these factors.

While Barr (2012) suggests that the laws of the market can be drawn into an analysis of welfare provision to demonstrate the limitations of the market, other criticisms of this pro-market stance rest on concepts previously explored: equality, justice and social solidarity. This draws our attention back to decommodification (why should price, and therefore affordability, dictate if you have adequate shelter or healthcare?) and wider debates around the socioeconomic structure, the social inequalities this produced and how these should be redressed. Thus, the state–market debate, which rests at the core of the majority of ideological debates about welfare, also rests at the core of crisis narratives.

We can draw out of this discussion a few key points regarding economic crisis narratives:

• The state is inefficient in allocating resources.
• If the state has a monopoly on welfare provision, there is no innovation.
• Conceptual arguments in favour of state provision are flawed, as there is no agreed definition of concepts; as such, they are political impositions on citizens, which curtail their freedom.

However, we should also consider that the market is also limited on each of these points. The need to purchase goods and services to secure your welfare can exclude citizens who have insufficient income. The market may be able to innovate, but it does not ensure equal access to high-quality provision (although we could debate whether the state is able to secure this). Finally, arguments in favour of the market rests on a conceptual analysis of freedom, equality and the needs/wants debate (to name just a few examples). Thus, the presentation of economic rationality behind the economic crisis narrative should not mask the often-ideological basis of the argument. Other crisis narratives, however, are more overt in their ideological foundations.

Additional 'crisis paradigms'

These other narratives are only given brief consideration here, as they have tended to be sidelined from political debate, and I wish to quickly return to our economic critique of welfare provision in relation to neoliberalism. However, the alternative crisis narratives are important sources of academic thought that you should explore in their own right. As such, a selection will be reviewed that emphasises crisis rather than more focused critiques regarding welfare provision. Consequently, attention is not given to feminist, anti-racist, postmodern, disability or sexuality-based critiques of welfare states, for they highlight limitations and biases within provision, rather than indicate the impending collapse of welfare (although students of Social Policy must also become familiar with these; see, for example, George and Wilding, 1994; Lewis, 2004; Carabine, 2009). Two accounts are explored briefly here: Marxist and environmentalist.

Marxist accounts of the development of welfare provision draw attention to efforts to control class conflict. The development of social security provision, for example, seeks to avoid the political instability caused by increasing poverty during the Industrial Revolution and the rise of capitalism (Deacon, 2002). This critique suggests that welfare is designed to support economic productivity, ameliorate the damaging consequences of capitalist developments and provide a mechanism for disciplining and controlling the population. For O'Connor (1973), however, the welfare state is not sustainable. He highlighted the potential '**legitimation crisis**' that would arise from tensions between state welfare and the demands of capitalist production. The state provides services and benefits that improve accumulation of capital and private profits – but these must also facilitate the acceptance of the capitalist system. The state cannot neglect either of these functions; to do so would undermine either economic growth or acceptance of capitalism. As such, social services are integral to capitalism and essential to economic and political survival. Essentially, this is the opposite to the economic crisis perspective, which suggests that welfare provision erodes freedom and market functions; here, welfare provisions help to foster the growth of capitalism.

However, this Marxist perspective does not divorce economic growth from political legitimacy. The popularity of capitalism rests in its improvement of living standards, not the provision of services. Developing similar ideas, Gough (1979) draws out the term '**fiscal crisis**' to describe the situation in which government expenditure outpaces revenues (spending is greater than income), resulting not from incompetence but the tension between accumulation and legitimation, alongside increasing public demand and unwillingness to pay necessary rates of taxation. This will generate the collapse of the capitalist system, as its growth is dependent on public expenditure. Roads, infrastructure, health and education are all key elements of a successful economy, but their costs continue to grow – unlike citizens' willingness to pay. Thus, a careful balancing act is required between these two pressures, which is difficult to maintain in practice (Figure 7.1).

Figure 7.1: Legitimation crisis

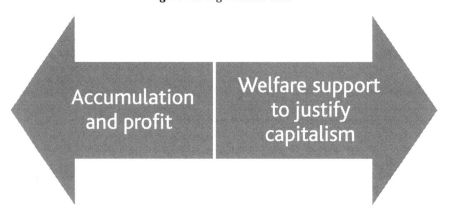

A similar sense of impending crisis has arisen from environmental concerns, illustrating the damage being done to the context in which human life is sustained. Essentially, the constant drive to produce and consume (**productivism** and **consumerism**) causes irreparable damage to the environment, which sustains human and natural life. Welfare states contribute to this because they are based on a productivist model of continued, and expanded, consumption. This threatens sustainability of the environment, and therefore human life. As Dryzek (2008:336) observes, suggestions of more radical reform highlight breaking away from the centrality of the sovereign nation state to focus on: '(a) dynamic, non–state forms of interdependent activity, (b) local governance, for example, in the form of deliberative democracy, and (c) coordinated global action'. Welfare provisions deal with the symptoms of a faulty economic system, not the root causes. Consequently, the New Economics Foundation (NEF) (2008) has suggested that there currently exists a 'triple crisis': a credit-fuelled financial crisis, accelerating climate change and soaring energy prices underpinned by encroaching peak oil. Bringing together environmental, social and economic concerns, such 'green' perspectives highlight significant flaws in the economy, society and design of welfare provision, and suggest a radical rethink of all three.

Despite these wider critiques, the predominance of the New Right analysis has been established. This could result from a longer ideological history and development alongside industrialisation than is the case with other crisis narratives. Evers and Wintersberger (1994) suggest that this economic crisis of welfare relates to misunderstandings generated through an implicit association with disease and recovery narratives. As others have illustrated in the discussion of the 1980s, such critique was neither necessarily accurate (George and Wilding, 1984) nor went without considerable challenge (Bean et al., 1985; Wilding, 1986). Yet, it did become the dominant frame through which welfare provision was reformed in the UK and many other western nations. This resulted from the rising prominence of neoliberal economic theory and the spread of globalisation as a source of economic and social change. These issues are explored in the remainder of this chapter. Combined, they produce a dominant narrative in relation to the economic crisis of welfare, which proposes the removal of state interference as the solution – the cure of the 'infection'.

Summary

This section has sought to orientate you towards the idea of crisis narratives. Earlier chapters noted some of the conceptual and narrative arguments that have caused shifts in how welfare support is provided. These have operated alongside a narrative of economic crisis, although a number of crisis narratives exist regarding welfare provision. Specifically, attention has been given to those that suggest some form of impending collapse of welfare, social and economic systems, resulting from either the tensions and production of capitalism or the imposition of political concepts that create pathways to totalitarianism. Such narratives, as Figure 7.2 illustrates, are drawn into debates about welfare, socioeconomic organisation and social policy objectives.

We can add here the discussion in the previous chapter. The discussion of stigma and troubled families illustrates how, for some, the idea of a **social crisis** can also be brought into policy narratives: inappropriate family formations, work-shy skivers unwilling to look for employment, and individualism or inequality are all

Figure 7.2: The welfare debate mix

types of social crisis that can be found in contemporary social policy commentary (Utting, 2009). Each narrative draws on various explanations of key concepts, either accepting certain definitions or refuting their existence. This, in turn, starts to inform new welfare system designs, which are pursued through policy and practice. Of the narratives explored, the economic claims of the New Right have gained dominance (not only in the western world but also globally), in part through the rise of neoliberal economics and in part through the development of globalisation. Both of these are considered in the remainder of this chapter.

Neoliberalism

This book intends to not only engage with concepts but also suggest that the dominance of certain political ideologies influence how these concepts are formed. Although we have not made ideology an explicit focus, there have been references to different ideological positions at appropriate junctions (and Chapter 1 explained this approach). However, for our discussion to progress, this chapter has started to give greater consideration to ideology – particularly that of the New Right. This results from the ascendency of neoliberal thinking, which has had a significant influence on welfare provision across the globe. As such, it is necessary to explore some key aspects of this theory – in particular its association with neoliberalism. This is important because this framework not only informs the aforementioned economic crisis narratives but also underpins the shifts explored in Chapters 5 and 6 – and, as such, has a significant influence on key concepts in Social Policy.

What is neoliberalism?

Harvey (2007:2) provides a useful definition for our purposes here:

> Neoliberalism is in the first instance a theory of political–economic practices that proposes that human wellbeing can best be advanced by liberating individual entrepreneurial freedoms and skills within an institutional framework characterised by strong private property rights, free markets, and free trade … State interventions in markets (once created) must be kept to a bare minimum because, according to the theory, the state cannot possibly possess enough information to second-guess market signals (prices) and because powerful interest groups will inevitably distort and bias state interventions (particularly in democracies) for their own benefit.

First, this definition illustrates how the theory contains a particular notion of how to secure human wellbeing (or welfare) through property rights, the free market and free trade. Arguments such as Hayek's (1944) and Freedman's (2002) are relevant here in promoting the preservation of individual liberty through the free market and non–interference by the state. State intervention into the market will disrupt market mechanisms, biasing them in ways that prevent their effective operation and thus eroding personal liberty. For Hayek, this was the essential problem of state planning of the economy. But before we continue, it is important to remember that *capitalism and neoliberalism should be treated as analytically distinct*. Neoliberalism refers to a particular political philosophy and set of beliefs regarding human nature and economics, and the particular policy programme this seeks to promote. Capitalism refers to social practices designed to accumulate profit; this may (or may not) be associated with neoliberal thinking. These have been entwined with each other since the 1980s, generating a revival of early–1900s ideological debates about the rise of the welfare state.

The gradual introduction of welfare provision by the state accumulated into the promotion of Keynesian economics from the 1930s onwards. This economic theory suggested that the role of government was to manage the national economy, linked to the responsibility for assuring its citizens a degree of economic wellbeing. Advocates of Keynesian economics suggest that the market cannot self-regulate; in fact, it sometimes makes decisions that result in inefficient macroeconomic outcomes, and require state policy to correct them. Thus, at times it is correct for the state to directly intervene with market functions. However, by the late 1970s, Keynesianism lost favour – partially due to recession and partially due to a renewed economic crisis, as outlined earlier. Consequently, dominant economic theory was soon established around neoliberal economic thinking (see Wapshott, 2011). Neoclassical economic thinkers such as Hayek (1944) argued instead for economic liberalisations, free trade and open markets, privatisation, deregulation and enhancing the role of the private sector in modern society. Consequently, theorists such as Hall (2005:19) have seen the rise of neoliberalism as 'the death-knell to the old notion of "the public realm", the social conception of the individual ... And the basic social-democratic idea of collective provision' – in essence, the end of universal, collective, rights-based welfare provision.

The prefix 'neo' is important, for it signifies the revival of classical liberalism of the Victorian period to fit a contemporary setting, in order to challenge the rise of collectivist ideologies – the perceived threats to freedom and individuality. It is essential to remember that neoliberalism is not a uniform paradigm. As Eagleton-Pierce (2016) elucidates, the arguments of Hayek will differ in certain degrees from those of Thatcher and Reagan in the UK and US respectively during the 1980s. However, certain core characteristics can be drawn out, as can the variations that develop. Essentially, this economic theory seeks to promote the priorities of the price mechanism, free enterprise, the system of competition and a strong and impartial state. The state is necessary, for it can ensure that security and fairness occur in transactions, and protect property/ownership rights and contract rights – but it should not stray into direct engagement with the market. Table 7.1 outlines the characteristics of neoliberalism.

However more recent usage has associated the term with globalisation as a shorthand for the negative consequences of neoliberal capitalism (Stedman

Jones, 2014). For the student of Social Policy, it is important to not simply label things as 'neoliberal' (or even 'capitalist'), without a more nuanced appreciation of its analytical accuracy. To develop this, it is possible to highlight variations in neoliberal praxis; that is, both the theory and the actioning of neoliberal ideas.

Neoliberalisation

Table 7.1: Characteristics of neoliberalism

Characteristics	Description
Role of the market	To organise all forms of human interaction so that they maximise freedom of choice and generate 'efficient' outcomes (consequently maximising welfare).
Role of the state	To ensure the efficient functioning of the market.
Inequality	Naturally generated by the market reflecting merit. Any arrangements or practices that generate outcomes that would not naturally occur from the market (e.g. redistribution) should be avoided.
Deregulation	The practices of reducing government regulation of any practices that might impact on profit making, freeing the banks and financial services from (claimed) intrusive state control (e.g. health and safety and environmental conditions placed on businesses).
Privatisation	The selling of state-owned enterprises, goods and services to private investors. The underpinning logic is the move towards efficiency through the market rather than state monopolies. This has happened to utilities (e.g. gas, electricity and water) and industries (e.g. the railways).

Peck and Tickell (2002) suggest that a process of **neoliberalisation** is occurring, through which states become increasingly neoliberal. This is potentially an easier way of grasping the implications of neoliberal thought, as many texts discussing the theory will do so through the lens of local political configurations. Taking the example of the UK, the integration of neoliberal thinking within the New Right in the UK has been well documented (Johnson, 1990; Waine, 1991; Wilding, 1992). This is not the application of pure economic theory but rather its mixing with existing (historical) ideological ambitions of political parties within the nation, to create a renewed challenge to state welfare and to reinvigorate welfare principles and objectives in terms of market and economic language and ambitions. Consequently, governments sought to reform the role of the state under the broader neoliberal economic agenda: privatisation of key utilities, the introduction of quasi-markets in health and education and the introduction of the ability to buy outright state-owned housing (Le Grand, 1992). Essentially, such developments were better classified as neoliberal hybrids: a blending of neoliberal economic theory with other political ideologies. Levitas (1988) illustrates this in the UK, suggesting that the ideas underpinning the New Right governments promoted the small-state neoliberal economic theory in conjunction with a conservative moral authoritarianism which, combined, produced the New Right ideology. The focus of this, in relation to welfare, was the promulgation of particular narratives of welfare recipients and welfare provision that promote fundamental change: a combination of the policy narratives in the previous chapter with the economic crisis narrative outlined in this chapter.

There is no 'pure' neoliberalism. Rather, the characteristics outlined above are drawn into national political and historical contexts to create varieties of neoliberal ideas that operate at the nation–state level (Larner, 2005). Subsequently, retaining the UK illustration, the New Labour governments' 'Third Way' ideology (1997–2010) offered a blend of neoliberalism and social democracy (David, 2000; May et al., 2005). We could suggest similar developments in the US and Germany in their move towards **Third Way** politics. These entanglements of different ideological and economic arguments have resulted in nuanced debates about what is being integrated. Thus, while Hall (2005) suggests of New Labour's hybrid that a dominant neoliberal agenda was blended with social democracy as the junior partner, Jessop (2004) suggests the pairing was of neoliberalism and Christian socialism, rather than social democracy.

For our purposes, this debate is semantic. What it illustrates is that neoliberal praxis is never based solely on neoliberal ideas; it is integrated into local economic, political and social contexts. This is important when considering the earlier discussion of nation-building. These new hybrid configurations create a new framework in which national identity is developed and pursued through policy interventions. This engineers a rearticulating of key concepts, as we have seen, and a reposition of welfare services – a process that pays considerable attention to global, as well as national, dynamics.

Reiterating the relevance to welfare and Social Policy, the work of Fourcade-Gourinchas and Babb (2002) highlights the variations in 'neoliberalism' around a central neoliberal political configuration. Peck (2004) supports this in his suggestion that qualitatively different geographical variations of neoliberalism have developed, and Larner's (2005) analysis places political struggle at the centre of variations in neoliberalism, highlighting how local political struggle impacts on how these variations are formed. Thus, while at the global level neoliberalism has spread, this integrates into national welfare debates to facilitate a shift in how nation states respond to the welfare needs of their citizens. This creates a new policy narrative around the intent and purpose of welfare, which is developed alongside the narratives explored in the last chapter.

Before taking this argument further, it is important to note that neoliberalism does not have agency; that is, the capacity to act independently on a set of beliefs. Rather, national and international actors – that's policy makers, campaigners, citizens – have agency and can act on certain beliefs. As such, *neoliberalism* does not change policy (nor does Marxism or feminism); rather, politicians, policy makers and a range of other stakeholders have to actively pursue policy and practice that place these theories at the heart of welfare provision.

Thus, advocates of neoliberalism hybrids integrate this framework into welfare debates, creating a new conventional wisdom of social problems and their solutions. Galbraith (1958) suggests that the term '**conventional wisdom**' can be used to describe ideas invested with a certain amount of esteem at a particular time, which then become an acceptable explanation of current affairs. He specifically used the term to highlight resistance in economics to ideas that did not fit with the neoliberal paradigm. Conventional wisdom therefore comes to gain an unquestionable status in public understanding based on the narratives (or stories) it tells about social problems (the lens through which constructions are formed). However, as Galbraith notes, this does not mean it cannot – or should not – be challenged (see our discussion of change in Chapter 10).

The establishment of this new conventional wisdom has created momentum for welfare reform, along with a number of other lines of development, many of which we have previously explored and to which we can now add this wider economic narrative. Clarke (2004) illustrates some of this in his discussion of the shift in the mixed economy of welfare (MEW). This shift instigates a change in social responsibilities – from the public sphere (government) to the private sphere (individuals and families) – and reliance, therefore, on the market. A similar suggestion is found in Drakeford's (2000) argument regarding privatisation: what was once seen as a collective responsibility is now the responsibility of the individual. Clarke (2004:30) further suggests that 'neoliberalism tells stories about the world, the future and how they will develop – and tries to make this come true'.

An essential element of this story is the end of history narrative. Presented by Fukuyama (1992), the suggestion is that economic and social progress has reached a point at which there are no further economic or social forms to develop; capitalist free markets and the democratic political system have won out. The claim of Marxists – that capitalism will eventually be overturned by the rise of Communism – has proven to be false. This is the meaning of the end of history claim: there is no further economic development to occur; neoliberal capitalism is the end state. Politicians, such as former UK prime minister Margaret Thatcher, have suggested that neoliberal reforms were necessary because: 'There is no alternative' (TINA). Adding support to these narratives, policy makers have highlighted the significance of globalisation as radically changing the economic and social landscape. These changes, it is suggested, necessitate the adoption of neoliberal ideas into national contexts to ensure the nation remains competitive and strong in the new global economy. Thus, the new conventional wisdom is presented as not an ideological argument but a response to a changing socioeconomic order. The ideological dynamics are consequently hidden.

Globalisation and neoliberalism

Globalisation and the ascendency of neoliberalism have been seen as parallel developments. Global organisations such as the World Bank and the International Monetary Fund (IMF) have adopted neoliberal thinking and promoted this on the global stage. The World Bank often attaches conditions to loans that require policy change by nations, often placing social policy safety nets as residual elements within a privately provided commercial welfare system – using the market to provide for welfare needs, as desired by neoliberal thinkers. The IMF has operated in similar ways.

For example, Genschel (2004) highlights the case of France in the 1980s, which sought to implement Keynesian-type economic and welfare policies but was required by the IMF to adopt the restraint and austerity approach found within neoliberal economic thinking. Additionally, a £2.3 billion loan to the UK government in 1976 came with conditions that required cuts to public expenditure. The European Union (EU) made similar demands of the Greek government; in the wake of the Global Financial Crisis of 2008, they were required to implement 'austerity measures' (significant cuts in publicly provided welfare services) as a condition of receiving financial support. The suffering of Greek citizens was clearly insufficient by itself (Matsaganis, 2012; Greer, 2014). Within developing nations, the IMF and World Bank have attached conditionality to loans to governments requiring that certain services are provided by the market rather than the state (Nelson, 1996).

Thus, global actors hold sway over how nation states seek to develop their own policy approaches, often requiring that nations adopt neoliberal practices, which starts to question the sovereignty of the nation state. But this, as just noted, rests on agency – the decision by policy makers to pursue these courses of action. There are, of course, wider debates around the availability of other choices and the levels of coercion that may be used – but these are generated by other actors with agency, who have opted to follow a particular ideological position. What is integral here is the close relationship between neoliberalism and globalisation (while remembering that they are not the *same* phenomena), which creates a new policy narrative driving welfare reforms.

To start to understand this conceptual entanglement, we need to revisit the nation-building discussion from Chapter 4. Globalisation, within a neoliberal framework, has promoted the idea of a competitive global market in which nations must compete with each other for business investment by international corporations. Presented as the most effective way for markets to operate, nation states have to alter their nation-building projects to pursue the creation of a competitive state, which is underpinned by neoliberal economics. Alongside wider economic changes, welfare provision is rethought, not only to reduce the size of the state (to remove it from interference in the market) but also to reposition welfare interventions to reflect a move towards a social investment welfare state (Morel et al., 2012). Welfare provision must be redefined in terms of **human capital** investment; in other words, improving the educational level of citizens, so that they become a highly qualified pool of potential employees to attract businesses to invest in the national economy rather than in other nations. This creates yet another policy narrative for reforms to welfare systems, which aligns with some of the broader principles we have already explored in relation to stigma/shame and the family: *welfare policy must seek to alter the behaviours and* *activities of citizens to align with the new global world order.* The argument goes along the following lines.

Globalisation processes have created new risks, against which the nation state cannot provide protection, for they exist beyond the control of nation states. As such, individuals must provide/secure their own sources of support. The state can assist to an extent with this provision, especially where it fosters individual responsibility for protection or helps with economic investment. But some forms of welfare support will radically change, aligning with the increased conditionality and residual provision explored in earlier chapters. As noted, this places a *changed socioeconomic context* – not a *different ideological view* – as the cause of welfare change. It is a response to wider changes rather than just one interpretation of those changes (as we will see when we explore globalisation in more detail shortly). In brief, the way in which neoliberalism has sought to explain globalisation has facilitated a change in welfare provision. Other ideological positions will offer different explanations.

Summary

This section has briefly sketched out the ideas of neoliberalism. Attention was given to key characteristics that have developed at a global level to form an influential paradigm, which is brought into welfare debates. But the argument has been a bit more nuanced than simply stating that 'neoliberalism' causes change. On the one hand, it is an ideological framework that interacts with other political, historical and social contexts. Subsequently, neoliberalism is not simply one form; there are varieties, or hybrid neoliberalisms, as Figure 7.3 illustrates. On the other hand, the changes that occur require political actors who engage with and enact these ideas. Change does not occur simply because of new (or revived) ideas, but rather because policy makers actively pursue these ideas in practices (praxis). It is possible to resist and challenge this praxis; however, as we will see, the contemporary context of globalisation makes such resistance difficult. Such challenges are difficult, however, in part because of the global nature of neoliberalism.

Figure 7.3: Neoliberal hybrids

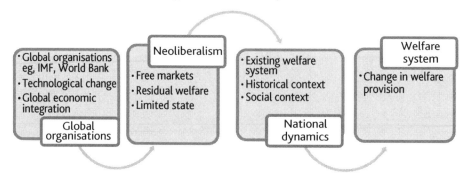

Globalisation

Although it is essential to keep the concepts of globalisation and neoliberalism analytically distinct, we did start by exploring the overlaps. This allowed for a discussion of a further policy narrative that has triggered conceptual changes, hinted at throughout earlier chapters. But it was suggested that neoliberalism is just one explanation of globalisation processes. As Clarke (2004) notes, this explanation of globalisation could really be a reflection of neoliberalism making claims of the world and trying to make them true. The discussion of globalisation that follows seeks to suggest some broader definitions around the *economic dimension* of globalisation, focusing again on the policy narratives this generates. It is not possible to also consider the social and cultural dimensions of globalisation, despite their relevance to Social Policy and Social Sciences more broadly (see, for example, Stevenson, 2000).

Economic changes: the rise of globalisation

The type of society found in the western world has changed significantly since the development of the welfare state. The post-Second World War period was classified as part of the **Fordist** era (associated with car manufacturer Henry Ford, this refers to the industrial method epitomised by large-scale mechanised mass production), where industrialisation relied on the development of production lines, allowing workers to be involved in the creation of one small part of a finished product rather than the production of the whole. This allowed for greater quantity and faster production, which drove economic growth and was later modified through **Taylorism**: a factory management system developed to increase efficiency by evaluating every step in a manufacturing process and breaking down production into specialised repetitive tasks to increase efficiency of output.

The welfare state is attached to this industrial era; indeed, some suggest it is an outcome of these changes. Yet, from the 1960s, economic crises narratives have generated a number of socioeconomic changes that have influenced welfare provision. As a result, Jessop (1995) argues that there has been a change from Keynesian welfare national state (KWNS) to a Schumpeterian workfare post-national regime (SWPR) (see Table 7.2). These changes set the context for contemporary debates around globalisation and provided the foundation for globalisation; accompanying this economic reconfiguration has been the rise of global economic integration, and an increased role of multinational corporations (MNCs) and transnational corporations (TNCs).

Thus, the concept of globalisation is drawn on to suggest the need for significant welfare reform because, it is argued, there has been fundamental change in the socioeconomic world. While this section offers a definition and account of globalisation (focused predominantly on economic considerations, in line with the rest of this chapter), it argues that the development of this idea within political

Table 7.2: From Keynesian welfare national state (KWNS) to Schumpeterian workfare post-national regime (SWPR)

KWNS	SWPR
Secure the conditions of full employment	Constant economic revolution and innovation, requiring flexibility for competitiveness
Welfare focused on generalising the norms of mass consumption and collective consumption	Focus on workfare rather than welfare
National focus: local, regional and international were subordinate to the national	Nation state hollowed out in three directions (up towards international agencies, down towards regional and local levels and sideways to cross-border governance)
Statist: MEW was shaped by state institutions	State plays less of a role in welfare provision compared to the private and voluntary sectors

and policy debates is *intentional*. Within the neoliberal paradigm, a specific notion of globalisation justifies the changes occurring as being out of the control of politicians: a natural development of a global, free market beyond the scope of nation states. As such, these economic changes (alongside social, cultural and technological changes) require policies that respond to and support the new context (rather than challenge or reshape it). Subsequently, it could be argued that this blend of neoliberalism and globalisation becomes the new conventional wisdom, ensuring that social policies implicitly accept the dominant neoliberal account of globalisation, which consequently reinforces the notion of economic crisis and necessary 'welfare' reform.

An economic focus on globalisation has remained one of the key issues of the debate and the efforts to define the concept. The rise of footloose capital and companies has facilitated economic integration across the world; simultaneously, neoliberal economics has come to dominate economic theory and foster a reconsideration of the market–state relationship. This economic context, as Farazmand (1999) explains, was presented as both the 'end of history' and the end of public administration; here, the state becomes irrelevant. This was presented as the natural progression of capitalism, and as such required that the state develop new approaches to delivering social services: the adopting of **privatisation** and what has been termed New Public Management (NPM) – the implementation of the private sector's managerial practices into the public sector, including new auditing and target regimes (see Clarke et al., 2001).

This gradual economic integration, therefore, has defined globalisation as a process. But the nature of the process is unclear. Clarke (2004) suggests a set of definitions that can shape our understanding of globalisation. The first presents globalisation as a *distinct causal process that is remaking the world*: the economic changes, alongside the political and cultural changes, are fundamentally altering the world we inhabit. For others, however, globalisation is the *result* of other processes: of changes such as new alignments of regions, nations and transnational interrelationships. Regarding politics, the argument presented is that the state has been hollowed out, as MNCs, TNCs and other forms of global governance start to dominate and direct national policy. There has also been the rise of global political actors, such as the IMF, World Bank, UN, EU and global non-governmental organisations (NGOs) (Yeates, 2008), all of which are involved in policy and politics in various ways.

In addition to the economic and political changes are cultural changes, which are perhaps one of the most overlooked aspects. This is the suggestion that the globe is shrinking in terms of temporality and spatiality, allowing cultural influences to rapidly and easily cross borders and creating cultural instability and mobility; consider, for example, how social media links the world in an instantaneous exchange of information. This has led Giddens (2002) to suggest that globalisation is new, revolutionary and goes beyond economic terms to impact on people's lives locally. Influenced by changes in communications technology, facilitating both business and cultural exchanges, this affects a range of things – from family structure to democracy. Such views have helped foster the promotion of globalisation as something new that has to be responded to; hence, the need for neoliberal praxis across economic, political and social spheres of life: nation states have lost control of their economies in this global world. However, for Hirst and Thompson (2004), this is not true; rather, nation states continue to regulate their economies differently, and so no unilateral global economy exists. Yes, there is an internationalised economy crossing political boundaries, but this has historically been the case for a much longer timeframe.

As noted, Clarke (2004) presents a number of ways in which we can understand globalisation. The second is a *distinction between a linear development and set of contradictory trajectories*. The former suggests an unfolding process occurring in one clear distinct and natural way. This implies homogeneity in the increase in the mobility of capital, investment, trade and information across the globe, thus dissolving outmoded barriers, boundaries and ways of life that block the development of a new world order. The latter suggests there is no even and clear path being followed; rather, the development is uneven, contradictory and full of tensions. Both illustrate how the concept of globalisation is seen as a process (or its end result) with a number of driving influences (economic, political and cultural), and that explanations of this process are more varied than is implied within neoliberal debates.

To this, Clarke (2004) adds a further set of definitions of globalisation: a *distinction between the apocalyptic change and unfinished tendencies*. The former views globalisation as a radical shift in the dimensions of human life, while the latter suggests it represents uneven and unfinished geopolitical realignments that are still taking place. It is important to note that Clarke is not suggesting that globalisation is explained by one of his three aforementioned distinctions. Rather, all three interact with each other in debates on globalisation. Similarly, Fitzpatrick (2001a) divides the globalisation debate into four groups of intersecting and overlapping sets of arguments, represented in Figure 7.4.

Figure 7.4: Fitzpatrick's globalisation groups

On the one hand, therefore, we can start to question the explanations offered in the neoliberal/globalisation narrative. If these globalisation practices are contemporary versions of pre-existing historical practices, or an ideological imposition of a certain interpretation of the world, then we are able to challenge and question the pursuit of welfare reforms in line with this policy narrative. However, perhaps a more challenging argument to question is the emerging view that these global trends – regardless of whether they are inevitable or pursued by political actors – are gradually eroding the nation state. This weakness manifests itself through welfare reform, as corporations become more powerful actors than states, placing the commercial sector at the forefront of welfare provision.

Does globalisation weaken the nation state?

As indicated, the rise of globalisation occurs alongside a shift from Keynesian to Hayekian economic ideas, resulting in a parallel analytical focus on globalisation and neoliberal economics and the integration of the two. Combined, this has not only resulted in a rethinking of the state–market relationship but also generated debate about the continued relevance of the state as a powerful institution in relation to economic and welfare policy. As indicated in relation to conditionality and financial support from the IMF or EU, this results from the ability of nations to resist the demands of global governance bodies pursuing neoliberal inspired practices. Additionally, as Massey (1999, cited in Clarke, 2000:213) suggests:

> the imagination of a globalization in terms of unbounded free space chimes all too well with that powerful rhetoric of neo-liberalism

around 'free trade'. It is a pivotal element in a powerful, political, fully-fledged discourse. It is a discourse which is produced in the countries of the world's North. It is a discourse which has its institutions and its professionals – the IMF, the World Bank, the World Trade Organization, Western governments. It is a discourse which is normative; and it is a discourse which has effects.

Thus, globalisation has created not only powerful global institutions influencing economic policy and practice but also a powerful discourse about the nature of socioeconomic change – changes that are relevant to welfare provision. However, before we can explore the relevance to welfare debates, we must first examine the broader argument.

Questions about the power of the state have gained significance as a result of the rise of MNCs and TNCs. An MNC is *one* corporation that operates across a number of different countries. These are different from TNCs, which develop as a result of mergers of *different* companies, which can be across different countries. These organisations have been considered the driving force of globalisation because they facilitate international economic integration, facilitating the claim that the new global economic order has fundamentally reduced the power of nation states. The global scope of these corporations and their incomes can easily be larger than the gross domestic product (GDP) of nations, which, it is argued, grants them considerable influence over nation states and international government organisations (IGOs): the World Bank, IMF and so on. In fact, many IGOs have incorporated business opinions into their operations, while they have yet to engage labour and civil society organisations to the same extent.

The growth of these corporations has resulted from the pursuit of neoliberal economic theory, which suggests trade barriers between nations curtail economic growth and therefore distort market practices. The removal of these barriers allows corporations to grow and expand their investment activity across multiple nations, and also facilitates cheap importation of goods, which allows market practices to efficiently use the world's resources. These economic policy changes have two relevant implications for social policy. First is the claim of a race to the bottom. Here, trade openness allows for business relocation where labour and production costs are cheaper, generating a downward pressure on wages and conditions of employment as whole sectors of businesses seek to become competitive in the global market. This has implications for not only the sufficiency of income to meet the accepted standard of living and new employment practices (such as zero-hours contracts) but also the potential increase in unemployment, as jobs are moved from one country to another. Mishra (1999) has suggested a policy response to this: an international agreement that ensures high social protection standards within the developed economies and support for developing economies to reach those same standards. Essentially, this is based on the view that the level of economic development dictates the level of social protection, with effort to bring everyone up to a certain standard.

The second underpinning process relevant to welfare provision is the aforementioned *weakening of nation-state power*. This is tied to the expanded role given to IGOs over policy issues. As Rieger and Leibfried (1998:366, emphasis in original) suggest: 'The movement towards and the trends in a globalised economy have been triggered, contained, differentiated or modified, weakened or strengthened, and slowed down or speeded up through *national structures of social policy and their developments*, to the degree that these could replace protectionism'. Such views underpin Genschel's (2004) argument that the globalisation of markets resulted in little choice but for governments to become market friendly. Thus, we can see the potential TINA argument being relevant here: neoliberalism is a response to these global processes, not the cause, so the argument goes. Such analysis seeks to suggest that state welfare provision is based on an outdated economic theory; that it follows certain ideas and practices around social protection that do not reflect contemporary employment practice, and is inefficient in its allocation of resources, especially as it is politically biased to promising to deliver more (for governments to win elections).

These narratives potentially alter definitions of the nation and welfare states explored previously. For some, the nation state is weakened by increasing economic integration, while others consider it to be strengthened. The weak state argument rests on a number of key claims, starting with the view that nation states have a decreasing ability to provide for their populations. On the one hand, there is a need to be competitive in the face of footloose capital; on the other, there are new pressures, requiring a fundamental change in public welfare provision (a social investment approach). Additionally, people now live (so it is claimed) in a borderless world, undermining the national, territorial basis of citizenship. Not only are nations economically integrated but also technological developments facilitate global cultural exchanges, and new political bodies have formed. As such, a powerful argument for economic and welfare policy change has dominated in political debate since the 1980s.

These narratives promote the idea that the international competitive economy requires a very different type of state: one that is not attached to significant levels of expenditure and redistribution, but facilitates the economic competitiveness of the nation. This results in a process known as **welfare retrenchment**: the rolling back of welfare provision to allow for a more dynamic and responsive market, and a smaller state that leaves the market alone. However, the analysis does not end there. Genschel (2004) summed up the next stage of the argument, which claims that the state–market debate has now been turned on its head. As such, there is an argument that the rigidity and inflexibility of welfare systems and their bureaucratic practices are the cause of their own failure. The weakness of the welfare state (and the state more broadly) is therefore self-inflicted. Thus, advocates of globalisation would argue that globalisation is a response to those weaknesses to hold the welfare state in check – to prevent it getting too big or responding to newly invented needs.

It is possible to pick out several arguments from those we have already examined:

- needs are a false political construction that politicians agree to in order to win elections – thus, they are never-ending demands on public bodies;
- the ideas of Hayek and Friedman have replaced Keynesian economics;
- only the free market can allocate resource efficiently;
- the state should not create jobs but invest in the human capital of citizens to attract business investment into the nation;
- welfare systems have flawed designs and lack the ability to innovate and respond to the changing socioeconomic world; thus, there is a need for increased market (or commercial sector) provision.

The influence of these combined arguments results in Genschel's (2004:614) proposal of a growing perception that the welfare state 'systematically encouraged attitudes and expectations that it was not in a position to satisfy. The institutional guarantee that social needs would be taken care of worked as an incentive of people to invent new needs.' Subsequently, there has been a gradual development of a number of different narratives around the (global) market–state relationship, which facilitate the shift in welfare provision that we have already explored:

- a change in the MEW towards increased use of the commercial sector and quasi-markets;
- the rethinking of entitlement and the consequential impact on welfare design (increased means testing and conditionality);
- a move towards ideas about a social investment welfare state and greater citizen responsibility for welfare (more on this in the next chapter).

But this argument has not gone unchallenged. In terms of the economic development argument, Hirst and Thompson (2004) contend that economic integration is not 'new' but comparable to pre-1914 levels of trade. In addition, this internationalisation of trade is not global; rather, it is concentrated in three regional trade blocs. Furthermore, MNCs find it difficult to detach themselves from a national base (they have to be connected to at least one nation state), and they also require assistance to develop their business from the state (an interesting analysis of state support of corporations can be found in Farnsworth, 2004). Thus, not only is there still a need for a level of political organisation to ensure market functioning but also efforts to organise cross-national regulation and monitoring of the markets have yet to be exhausted: history has *not* ended. The immediate response to the global financial crisis of 2008 is an example of nation-state efforts to develop such international regulation (Wintour, 2008a).

Regarding the political process and weakening of the state, Weiss (1998) puts forward the view that globalisation is not undermining the nation state; rather, state power adapts to the changing economic context, and nation states therefore remain influential. This view is based on two key claims:

- that a national home base remains the rule rather than the exception for MNCs;
- that political leaders play a large role in claiming and contributing to the view that governments are helpless (essentially, how they present and explain globalisation is more impactful than globalisation per se, and it also reminds us of the need for agency in order to pursue ideas in welfare practice).

This latter point is important because it suggests that the state – not economic and technology changes – has driven globalisation. Thus, the desire for political change has resulted in the current dominant narratives around neoliberal economic practice and the globalised world. Other narratives and alternative choices based on different interpretations of socioeconomic change are possible, but there must also be political will to pursue these. Thus, Weiss (1998:20) argues that 'the state is constantly seeking power sharing arrangements which give scope for remaining an active centre, hence being a "catalytic" state'; rather than being passive, the state has actively pursued changes in welfare that allow it to retain power. These can be found in a range of design features embedded in welfare systems; NPM techniques, devolution and pluralism in welfare provision (the use of the private and third sectors) – accompanied by auditing, regulation and determined targets of the outputs of different sectors by the state – illustrate that, rather than directly controlling welfare, the state now steers welfare provision in the direction that it desires. Thus, the state is not weak; it is merely using different tools to provide welfare services, which do not involve direct state provision.

Repositioning Social Policy debates

The foregoing illustrates that socioeconomic changes generated in response to globalisation are largely *political choices*; decisions informed by neoliberal economic thinking. Changes in the perceived power of the nation state and its ability to provide welfare are a reflection of those political decisions (Genschel, 2004). These changes have consequences for nation–building and welfare system design, as well as for relocating the response to social problems to the global level.

New nation-building projects are not created around protecting social rights as a response to the consequences of industrialisation, but rather around attuning social rights to the needs of the nation within a globally competitive economy. This is illustrated in the World Economic Forum's annual *Global Competitiveness Report* (which ranks nations in terms of their competitiveness) as well as within political speeches: 'But I say – there is a global race out there to win jobs for Britain and I believe in leading from the front. So, I make no apology for linking Britain to the fastest-growing parts of the world' (Cameron, 2014).

The nation must be competitive, and this has resulted in a shift in how welfare provision is thought. As Powell (1999) illustrates in relation to New Labour, and Morel et al. (2012) in relation to Europe more broadly, 'good' forms of welfare invest in people to build up their human capital: the skills, knowledge and capability of individuals. A skilled and highly qualified workforce enhances the competitive advantage of your nation. As such, investment in health and education, and increasing higher education participation, are examples of 'good' welfare spending. Paying social security to the unemployed is 'bad' welfare spending. But 'bad' forms of welfare provision can be reformed to diminish their impact. Such changes require a redesign of welfare provision, which needs to be established on a re-articulation of key concepts. In part, this is about a justification for reduced state provision and a shift in the MEW towards the commercial/market sector. This has been illustrated throughout the foregoing and the previous three chapters. However, we now have a broader conceptual framework for understanding some of this change. In part, this is also about a rethinking of welfare provision – away from needs and survival/participation within your society, towards equipping citizens to take care of themselves – and rethinking state provision in relation to this. Consequently providing a framework for facilitating change to welfare entitlement.

Associated with this is the discussion of decentring Social Policy, which influences the wider MEW. Globalisation has resulted in a rise in a number of policy actors. The World Bank, IMF, UN, EU and WHO are some examples of governmental organisations that interact with policy making. As such, the study of Social Policy must, as Deacon et al. (1997:195, cited in Yeates, 2008:11) suggest, consider the 'practice of supranational actors [which] embodies social redistribution, global social regulation, and global social provision and/or empowerment, and ... The ways in which supranational organisations shape national social policy'. This can have a number of impacts. For example, the EU uses the open method of coordination to develop overarching policy aims and objects, to which its member states should subscribe. However, this does not impose policy solutions; rather, policy design remains within the purview of individual nations to determine (Daly, 2008). Thus, in relation to social policy, the EU has an influence in *framing the debates* around welfare, but less influence in the *design of policies* to secure welfare (similarly to how human rights exist universally, but are protected in various different ways at the national level).

Globalisation highlights how classic Social Policy issues – redistribution, social rights and so on – have been brought into the supranational level. There are growing calls for developing a social protection through supranational actors, but:

> there are also many common problems that require a common resolve. Think about the legacy of public and private debt, and about fiscal and current account imbalances. Think about the reforms needed to make the financial system safer and bring it more into the service of the real economy. Think about rising inequality, environmental degradation and the long-term challenges of climate change. These are not abstract challenges. It is only by addressing them that we can ensure future prosperity for all and meet the rising aspirations of our global citizens – for jobs, for security, for opportunity, for dignity. (Christine Legarde, Managing Director of the IMF, June 2014)

The suggestion here is that social problems require joined-up, global solutions. Additionally (and not discussed here) there are issues around **migration**; this can increase the pressures on national welfare provision, which questions the territorial-based assumptions of much social welfare, undermining traditional nation-building projects.

Nevertheless, some views of globalisation claim that the changes proposed are overstated. This suggests that, even if economic globalisation is occurring (as the sponsors suggest), there is still a need for welfare state provision. It will not be removed; rather it is altered to fit new purposes. Pierson (1998) argues the focus on globalisation is looking in the wrong place to explain the changes occurring. Slower economic growth, rising service sector employment (and decreasing manufacturing employment), population ageing and the expansion of government commitments to social welfare are the real cause of the problems faced by welfare states, and these correlate with globalisation– but *correlation is not causation*. While the welfare state has a 'stickiness' that means it will be hard to dissolve, its limited ability to respond to change creates the tensions and debates that eventually give way to reform and change. But these changes have more to do with ideological projects of governments (national and supranational) than restricted choice imposed by external forces (Rieger and Leibfried, 1998). Consequently, newly forming political ideologies are generating the change they claim has occurred. Political choice is the driver, and different choices can be made.

Austerity: a new economic crisis narrative

Arising out of this complex weave of globalisation and neoliberalism, a further crisis of welfare has formed. The global financial crisis of 2008 started when mortgage-related securities within the global financial system suddenly collapsed. This rapidly moved from a mortgage crisis to a financial crisis, as banks withdrew lending in order to build up reserves (Kotz, 2009; Farnsworth and Irving, 2011). The combined narratives of neoliberalism and globalisation promoted a specific explanation for the crisis, which hindered efforts to reinvigorate Keynesian thinking for the global stage (Farnsworth and Irving, 2011). Consequently, a renewed neoliberal critique of state intervention, in particular state expenditure, has been found in the concept of **austerity**.

Exploring the consequences of this new narrative, Clarke and Newman (2012:300) explain that the UK's response to this austerity crisis moved 'from an economic problem (how to "rescue" the banks and restore market stability) to a political problem (how to allocate blame and responsibility for the crisis): a reworking that has focused on the unwieldy and expensive welfare state and public sector'. This reworking of the crisis into one of public finances has underpinned narratives that seek to reduce state expenditure, such as that found in the UK. For Gough (2011) this generates a fiscal crisis in the Marxist sense: the financial resources for welfare have dried up, and the dominant narrative has convinced voters they should desire reduced expenditure. This generates a demand for policy reforms that facilitate reduced public spending and the removal of the state; but new conceptual narratives and justifications are required for this course of action. The neoliberal dimension remains relevant here because a demand for 'austerity' by itself is insufficient. Post-Second World War, there was an acceptance of austerity in the household while the nation rebuilt and created a collective resource for securing welfare via the welfare state (Farnsworth and Irving, 2011). In its contemporary guise, austerity is used to produce a narrative in line with neoliberal and globalisation arguments. Austerity is again something to accept for the national interest – but now it is about dismantling the welfare system, which provided protection of social rights. Similarly, leaders across Europe have called for austerity to be a permanent feature of UK policy to ensure a leaner state. For example, German chancellor Angela Merkel has argued for continued economic restructuring and imposing 'austerity measures' in nations such as Greece (Wearden and Elliott, 2013).

However, such an account cannot overlook the potential diversity of responses. As Farnsworth and Irving (2011) suggest, there is actually a 'variety of crises'. Individual nations have responded to the economic crisis in different ways. China has increased its social security provision; the US and Canada have not radically revisited their social safety nets; whereas in Iceland, the financial sector – central to its national economy – faced a period in which financial resources were not available to meet increasing demand for welfare interventions based on solidarity, egalitarianism and the role of the state. This reminds us that global ideas must still be filtered through national political and historical debates (as illustrated by the neoliberal hybrid discussion earlier in this chapter).

That said, within the contemporary setting, austerity is presented as an 'urgent truth'. The global financial crisis of 2008 has generated a need to reduce public spending and reform welfare services, facilitating an intensified neoliberal policy agenda (Grimshaw and Rubery, 2012) that seeks to withdraw state provision. The austerity crisis can be seen to have resulted in entrenchment of neoliberal economic theory through the new fluidity of economic globalisation. The outcome of this shift is an intensified neoliberal policy emphasis, which seeks to redefine both minimum standards of welfare provision and social need (Grimshaw and Rubery, 2012).

Chapter summary

This chapter has explored the idea of crisis narratives as part of the broader discussion of how the socioeconomic context influences the formation of welfare policies, and subsequently, the use of certain concepts to support these claims. Particular attention was given to the concepts of neoliberalism and globalisation. Opening this chapter were two quotes highlighting two sets of constraints on welfare provision – neoliberalism and globalisation – as illustrated in Figure 7.5. Essentially, these pressures have shifted welfare support away from state-provided services, income transfers based on social rights and the promotion of equality through redistribution. In its place is increased reliance on the commercial for-profit sector to provide services, a reliance on the state to provide the bare minimum for survival for those unable to make their own private provision, and the promotion of the free market in not only the economic sphere but also social life more broadly.

Figure 7.5: Contextual pressures for welfare reform

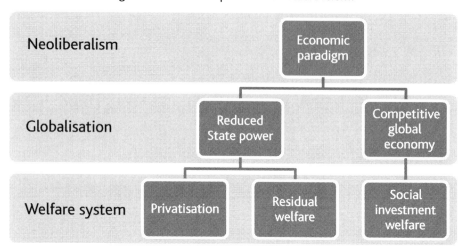

This chapter has provided an introduction to a concept that refers to the *context* of welfare provision, rather than a concept directly involved in *debate* around the nature and design of provision. As with the previous chapter, we continued to shift our focus to *narratives* around policy. In this chapter, 'crisis narratives' were highlighted to indicate a shift and change in the socioeconomic context that radically alters debates about welfare. We can see the dominance of economic crisis narratives, which can be linked to neoliberalism, marginalising other explanations of change and potential crisis (found in Marxism and environmentalism). As hinted at throughout the chapter, these narratives have been supported by another broader shift: encouraging citizens to take on greater responsibility for their welfare. This is the focus of the next chapter and our exploration of risk.

Critical thinking activity

Evaluate the claim that globalisation is weakening the nation-state's ability to develop welfare provision.

Further reading

Greve, B. (2015) *Welfare and the Welfare State: Present and Future*. Oxon: Routledge.

Harvey, D. (2007) *A Brief History of Neoliberalism*. Oxford: Oxford University Press.

Wilding, P. (1997) Globalization, Regionalism and Social Policy. *Social Policy and Administration* 31 (4) pp410–428.

Yeates, N. (2008) *Understanding Global Social Policy*. Bristol: Policy Press.

Don't forget to look at the companion website for more information.

8

How does risk change the welfare state?

> People who are poorer should be prepared to take the biggest risks – they've got least to lose.

> Dependency on the state cannot continue. We need individuals to take on greater responsibility for their own welfare.

Key concepts in this chapter:
risk • resilience • social exclusion • social investment welfare state

Our discussion has started to shift to focus on concepts that inform debate about the wider context of welfare. Welfare systems are therefore always open to reform through changes in these conceptual debates. The previous two chapters also drew attention to how these debates inform narratives around welfare provision. Neoliberalism and globalisation are particularly important because they generate a sense of global change and crisis that requires urgent action. The previous chapter hinted at the nature of those reforms, which brings us to our next concept – **risk** – which has provided a new analytical lens to the study of Social Policy. Risk has been expressed in a number of ways (as we will soon see). Our specific focus is partially summed up by Lord Freud (cited in The Telegraph, 2012) a Member of the House of Lords who oversaw a range of reforms to social security provision under different governments in the UK:

> We've got the circumstances now where ... people who are poorer should be prepared to take the biggest risks – they've got least to lose. We have, through our welfare system, created a system which has made them reluctant to take risks so we need to turn that on its head and make the system predictable so that people will take those risks. I think we have a dreadful welfare system.

We have examined debates around dependency, deserving and undeserving recipients, and a shift in nation-building towards a competitive global economy. Risk is a means by which these debates can be brought together to facilitate welfare reform. As with the previous chapter, a narrative for policy change will become apparent, which alters how entitlement concepts are presented to the public. Through a discussion of the risk society thesis, it becomes possible to reflect on its implications for the development of social policy as an activity of government and Social Policy as an academic discipline. This, in turn, allows us to explore how the concept of **resilience** enters into welfare debates; that is, the need to ensure citizens are capable of coping in the changing socioeconomic world – especially where the state takes a reduced role in direct provision of welfare.

What is the risk society?

The introduction to risk needs to start with an exploration of social theory. This allows us to understand both the concept and its relevance in relation to a changing context of welfare debates. Social theory has always sought to *explain* the world (a key difference with Social Policy, where we also want to *change* it). The early development of Sociology drew attention to explaining the development of modernity, which was seen to facilitate the development of scientific, objective knowledge to explain the nature of the world we lived in. Social policy itself is part of the modernist project: an attempt to improve human wellbeing through the collective. But societies do not stand still; they constantly change and evolve. Thus, Sociology has entered into a debate about the nature of contemporary society. We briefly explored one possible explanation in Chapter 5: postmodernism. An alternative explanation, which has relevance to the concept of risk, can be found in the suggestion that we have moved towards a different type of modern society: reflexive modernity.

Reflexive modernity

Beck (1992) promotes the idea of reflexive modernity, suggesting that the darker side to scientific and technological development generates new risks and hazards. We know that economic and social progress, the latter of which gave rise to the welfare state, can have positive and negative consequences. However, Beck suggests that these are *new* risks because they are no longer limited in time (potentially affecting future generations) or space (these risks are far-reaching and global in nature). These changes are manmade and can take a number of forms. They can be *social and economic*; for example, unemployment due to technical advances and global competition, or insecurity of home ownership due to the swings in interest rates. These new risks can also result from *intervention into the environment* (acid rain and global warming). A further consequence of these risks is that they do not fit the distributional logic found in the consequences of modernity. In modern societies, the risks people experienced were related to their class position: the lower your class, the greater number of risks you were likely to face (for example, the social gradient in health). The consequences of new risks can fall on anyone, regardless of class position.

So, why does Beck refer to this as 'reflexive modernity'? Beck (1992) argues that science and technology may generate risks, but they also produce actors who claim to assess the potential for negative consequences and seek to limit these. Subsequently, technical experts gain significant power, and can influence politics and policy agendas. As scientific knowledge grows, the power of these groups expands and informs a whole range of decision-making processes. This is where reflexivity comes into the discussion. Reflexivity refers to the ability to pause and consider the possible consequences of particular courses of action. Beck's critique of modernity suggests that science excludes reflexive thinking, as it divorces itself from social and political debates through claimed objectivity. Scientists have an idealised model of the risk system, reflected in the exclusive focus on laboratory knowledge. Such knowledge, however, does not adequately reproduce the external conditions of the world outside of the lab, creating a non-reflexive imposition of their knowledge as scientific knowledge is transferred from the lab to the real world. Science operates in a bounded world. This means that there are clear boundaries, which allow for an investigation into cause and effect, as everything can be accounted for. However, due to its complexity, the social world is unbounded; it does not have clear boundaries around an intervention, so consequences cannot be easily contained. Thus, in reflexive modern society we must question science from other knowledge paradigms, such as Sociology, Politics, Philosophy and so on. Natural scientific knowledge is not the only source of knowledge underpinning human development.

In a similar way, Giddens (1998) offers an overlapping account of the changes under the term late modernity. According to Giddens, the world is characterised by internally produced or manufactured risks, which contrast with the external risks of the natural world – the unintended side effects of science and technology. Socioeconomic changes have generated an expansion of choice and the dissolution of traditional norms and social boundaries, which can be enhanced through technological developments; hence his argument (see Chapter 6) about the need to consider relationships rather than families, as well as wider arguments about consumer societies and the breakdown of 'traditional morals'. Not all of these arguments are attributable to Giddens, but we could potentially sketch out overlaps between a number of debates we have examined in various chapters. Thus, for Giddens, technological changes associated with globalisation assist this process of late modernity, and this requires that we rethink the operation of welfare systems.

Criticisms of reflexive modernity

There are, of course, critiques of these theories. Steurer (1998, cited in Kemshall, 2002) offers three critiques of the 'manufactured uncertainty' presented by Beck. First, while Beck suggests that technological and scientific advances occur without appropriate regulation of these activities, Steurer argues that this overlooks the *growth in risk assessment management* within, for example, social care and social policy practice. Failures in policy quickly gain the attention of regulatory bodies and the media, often generating rapid policy change in response to perceived scandals (see, for example, Butler and Drakeford, 2005). Steurer's second critique questions the suggestion that traditional social inequalities do not reflect risks. Rather, *the class position people occupy still influences where risks fall*: a position supported by analysis, which suggests that class background still influences the life chances available to young people as they transition to adulthood (Furlong and Cartmel, 1997). Thus, the risk society thesis presents the illusion of more choice, allowing the repositioning of social problems as private concerns. Similarly, Taylor-Gooby (2001) suggests that the risk society is class ideology masquerading as social theory. Different social groups may be aware of the new risks they experience, but these groups exhibit varying levels of confidence in their capacity to deal with them. Thus, in a similar way to responses to globalisation, an ideological argument (such as neoliberalism) is underlying the dominant explanations of social change.

Finally, Steurer questions the claim that risks have increased, suggesting we are just better at detecting them now. However, Beck's argument can be more accurately described as claiming a *multiplicity of risks* exist. It may be unclear whether risks have increased, but they do contain new features – global scale, low probability but high consequence, indiscriminate impact – and they originate in political and organisational processes of decision-making on risk, which are attributable to human agency, not fate. More broadly, it has been suggested that Beck's arguments might better capture reflections on the circumstances of post-war Germany; that is, they may be a better reflection of the context in which he was writing than a generalisable theory (Dingwall, 1999).

Summary

As with the previous chapter, the foregoing suggests that a number of changes have occurred within society that relate significantly to the pursuit of welfare (illustrated in Figure 8.1). This has grown out of an investigation of changing socioeconomic contexts: beyond what is often described as 'modernity' (the industrial, capitalist world) and towards a form of society that has, in some way, moved beyond this historical point of development. These changes in the socioeconomic context, in turn, require a rethinking of welfare provision. As with globalisation and neoliberalism, this paves the way for a redesign of welfare systems in relation to the wider mixed economy of welfare (MEW); namely, a move away from the state (which is seen as inadequate or inappropriate for this new context) and towards provision through other sectors of the MEW. As we will see, this leads to a suggestion of the need to refashion welfare provision to promote prudential or responsible citizens, who are willing to secure their own welfare and take the risks required to pursue their welfare goals.

Figure 8.1: Towards the risk society

Changing welfare debates

Beck (1992) and Giddens (1998) suggest that the changed social context requires a reallocation of how to respond to these new risks. The state cannot always control the context of our lives, but it can be refashioned to facilitate our resilience and ability to cope within this changed world. Welfare provision, therefore, should facilitate the development of positive risk-takers because of the changes required by individuals to manage their own risks. Consequently, welfare provision is reformed: away from the traditional welfare state and towards a new welfare system suitable for late modernity. Thus, the risk society thesis has a number of implications for social policy and the welfare state.

Promoting risk-taking

Giddens' (1998) contribution to the development of the 'Third Way' argument underpins much of this discussion on risk. It suggests that the welfare state previously managed economic risk through collective provision, establishing minimum standards (a level of need) below which no one should fall. However, this fostered dependency on the welfare state, and encouraged people to become risk-averse. This is perhaps best illustrated in the assumption that those on unemployment benefits are unwilling to take new job opportunities because of the uncertain impact this may have on their incomes, whereas remaining on social security support ensures their incomes remain stable. This is, of course, not an uncontested view; but it highlights how the *individual* is seen to be at fault, rather than the lack of secure forms of employment in the *economy*, which are beyond the control of the individual. In late modernity, the welfare state needs to be repurposed, focusing on the individual to encourage 'positive risk-taking'. To address the risk-averse nature of welfare recipients (claimed to be dependent on state welfare provision) necessitates a redesign of welfare provision. Thus, conditionality in social security support for the unemployed becomes viable when framed as supporting the unemployed to engage in job-search activity and training. This ignores the potential consequence of sanctions for failing to meet these conditions, and says nothing of the reduced-value income support resulting in having less income to live on.

Subsequently, a focus on risk has eroded confidence in and legitimacy of the welfare state, as the rationale for state welfare in its original form contradicts the new conventional wisdom of contemporary society (Kemshall, 2002). Questions arise regarding the appropriate coverage and resourcing of the welfare state, overlapping with both economic crisis narratives and the distinction between deserving and undeserving citizens (illustrating a potential ideological strand in the debate around the risk society). This suggests the need to rethink how key concepts, such as need and citizenship, are considered. Welfare support should not just meet needs; rather, it must encourage citizens to become active agents in shaping their world (making choices that affect their life-course) through calculating the risks and opportunities attached to those decisions (for example, making decisions about the costs of attending university to gain a degree and the potential long-term benefits of having a degree).

Thus, social policy within risk societies focuses on *identification* and *intervention*. Freeman (1992) claims this occurs with four key purposes in mind, which illustrate potential ideological justifications for the promotion of the risk society thesis:

1. Management, rather than elimination, of social problems;
2. Maintenance of the status quo;
3. Protection of vested interests; and
4. Reconstruction of social problems as individual choices and responsibilities.

From this, it is possible to suggest that social policy is no longer about the alleviation of individual needs or the pursuit of collective goods. Welfare is refashioned to move the prevention of risk and displacement, or risk-management responsibilities, onto the individual: the **entrepreneurial self**.

Changing language

To ensure you understand the driving arguments for change, we need to explore this theoretical change a little further before directly discussing its welfare implications. Often, it is possible to find terms such as 'moral hazard', 'dependency', 'scroungers' and 'perverse incentive' in contemporary debates around the welfare state, especially in relation to social security. While the development of the welfare state was successful in overcoming the division of deserving/undeserving through the provision of universal welfare, this position has been reversed since the 1980s. For Giddens, this does not reflect a throwback to an earlier time, but rather a response to the changes in society that are impacting on local life and global order. It is about finding new solutions to social problems that are not only financial but also relate to the legitimacy of provision (the wrong people are having their needs met) and the flexibility of welfare services (a need to move away from bureaucratic organisations). Kemshall (2002:40) provides a useful table that helps to explain the consequences of this (Table 8.1).

The risk society thesis thus promotes a shift in key notions of state welfare provision. Universal welfare has transitioned to a residual system, whereby only the barest minimum welfare support is provided to those who have proven incapable

Table 8.1: Welfare and risk societies

Welfare society	Risk society
Universal welfare: as described in previous chapters	*Residual welfare*: a form of provision by the state, which ensures meagre survival of citizens who have not made their own provision
Risk protection: based on the recognition that the risks of problems are ubiquitous and citizens require protection through collective pooling of resources	*Risk promotion*: the redesign of social welfare support to encourage citizens to take risks to change their circumstances, suggesting that the individual (for example) is the barrier to their unemployment
Social insurance: the principle through which collective pooling of resources is pursued	*Social justice*: as described earlier, a concept in Social Policy
No-fault exposure to risk: the individual is not to blame for experiencing social problems	*The prudential citizen*: the individual must adopt certain behaviours that protect them against various social problems (e.g. working hard in school to secure good qualifications; developing their own savings to protect from unemployment or old age); the experience of social problems, therefore, becomes the fault of the unprepared individual

of protecting themselves. This represents a change from the initial conception of risk as *structural* (for example, unemployment caused by the wider economic context) towards a revised notion of risk as 'a fact of late modern life, a source of opportunity as well as a threat' (Kemshall, 2002:40). Citizens are expected to take risks to improve their circumstances, but are also assumed to have the capacity to make judgements between the positive and negative consequences of such risks. We should ask whether this is any different from Murray's argument that fear motivates people to lift themselves out of poverty – and, furthermore, if this is an appropriate basis for welfare provision.

Further changes mapped by Kemshall (2002) (see Table 8.1) include the view that traditional welfare provision sought to protect citizens through social insurance provision. This was achieved through National Insurance contributions, which protected citizens against the possibility of unemployment, ill health and so on. Within the revised context influenced by the risk thesis, welfare now seeks to promote a notion of social justice: the *ambition* to ameliorate the worst effects of capitalism, requiring a redirection of state funds towards education and skill development, and away from the alleviation of misfortune and redistribution of social goods. Such ideas overlap with the response to globalisation: an investment in human capital. Finally, there is the move from no–fault exposure (it is not your fault you are ill or lost your job) to a focus on prudential citizens (you have adopted the wrong lifestyle). Combined, these changes illustrate a significant repositioning of welfare provision.

Thus, there are three key developments to consider. The first is a move towards a *social investment approach to welfare*. Here, the intention is to 'modernise the post-war welfare state so as to better address the new social risks and needs structure of contemporary societies' (Morel et al., 2012:1). Policy effort focuses on investment in human capital, such as early childhood intervention, education and the idea of lifelong learning; jobs are no longer for life, so the workforce requires generic transferable skills and the ability to retrain as appropriate. Alongside these efforts are policies to make the best use of human capital, such as childcare to support women's employment and anti-discrimination regulations and frameworks to ensure more citizens can gain employment opportunities. Finally, the wider reforms require that welfare policy fosters greater social inclusion (examined in detail shortly), which, focused on employability, ensures all citizens are considered a productive factor in economic growth. This creates a new narrative around welfare provision, positioning it as a *benefit* rather than a *cost* to the economy: there will be no more 'bad' forms of welfare expenditure.

The second key development for a consideration has been the focus on **prudential citizens**. In his discussion of state power, Garland (1996) used the term **responsibilisation** to present the changes that emphasise new expectations of citizens' behaviour (see also Chapter 9). Under this notion of responsibilisation, it is now the duty of the citizen to take on increased responsibility for their own welfare and to protect themselves from various social risks – through actively seeking work, saving in a private pension and making appropriate educational and training decisions to maintain one's employability. Recall the Titmuss quote in Chapter 3, partially reproduced here in relation to welfare support: 'they represent partial compensations for disservices, for social costs and social insecurities which are the product of a rapidly changing industrial urban society. They are part of the price we pay to some people for bearing part of the costs of other people's progress'. The arguments in favour of a risk society have abandoned these assumptions; the aim for policy is not to directly respond to social problems but to mobilise non-state agents to develop solutions. Within social policies, such practices can be found in asset-building policies (Rowlingson and McKay, 2012), conditionality on social security, and homelessness policy (Whiteford, 2010). This links to the later discussion of resilience.

Finally, the promotion of the risk thesis highlights a tension in welfare provision: on the one hand, the protection of service recipients from risks; on the other, those same recipients' rights and ability to make choices. High-profile welfare scandals, such as the death of Baby P and Victoria Climbie in the UK, bring to the public's attention the complex and risky situations in which welfare professionals find themselves. In relation to social work, Webb (2006) argues that such situations generate a movement towards elaborate rule systems and procedures, which reduce the scope of professional judgements by social workers. Recognising that individuals wish to pursue their own choices regarding their lives leads them to requiring a secure environment in which to pursue opportunities. But where crisis and failure occur, governments create more systems of accountability to establish systems that not only shape but also control policy and allow the prediction of risk. Webb suggests this is a symbol of the risk society (although one could argue it is actually a symbol of the perception that the risk society is real, rather than evidence of its existence).

As such, frontline social workers must now operate with increased awareness of risks, and pursue assessments of risk in their work. Herring and Thom (1997:233, cited in Kemshall, 2002:75) illustrate this in relation to the tensions around rights, arguing that risk management results in 'consideration of protection, of the appropriate balance between protection and freedom and the right of individuals to choose how and where they live'. But unlike the commercial sector (organisations such as banks), welfare organisations have no clear measures of risk, which adds to the challenge of this work. New service targets, performance measures and lists of procedures form part of the toolkit for assessing risky situations, but this does not resolve the tension for welfare recipient choice. Furthermore, these assessments take place within services often experiencing financial changes and service re-organisations, which creates uncertainty regarding what services will be available to help users manage risk in future. Once again, this creates a policy space in which citizen resilience to uncertain contexts is presented as the primary response to risks.

Summary

The promotion of the risk society thesis has shifted welfare debates. As with the previous two chapters, it has given rise to a new narrative that increasingly focuses on the individual, and their own contribution and efforts to alleviate their disadvantage and experience of social problems. Welfare provision changes, as the central arguments of entitlement change, to reflect the new insights into the context of our lives – as the risk society thesis explained (Figure 8.2). The response is to use welfare systems to create prudential citizens, who prepare in advance to protect themselves from the potential harms of contemporary society. Concepts of need, citizenship and equality fundamentally shift away from the ideas portrayed in the 1940s, which recognised individual and societal needs and protections against an ever-changing socioeconomic structure outside the control of individuals and the communities in which they live. Instead, as noted with globalisation, the context has changed and is beyond the control of the nation state. We are told there is no alternative to this, and so welfare provision must change. Thus, rather than trying to alleviate and prevent disadvantage and social problems, the welfare system seeks to help citizens *manage uncertainty* when it impacts on their lives.

Generating policy change

The foregoing discussion suggested that the risk thesis has been integrated into an analysis of the socioeconomic context, facilitating a change in approach to securing human welfare. No longer should a welfare system seek to provide protection; instead, it should enable citizens to take greater responsibility. A number of

Figure 8.2: Reshaping welfare support

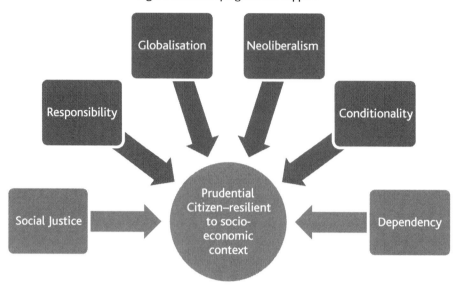

approaches follow on from this stance: the use of education as an investment in one's future, the development of savings products (such as non-state pensions) and the development of re-employment initiatives. Welfare policies are deployed through the wider MEW to facilitate citizen responsibility. Such changes rest on rearticulating certain concepts and introducing (or revitalising) others. Such changes are now explored in relation to need, as well as the idea of resilience.

Are we moving away from the concept of need?

In Chapter 3, different theories of need were introduced as part of a wider discussion of the entitlement triangle. Since the 1980s, the concept of need has come under significant critique as part of a political project to reduce state provision of welfare support, due to the dominance of economic crisis narratives and the rise of neoliberal economic theory. Langan (1998) argues the concept of need itself was reconceptualised. This is the suggestion that policy makers explicitly moved away from definitions of need related to public opinions, or even generally accepted standards in society, and towards defining needs quite explicitly. Langan (1998:28) illustrates this with the following example from a (now-dated) Department of Health document, released in 1991, which discussed needs assessments for community-based care: 'In this guidance the term ["need"] is used as a shorthand for the requirements of individuals to enable then to achieve, maintain, or restore, an acceptable level of social independence or quality of life, *as defined by the particular care agency or authority*' (emphasis added).

The context for this change was not only the analysis outlined in this and previous chapters but also the perceived influence of public demand in relation to the concept of need. Consequently, needs were seen to be driven by public demand, and were no longer a true reflection of the minimum required for survival. As we have discussed in relation to social divisions, diversity of citizens highlights specific needs for certain groups; this creates new demands for needs to be met to ensure all citizens secure their welfare. Langan's quote illustrates an attempt by policy makers to challenge this perception. Thus, how needs were to be defined was to be returned to specialists and experts, not subject to the political whim of the electorate. The shifting notion of need was integral, therefore, to the move towards increased use of the commercial sector in welfare provision; primarily, outright privatisation and the use of quasi-markets. People would only satisfy true needs within the price system of the market, which could respond effectively to demand through competition for consumers. This ignored significant critique that such approaches ignore inequalities in socioeconomic conditions, which make some more vocal and powerful consumers than others.

Langan (1998) goes on to argue that the development of needs-led welfare is based more on the demands of a chronically declining economy than the casualties of that decline. Needs were subsequently defined by state actors, and defined in a restrictive way, with the addition of conditionality, to tackle perceived behavioural faults. Need, as with the broader concept of social rights, is therefore subject to the dynamics of financial constraint rather than a sustained discourse of entitlement. And, despite claims to be challenging the political influence of the concept, this very change is a reflection of a political decision to pursue an ideological agenda underpinned by neoliberal arguments (as explored previously).

This shifting ground over the concept of need continued in the 1990s, when the concept of **social exclusion** started to gain credence. In part, this term sought to draw policy makers' attention away from income and expenditure (and a number of other social problems) as the root causes of poverty and towards a range of dimensions that might exclude citizens from their local community/ society. Levitas et al. (2007:9) offer the following definition of social exclusion:

> Social exclusion is a complex and multi-dimensional process. It involves the lack or denial of resources, rights, goods and services, and the inability to participate in the normal relationships and activities, available to the majority of people in a society, whether in economic, social, cultural or political arenas. It affects both the quality of life of individuals and the equity and cohesion of society as a whole.

The breadth of the concept sought to draw out the multiplicity of different aspects of our social, economic and political lives, which influence our engagement and participation in society. Bradshaw et al. (2004) identify a range of drivers to social exclusion, which include macro drivers such as demographic changes (ageing populations, youth unemployment and so on), the labour market (not only unemployment but also changes in work itself in terms of security, type of work and pay) and the policy context (how social policy reacts to these changes to limit – or exacerbate – experiences of poverty and hardship). However, they also provide a focus on individual risk factors that signal the increased vulnerability of certain categories of individual (such as disability, age and low education qualifications), as well as triggers (events that precipitate social exclusion, which they link to homelessness). The idea of vulnerability is explored in a bit more detail in the next chapter.

Essentially, these ideas create a multidimensional dynamic to social exclusion, which illustrates a broader range of factors that impact on participation in one's society. It is, of course, important to note that each factor does not operate in isolation; they criss-cross and overlap, reminding us that social problems really are **wicked issues**. For example, the British dimensions of social exclusion highlighted by Levitas et al. (2007) highlights three broad dimensions, each with different elements (see Table 8.2).

Table 8.2: Dimensions of social exclusion

Dimension	Elements
Resources	Material/economic resources
	Access to public and private services
	Social resources
Participation	Economic participation
	Social participation
	Culture, education and skills
	Political and civic participation
Quality of life	Health and wellbeing
	Living environment
	Crime, harm and criminalisation

A range of circumstances are therefore drawn into an account of social exclusion. Such experiences are considered problematic because of their human cost in terms of underachievement, mental ill health, stress and low income (to name a few). In addition, there are seen to be societal impacts: in the forms of higher crime, reduced social mobility and reduced social cohesion. Where an individual or community is excluded in several of these domains, they are considered to be in 'deep exclusion', or multiple deprivation. As this term has gained prominence, the focus on 'needs' has diminished, as noted.

Reiterating the importance of certain policy narratives, established on conceptual debate, Levitas' (1998) identifies a number of discourses of social exclusion. The first of these is the social inclusion discourse (SID), which focuses on moral integration and social cohesion, to be achieved through participation in the economy – specifically, paid work in the labour market. This has become the dominant form through which social exclusion is explained and addressed. The influence of the concepts of risk and globalisation ensures that this form of economic participation becomes the best route for inclusion, largely ignoring all other social activities that bring value and can foster a sense of inclusion. Specifically, it underpins the notion of social investment through the promotion of education as a lifelong process, and work as the best route out of poverty. Employment ensures citizens are able to take the necessary risks to satisfy their needs, discharge their duties and facilitate their participation in society.

The second, mentioned previously, is the moral underclass discourse (MUD). The emphasis here is on the alleged moral, cultural and behavioural deficiencies of those excluded from society and labelled as an underclass. This concept of an underclass, as noted, draws attention to individual faults – and the responsibility of the individual to change their behaviour. Such analysis is in line with the shifts in Social Policy debate resulting from the risk perspective. Yet, as Titmuss (1971) argues, our consideration of the definition of need must also pay attention to the organisation of resources to address this need. The MUD underpins a welfare system that is more punitive and punishing of those perceived as not conducting themselves appropriately, and that provides only a residual social safety net focused on providing 'subsistence needs', which further acts as a disincentive to claiming support. Stigma is a mainstay of such approaches (see also Chapter 9).

This contrasts with the third discourse – the redistribution discourse – which accepts the multifaceted nature of social exclusion and argues for policy intervention beyond poverty alleviation alone. Attention is given to a wider range of processes that cause inequality. It pursues forms of welfare support that do not seek a minimal amount of inclusion but rather encompass social, political, cultural and economic citizenship within a broader critique of inequality, which creates space for activities other than paid work to be considered by policy makers. Consequently, how social exclusion is phrased alters the underpinning meaning of the term and its applicability to policy making. While arguments have been made from this position, so far there are no clear policy developments to which we can attach these views; MUD and SID have dominated the political stage.

In his review of social exclusion, solidarity and globalisation, Room (1995) suggests there are five changes that reconfigure debates around poverty to align with social exclusion (see Table 8.3). Room is sceptical of this reframing of poverty to focus on social exclusion. In relation to the first three reconfigurations, he suggests these issues were already under investigation within poverty studies. Subsequently, the 'excitement' offered by social exclusion as an analytical concept for exploring these changes is somewhat misplaced. His account of the relational dimensions again suggests that some poverty studies sought to move into this territory, but a number of problematic dynamics remain under-theorised. One such topic requiring further investigation is how relational elements of social life are renegotiated over time and place.

Table 8.3: Changes to poverty debates

Reconfiguration	Explanation
A refocusing from financial to multidimensional disadvantage	This recognises that financial matters, while important, are insufficient for an understanding of hardship; rather, a more nuanced exploration of interconnected dimensions is required. This entails analysis that seeks to understand the relationship between e.g. poverty and housing, or lack of qualifications with performance in the labour market.
A move from a static to a dynamic analysis	This focuses on efforts to explore the triggers and causes of exclusion, and how these impact on its duration. It suggests that the risks exist across a number of contexts, but do not necessarily generate poverty. Thus, the term 'social exclusion' offers a means by which we can explore multidimensional aspects to understand when the risks become lived reality.
A consideration of the resources of the local community rather than the individual or household	Suggesting that a household focus is insufficient for understanding poverty and a need to reflect on the deprivation of the wider community. Facilitating a focus on community self-help initiatives and mutual aid on the one hand, and local cultures that limit participation and engagement on the other, this change facilitates a broader analysis of context of poverty than a narrow focus on households.
A move away from distributional to relational dimensions of stratification and disadvantage	This links to the discussion at the end of the last chapter regarding relational welfare. The focus here is a shift away from distributional issues (wealth and income) to a consideration of participation: people's social relationships and engagement in society.
A shift away from a continuum of inequality to 'catastrophic rupture'	The suggestion here is that social exclusion creates a catastrophic rupture in people's relational engagement with society. Not all groups experiencing disadvantage will experience this exclusion – this is the purpose of empirical investigation – but where it occurs, it results from the multidimensional nature of social exclusion, and its effects are irreversible.

Finally, Room (1995) highlights the important parallel development to social exclusion, whereby middle and upper classes have the ability to *choose* to exclude themselves from society – especially from interaction with those groups they wish not to interact with. They can avoid many of the duties and requirements placed on poorer citizens, making a mockery of government efforts to pursue inclusion. Only certain groups are considered to be of significant concern and in need of re-engagement; these are often the same groups isolated through stigmatising narratives from mainstream society. A pertinent question, therefore, is to always ask from whose perspective certain 'troublesome citizens and groups' are being defined.

Resilience and welfare

Responding to risk and social exclusion requires that individuals not only take on an increased responsibility for securing their welfare in the present but also protect themselves against future risks. The focus on resilience in relation to policy and practice has gained increasing attention as a means of achieving this. While recent work has sought to add theoretical depth to the concept of resilience, the term has a long-established association with environmental issues, including explorations of the relationship between ecological and human resilience, as well as environmental management (Adger, 2000). This focus on ecological resilience has grown alongside a focus on 'community resilience' and the role of the welfare state and social work professionals in promoting resilience (Bonanno, 2008). Further consideration has started to critique the concept of resilience for being framed in governmental terms – which often place responsibility for social (and environmental) problems onto individual and community actors, thus limiting wider structural reforms – and the misapplication of resilience in its ecological sense to social relations (Gregory, 2014).

Three changes were discussed earlier in relation to welfare provision and risk: the development of social investment, creating prudential citizens and changes in frontline practices to reflect increased awareness of risk. Combined, these require welfare policy to focus on building the resilience of individuals to avoid or cope with adverse circumstances. Here, there remains definitional problems as to what resilience actually involves. Does it require a focus on protective factors, such as family characteristics, schooling and educational attainment, the development of aspirations and the promotion of human and social capital? Or is there an unknown factor at play – perhaps what we assume to be resilience is actually the absence of a risk factor that research has yet to uncover?

In welfare debates, the former view on positive factors has come to dominate, promoting an asset approach: a consideration of the characteristics and capabilities citizens already have that allow them to overcome adversities, rather than a focus on what they lack (a deficit approach to policy). An asset approach can be achieved in a number of ways. First, in line with the social investment perspective, there is greater attention to 'good' forms of welfare – such as health and education. Policies can target a range of personal, social and economic circumstances that could promote resilience, including: reducing child poverty; targeted home support for vulnerable families; literacy skills; effective personal; social and health education; and school funding targeted at the poorest. Additionally, the central state may design policies to contain conditionality: requirements to be met in order to receive welfare support. Such conditionality may seek to promote behavioural change, such as ensuring children attend school, to develop future resilience through the promotion of human capital. But such policies need to be carefully designed, as interventions can also create perverse incentives, which have different behavioural effects (Bastagli, 2009). Other policies, such as asset-building policies, seek to encourage the formation of prudential citizens, who take measures to protect themselves from future risks (such as developing adequate pension provision for old age). Finally, Fraser et al. (1999) show how the focus on protective factors forms part of a 'risk and resilience' framework in social work practice, conceptualising problems and designing interventions and measurement tools that fit into these debates. Social workers must understand the risk factors and required protections for their clients, and engage with evidence-based interventions, to build the capabilities of clients to ensure their resilience.

Resilience has been defined as coping with shocks and traumas, helping individuals and/or communities to maintain healthy, 'symptom-free' functioning (Bonanno, 2008). The research on resilience locates **social capital** as a central resource for creating and protecting communities; as such, the intention is to build community networks and individual capabilities to survive shocks; for example, helping someone survive unemployment by having not only prepared their own savings against such an eventuality but also built up their own skills and education to allow transfer into new employment. The prudential citizen ensures they are protected, rather than taking the risk of not having protections against unforeseen eventualities. Yet, as Norris et al. (2008:146) state: '[i]t would not be too difficult for the concept of resilience to erode into one more way of stigmatising suffering individuals and communities'. It is drawn upon in relation to the risk thesis as a means of developing citizens equipped to not only make life–course decisions but also cope with the risks associated with those, be they personal or financial. This has generated a renewed interest in the concept of **self–help**.

Reinvigorating self-help

Historically, welfare provision operated outside of the state through the family, private commercial provision, collective friendly societies and philanthropic donations. State intervention (reluctantly, at first) grew out of a recognition that such provision was not always sufficient, did not ensure equal access for all citizens and did not offer an adequate response to the structural causes of social problems; hence, the rise of state involvement in welfare provision (as discussed in earlier chapters).

Yet, the repositioning of welfare and contemporary society within the debates of globalisation, risk and (ultimately) neoliberal economic thinking has questioned a number of these collectivist assumptions. Resilience has become the new focus of many interventions, providing a window of opportunity into which a reinvigorated notion of self-help gains credence. This term encompasses a range of activities conducted by individuals or communities for themselves or their families, which is reciprocal, not carried out by professionals and draws upon local people's skills, power, labour and knowledge (Burns and Taylor, 1998). While some suggest that the rise of welfare systems largely removed self-help provision, others have proposed that policy makers draw on self-help solutions when formulating policy, for a number of reasons:

1. To reduce demands on rising welfare budgets;
2. To counterbalance the breakdown of social cohesion (re-establishing moral and social responsibilities); and
3. To help cushion the impact of poverty. (Burns and Taylor, 1998)

Reasons 1 and 2 are important to the discussion here.

Neoliberal projects, on the political Right, have an inherent tension in their ideological foundation. On the one hand, their economic base requires a limited state (Reason 1 in Burns and Taylors' list); on the other, their social-authoritarian morality requires a strong state to re-establish moral/social responsibility (Reason 2). In the UK, there have been efforts to bridge this division through the development of the ideas of a 'Big Society' and **localism**: arguments for greater local involvement in service provision, reducing state services in favour of locally developed, community-based interventions. There are a number of debates and critiques of this that we cannot discuss here (see Taylor, 2011; Alcock, 2012); the key point is how participation, through self-help, was used to inform policy development. Promoters of the Big Society are interested in community self-help to establish 'little platoons' (Cameron, 2009) that take services out of public sector hands. But here, the concept of self-help becomes a little problematic.

Burns and Taylor (1998) argue that there are a number of uses of self-help initiatives. They can be a solution to social problems, a springboard into other forms of participation or an alternative to state provision. Additionally, they can be compatible with state policy (such as the Big Society), part of a continuum of activity (with the state at one end and self-help at the other) or in conflict with state activities and ideologies (attempting to promote an alternative form of living). This latter point is at the core of some efforts to promote various self-help initiatives within anarchist and feminist critiques of contemporary society (see Ward, 1996; Bryson, 2007). Consequently, there are different interpretations of self-help activity and the participation involved. Some view the schemes as primarily about encouraging citizens, instead of the state, to deliver services. Others argue that such initiatives are alternative to state interventions, and are based upon different ideological underpinnings; they present an alternative set of values and way of conducting life, which cannot be secured through state-promoted self-help.

Room (1995) suggests that research has already identified the limitations with community self-help approaches in poor localities, but these have been overlooked within this new analysis. Such limitations include the self-help initiatives being incredibly volatile and often short lived; they can collapse if key actors leave or move on, or if funding supporting the initiative comes to an end or is withdrawn. Following on from the foregoing distinction between ideological foundations, some self-help practices can be **co-opted**; that is, brought into a different ideological framework to support different intentions and practices (see Gregory, 2014). Finally, the association with community often presents such schemes as inclusive and all-encompassing, when exclusion and division can exist within community initiatives just as easily as in others. Yet, self-help and participation are linked with not only active citizenship (involvement is often how citizens, especially young people, are active) but also social exclusion. However, as Dinham (2005:304) suggests, 'it is anticipated that areas will become reconnected as communities, the socially excluded included and the renewed local relevance of democracy ensured as people experience and exercise their power in decision-making and the delivery of local services'. Participation is therefore seen as generating three effects for the socially excluded:

1. Transformation of attitudes from passivity to responsibility (linking together active citizenship and concepts of risk);
2. Regeneration of disadvantaged areas by harnessing new sense of responsibility to meet targets for change; and
3. New partnerships between the state and individual, based on power sharing, labelling individuals as 'stakeholders' rather than citizens. However, we can question if this power sharing is truly equal or not.

Summary

The concept of risk has been exercised in policy debate to rethink welfare services. As with the debates around stigma, neoliberalism and globalisation it has served as a tool for repositioning arguments around the responsibility of securing welfare and the purpose of state-provided support. The state is no longer focused on providing welfare services and income maintenance per se, but rather on facilitating citizens in their efforts to secure their own protection. This requires a range of policy changes, the context of which has been outlined here. It is possible to find more detailed accounts of how responsibilisation and social exclusion impact on social welfare provision (see also work that explores pension reform along the lines of financialisation [Finlayson, 2009]). Removing the risk-averse citizen necessitates wider changes to the welfare system that run contrary to earlier justifications for state involvement in welfare support.

Chapter summary

As with globalisation, the focus on risk and resilience has developed within a neoliberal economic paradigm, which facilitates a shift from collective risk and provision towards individual risk and responsibility. Drawing on the argument from this chapter and the previous, it is possible to reposition how these debates impact on welfare provision (see Figure 8.3). This narrative generates the sentiments expressed in the quotes opening this chapter: the need to take risks, and the need to end perceived welfare dependency. Promoting the idea of a prudential citizen has combined with the movement away from the 'traditional' welfare state model to promote social investment and responsibilisation. The risk society thesis has argued that we now live in late modernity: a view that industrial society has not 'gone away', but has fundamentally changed, creating new risks against which we have little protection. This requires that the system used to protect citizens against the old risks be modified in response to this new world we inhabit, necessitating fundamental changes in how welfare is provided. In part, this results in a desire to promote social investment, asset-building and interventions that promote the coping capacity of the vulnerable.

Figure 8.3 Refining contextual pressures for welfare reform

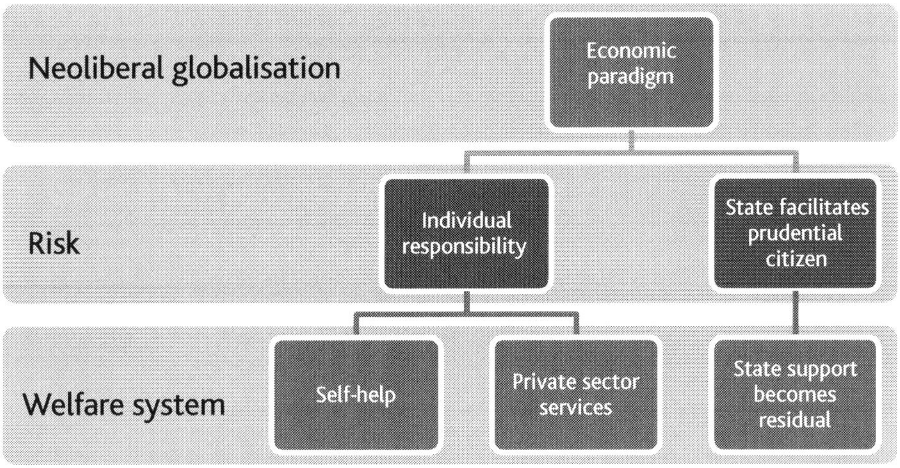

This is where the idea of resilience has gained significant support in policy making; it allows a refocusing of welfare efforts into investment approaches, particularly in relation to education and early-years interventions, and a greater reliance on citizens to make their own provision and self-help. Combined, the outcome of these conceptual debates has sidelined structural causes in favour of individualised (and pathologised) explanations of social problems. For some, however, such changes are the result of ideological arguments that seek to reduce the role of the state and require citizens to make their own provision. This is done within an increasing regulatory framework, which claims to help protect citizens from risks, but for some is about installing a new moral order on society. As such, 'risk and resilience' (again, as with globalisation) can be seen as one interpretation of contextual changes that has gained dominance in political and policy-making debates; other interpretations do, of course, exist.

Such arguments foreground a longer debate in Social Policy regarding the intent of policies to influence citizen behaviours and lives. Risk narratives have sought to change our analysis of social problems: how they are experienced by citizens, and how they should consequently be addressed. However, there is a critique of the presumed individualisation attached to this discussion of a risk society. Citizens may be aware of the changes occurring in their everyday lives and the changing policy responses; we cannot automatically assume there is diminished support for the collective state. Evidence from Taylor-Gooby et al. (1999) illustrated that while citizens recognise the shortfall in government provision, and people do make their own additional provision (pension savings and homeownership), these pragmatic strategies illustrate a willingness to take some risks *alongside* a belief that any negative consequences can be managed. It is not evidence for a diminished role of the welfare state.

Yet risk narratives, combined with those of globalisation and neoliberalism, remain dominant. Such analysis, it could be argued, seeks to control citizen actions and behaviours in a number of ways. As noted in relation to globalisation and neoliberalism, risk draws attention to the contextual debate: a debate that has informed much of the discussion in earlier chapters, and facilitated a change in how concepts are used to promote welfare systems. This concept also makes explicit how narratives for policy change have been accompanied with ideas of increased citizen participation and empowerment. This balance between social control, participation and empowerment forms the focus of the next chapter.

Critical thinking activity

Assess the relationship between the idea of a risk society and social welfare.

Otherwise change from question to assignment, for example?

Further reading

Dingwall, R. (1999) 'Risk Society': The Cult of Theory and the Millennium? *Social Policy and Administration* 33 pp474–491.

Kemshall, H. (2002) *Risk, Social Policy and Welfare*. Buckingham: Open University Press.

Levitas, R. (1998) *The Inclusive Society? Social Exclusion and New Labour*. Basingstoke: Macmillan.

'Resilience and Social Exclusion'; themed section of *Social Policy and Society* 8 (1) pp59–144.

Don't forget to look at the companion website for more information.

9

Is social policy about control?

Social policy is not just about securing people's welfare. It is also about trying to change behaviours or circumstances.

Welfare is meaningless if we don't empower people to pursue their desired preferences and goals.

Key concepts in this chapter:
empowerment • participation • personalisation • social control

So far, this book has demonstrated how key concepts have been integral to the formulation of policies, involving significant debate of not only what those concepts mean but also how they inform an understanding of welfare. We have explored justifications for welfare interventions, the establishment of entitlement criteria and debates about delivery and design of services. Recent chapters have shown us how policy narratives can develop around a range of issues, which also inform how policy makers and the public think about welfare provision. Within all of these debates, concepts are fundamental to the discussion. These debates are not just academic; they also have an impact on our lives and the lives of those around us.

Thus, conceptual debates influence the design of policy, which in turn seeks to alter or control some factor that causes diswelfare. This is achieved through various mechanisms and strategies of policy, which draw on key concepts to justify the changes sought. Essentially, policy seeks to intervene in the social, economic or even political structures in which we live our lives. However, as illustrated in the previous chapter, the focus has increasingly shifted to the individual. Consequently, policy is infused with three further conceptual debates, which interact with each other in various ways and form the focus of this chapter: **social control**, **empowerment** and **participation**. We will start with a discussion of social control, using participation as a means of moving the discussion towards an account of empowerment. This will relate, where appropriate, to other concepts and debates explored in previous chapters.

Social control and social policy

As a concept, social control has an implicit negative connotation in relation to interference in people's lives; a curtailment of freedom. However, it highlights a number of important considerations. On the one hand, it can refer to how social systems and structures create mechanisms for controlling citizens' behaviours, thoughts and actions. This can be seen to restrict the freedom and choices individuals have. The disadvantaged and often discriminated positions that some citizens occupy (as identified in relation to social divisions) can be the result of these structures: failure to accept the expected norms and behaviours resulting in stigma, sanction and potentially criminalisation. On the other hand, social control is also required to facilitate co-operation, communication and co-existence. This can also influence citizens' behaviours, thoughts and actions via the socialisation of newborn citizens through childhood (and often into adulthood) into the expected norms and values of citizens.

Policy can be used across either of these aspects of social control, with significant influences on the attainment of welfare. Consider, for example, the discussion of state-sanctioned notions of citizenship in Chapter 3. Policy has always been about control and order in some form: an explicit attempt to intervene in the world and create a change. New initiatives and interventions are responses to social problems; as such, they seek to promote change and remove diswelfare, often through an attempt to control the various factors which cause the particular social problem being addressed (be it the workings of the economy or the actions of a single individual). However, following the previous set of chapters regarding policy narratives, our concern here is primarily how policy is used to control and direct the behaviour of citizens, rather than the social context.

Social control

From the outset, it is important to consider how social control exists within a range of situations; for example family, work and doctors' practices. These contexts reflect differences in terms of formal and informal control. Formal control refers to legal or medical practices, whereas informal control refers to the integration of citizens into the behaviours and norms of the society in which they live, usually through processes of socialisation. As with the concept of risk, we are going to have to explore some sociological theory first, before moving on to more explicit welfare debates.

Chriss (2013) reviews a range of social theories that inform debates regarding social control, suggesting that a distinction can be drawn between direct control (all actual and possible restraints against deviance), internal control (systems of socialisation) and indirect control (the warm and secure bonds of attachment to others, such as family, which operates control from a distance). While theories of social control have highlighted a diverse range of focal points, they have generally considered the necessity of control for social function. Society requires coordination of its diverse parts to maintain itself and survive. Embedded in the earlier **functionalist** perspectives, social control acts as a form of regulation of society; there is a need for a system of sanction/punishment of those who do not comply with social norms.

Socialisation, as noted, is a starting point for guiding behaviours. Yet, as Parsons (1991) notes, different forms of social control can develop in relation to particular circumstances along four dimensions: situational, normative, individual and group.

- *Situational/individual:* where a person lacks the capability to perform a specific task or role within a specific situation and, as such, the person is identified as ill or sick; this leads to medical control.
- *Normative/individual:* highlights the failure of the individual to align with particular values, generating religious control.
- *Group/situational:* where there is a disturbance of group expectations within a particular setting, creating perceptions of disloyalty or detachment from the group, informal social control becomes apparent.
- *Group/normative:* reflects legal control as the mechanism for intervention, resulting from a perceived lack of commitment to legal norms.

Such forms of control can operate in a range of different ways through both formal and informal mechanisms. Thus, there can be instances of self-control, where individuals hold themselves in check due to not only external sanction but also internal feelings of disgust, shame, embarrassment and self-loathing. This overlaps with the discussion of stigma and shame in Chapter 6.

Providing a useful starting point for understanding the different types of social control, Chriss (2013) suggests three types of social control: medical, legal and informal. Combined, these 'amount to a range of normative prescriptions and proscriptions covering the areas of interpersonal relations and group living (informal control), behaviour more generally irrespective of the nature of the ties between persons in interaction (medical control), and the law and legal systems (legal control)' (Chriss, 2013:36–7). There is, he suggests, fluidity between the three. He illustrates this with the example of a man in a fast-food restaurant who is staring at another patron. If the latter moves to another part of the restaurant, this reflects informal social control: avoidance is the sanction being pursued. Alternatively, a complaint to the manager regarding disturbance by the 'weird guy' could be used. If the manager asks him to leave, this is still informal control, whereas calling the police to respond changes this to legal control. However, the police investigation could indicate a medical reason for the unusual behaviour, which moves the situation to one of medical control if the officers determine a need for a medical intervention. What we need to draw from this example and debate is that a range of types of social control exists; these are fluid forms of interaction which, we should remember, are not isolated from other social interactions (based on class, gender, ethnicity and so on).

Thus, social control refers to a range of interventions into social order: some through formal state mechanisms, others through interaction and the informal transmission of culture and values. Social policy plays a central feature within these forms of control. Policy can demand you meet certain conditions to secure welfare support (and punish you when you fail to meet these), or it can create incentives to act in certain ways (such as tax benefits for private pensions). It can also indirectly control through its underpinning assumptions (such as my often-used example of gender bias in the creation of a social security system predicated upon a male breadwinner family model). However, in relation to social control, significant attention in welfare debates has been given to control as discipline, emanating from the discussion of undeservingness and the work ethic. The Marxist critique of social rights as a means through which the working classes can be controlled also has relevance here.

If we return to Jensen and Tyler's (2015) earlier discussion of 'benefit brood' (Chapter 6), we can recall how stigmatised/shaming narratives develop particular images of certain groups, which facilitate welfare system reforms to intervene in the lives of certain citizens. Jensen and Tyler suggest this forms part of a move from a '**nanny state**' to a '**daddy state**'; the perceived caring and supporting approach of the 'nanny' is replaced with increased efforts to promote duties, sanctions and conditionality. Consequently, alongside new forms of conditionality there are efforts to promote active citizenship as another example of a policy shift that is relevant here. These changes create a new conventional wisdom around the daily life of certain citizens, ensuring public support for welfare changes to heighten not only control over but also discipline of citizens.

Is control about discipline?

The association between social control and discipline draws out a concern that the state uses welfare policy as a means for controlling a population and ensuring certain (elite) groups are protected within the socioeconomic structural arrangements of society (Lister, 2010). To an extent, this is predicated on a concern for achieving social order: the aforementioned functionalist accounts. However, from a Marxist analysis, such policy is pursued to facilitate state-centric forms of control designed to maintain capitalist society through labour discipline. Labour discipline is a key concept here, although potentially a little misleading. The traditional use of the term 'discipline' implies punishment for a perceived wrong. Here, the term retains some of this character, but refers more broadly to efforts to ensure the workforce maintains a certain work ethic to support the ends of capitalist productions. As such, 'labour discipline' contains elements of compliance, persuasion and moralistic/ideological pleas alongside tools of force and repression. This has been hinted at within the discussion of citizenship through the valorisation of work (as the primary duty of the citizen), the notion of social exclusion (inclusion in society is dependent upon paid work) and the deserving (hard-working/willing to work) versus undeserving (idle/work-shy) debate.

Such accounts tend to focus on the state's activities to seek to control and discipline (in that broader sense of the word) citizens to act in certain ways. These ideas are different from the more recent work of Foucault (1990, 1991), whose notion of power, reflected through control and order, is associated with not only government actions but also a range of non-government bodies. Foucault outlined a range of techniques and mechanisms for regulation and discipline, as well as the various levels at which this is enacted, and distinguished between three types of power (Table 9.1).

Table 9.1: Foucault's types of power

Power	Description
Sovereign power	Historically centralised power exercised by a sovereign individual, such as a monarch, which in contemporary society is held by a particular state or ruling class
Biopower	Power over life and death and the health and productivity of bodies, referring to medical and welfare professional power in particular
Disciplinary power	A range of different techniques to produce 'docile bodies' that can be (re)shaped, transformed and improved through compliance with institutional practices and discourses

In a series of books, Foucault examined significant changes in society to reflect on questions of power and control. Within *Discipline and Punish*, Foucault (1991) argued that, to a certain extent, changes in punishment for criminal transgressions not only reflected enlightened reform but were also generated by a shift in the use of power. Previously, punishment for transgressions were violent and public (flogging and hanging, for example); but such acts, by their violent and repressive nature, encouraged violent revolt. This started to change in the 18th century, when punishment was more carefully calibrated to fit the crime, as well as the intentions and social prospects of the criminal. The aim was to set a moral example and induce obedience through respect, rather than fear, and not to inflict a greater crime in the name of justice. Consequently, instead of retribution, the reform and correction of the criminal was the primary goal: the criminal must be 'saved'.

Initially, such ideas were retained within the criminal justice sphere; but through the idea of disciplinary control, Foucault suggested that concern with deviant behaviour (and its correction) should become a primary focus of activity. Yet, such power is not exclusively held by powerful elites; rather, Foucault (1990) argued, it is diffuse and ubiquitous. Power resides in a range of institutions in society, each of which acts in ways to discipline citizens into acceptable behaviours. Bringing this into some welfare policy illustrations, we can consider, for example, schools and hospitals. Schools are not simply the venue for intellectual engagement; they are apparatuses for the uninterrupted examination, measurement and stratification of all students and performances. Similarly, hospitals and healthcare have become organised around principles of hygiene and health promotion.

Health is transformed into healthiness – a lifelong attitude of responsibility for maintaining one's physical fitness, and the life-cycle itself, has been medicalised.

Foucault's argument is that power is *productive*: it creates certain types of subjects. We exist in a society in which we are under constant surveillance of various types; while initially targeted at the body, this eventually takes hold of the mind. Consider health messages around 'five-a-day' fruit and vegetables, the pressure to achieve educationally or family formation. Accordingly, through disciplinary power there is constant surveillance, which becomes internalised by individuals, who then produce self-awareness around these discourses, which then becomes the foundation of individual behaviour and actions.

Intervention into welfare can seek to integrate and harmonise social groups, but may also seek to divide, and to allow some groups to rule. Much of the debate about universal and selective services implicitly refers to this, drawing on concepts such as stigma to highlight the potentially divisive and detrimental nature of the latter compared to the former. This is, essentially, a matter of social order and control. Consider the discussion in Chapter 6; policy has been designed to encourage particular family forms and gendered roles, suggesting that a certain family form is morally correct. Yet this disadvantaged women, placing them in an inferior position to men. Thus, welfare policy not only promoted middle-class (Victorian) respectability but also created a division between men and women – outcomes that were then reinforced through the policies implemented.

In his analysis, Foucault was reluctant to support the progressive and benevolent discourses at the heart of welfare interventions and social reform. Rather, he emphasised that such discourses are entangled in power relations, which seek to foster discipline through welfare provision. Consequently, his ideas are often uncomfortable for students and academics within Social Policy, for they question the very assumptions of social progress. However, as Lister (2010) noted, Foucauldian analysis provided insight into not only discipline and control but also acts of resistance (a short discussion of which can be found in the final chapter).

Squires: anti-social policy

Offering an interesting account of social control within social policy, Squires (1990) draws on a number of these themes in his analysis of 'anti-social' policy. His work is worthy of a detailed consideration here.

He starts with the suggestion that a fundamental aspect of social policies is that, by their very nature, they are a 'double-edged sword'. That is to say, social policy often has a focus on integration and harmonisation of social groups, but at the same time can divide and rule others: what is a benefit for some can become a barrier for others. Thus, what is important here is not an automatic claim that some ideological positions lead to anti-social policies; after all, while some observers present the move from social-democratic to neoliberal ideas as a negative change, for others this change promotes freedom and choice. Rather, the term anti-social policy, Squires (1990: 6) suggested, is used to identify 'policies that create avarice and discontent, institutions to foster inequality and discrimination, structures to centralise power and cultivate authoritarianism and, perhaps above all, welfare that ignores needs and responds only to consumer demand backed by hard cash'. His focus was coercive elements of state intervention and the disciplinary relations of policy that develop alongside the positive and enlightened ideas of welfare provision.

The rise of the welfare state is mapped on top of the development of vast industrial changes in the western world, which had significant impacts on social and economic contexts of life. Such changes generated concerns with 'social questions', which motivated a range of reformers (drawn from the middle classes, who had the time to concern themselves with such intellectual matters and pursuits) and demonstrated concern for issues such as health, morality, idleness and poverty. As such, different social interventions developed to address the problems identified by reformers; but these suggested reforms were entwined with the need for labour discipline: an instilling of a work ethic suitable for the new industrialising world. As Garland (1981) argued, the development of social policy has sought to develop practices around welfare that support capitalist forms. Essentially, this means that policy had to help foster the development of labour power, to facilitate the move of the working classes from the fields to the factories, so that capitalist market practices could develop. Infused at the time with classical liberal economics (and resurfacing in the 1970s as neoliberalism), this required social policy to complement the labour market.

This developed in a number of ways. The early reformers, concerned with social questions, tended to rely on philanthropy to facilitate interventions to address problems through moral education. In its early development, social work very much reflected this idea; privileged middle-class women, through organisations such as the Charity Organisation Society, went out into communities to help reshape the social world. This was achieved through a particular discourse and with a specific purpose in mind: to re-educate certain groups and communities to give up their 'vices'. Similar analysis can be made of state intervention during the same time period. Thus, the UK's workhouses sought to discipline and punish those in poverty, who would willingly accept their destitution (resulting from personal failings) being corrected. The intention was to address idleness and **pauperism**; here, the importance and virtue of employment, and its attachment to moral worth, were overtly promoted. Both sets of activity sought to engage the individual in their own reform; re-moralisation relied on the active engagement of those perceived as lacking the right moral and ethical framework, while gainful employment and abstinence from vices sought to undermine it. As such, ideas of self-help, resilience, thrift and duty were key aspects of policy interventions.

Thus, the development of welfare provision within the industrial world originates from different influences. At the surface level, we see the ideas of the Enlightenment and human progress seeking to relieve suffering: the promotion of wellbeing. Beneath this surface, however, rests a range of intellectual ideas and opinions, which argued for a re-moralisation of character (with a particular middle–class interpretation of what that morality should be) alongside the need for a suitable labour force for the emerging capitalist system. Squires (1990) argued that concepts such as need were developed to reflect these ideas and requirements of capitalism, and have continued to inform a range of welfare developments. There is similarity here with the Marxist conception of social rights.

It is within such frameworks of analysis that we can give particular attention to the development of means testing. The means test reflects official endorsement of particular parents or relationships, responsibilities and expectations of citizens, while sanctioning and condemning others. It implies that there are certain instances where support is to be provided; not purely on the basis of rights or needs, but following a demonstration of deservingness. Consider the complexity involved where a single parent, particularly a mother, co–habits with a new partner. Lone–parent benefit, where means–tested, will often require (usually) the mother to inform the relevant agencies of her new partners' co–habiting status. Why? Because this impacts on her entitlement to social security; her benefit can be reduced, as the new partner is assumed to be providing support. But at what point in a relationship can such support be assumed, or even provided? Could we assume support is provided if the relationship is stable prior to co–habitation? Essentially, how the state defines your relationship may not be the same as how you define it. According to Squires (1990), the means test becomes a useful bit of 'political technology'; it supports or penalises certain forms of relationships, is based on state-sanctioned notions of need and social problems, and can be used to embed disciplinary practices within the core of day-to-day existence for the working classes.

Furthering the use of welfare to meet the needs of capitalism, there have been efforts to encourage the working class to give their labour freely. Yet, policy has been used to ensure disciplinary practices exist to unlock this labour for capitalist production. Already noted in earlier chapters, deservingness and the duty to work are two particular narratives used to generate feelings of stigma and shame among those not seen to be doing their 'fair share'. Thus, policy interventions seek to influence the behaviour and actions of certain groups of people, which starts with the use of state interventions into the social world. Over time, the locus of this discipline starts to shift and change; eventually, citizens become bearers of their own discipline, and self-discipline starts to be encouraged. This reflects Foucault's discussion of the internalisation of discipline: the need to emphasise how one is a striver not a skiver, the need to work for high levels of attainment in education or the efforts to which we are expected to go in order to maintain our health. The key point is that control and discipline develop alongside progressive intervention into the improvement of wellbeing.

Adding a Marxist dynamic to this analysis would emphasise class differences, a feminist critique would explore gender differences, an anti-racist critique would elucidate the experiences of different ethnic groups – or we could apply elements of all of these analyses. The intent here is to make us aware of control and discipline and, in our studies of Social Policy, to question the language used to describe problems and the interventions designed in response.

Control, vulnerability and policy

In the 1970s and 1980s, policy debates in the US and UK significantly shifted to focus on law and order rhetoric. Hall (1980) highlighted the increasing attention given to disciplinary legislation within parliamentary time and political debate as an indicator of a shift to a law-and-order society. His focus was on the 1980s, but we can see a continuation of this; for example, under New Labour, which introduced 3,000 new criminal offences in just nine years in office (compared to 500 new offences in the 18-year period of the Thatcher and Major governments). Hall suggests this occurs alongside a critique of the state's intervention in the market; so, a narrative develops where the state is removed from the market, while it seeks to mitigate against the fallout (in terms of increased social conflict) of a free market.

Articulating similar arguments to Squires (1990), Hall (1980) suggested that the history of welfare state provision obscures the development of disciplinary state interventions, as there was a brief period of affluence and development post-Second World War. Thus, state control and discipline of citizens has always been a function of policy. This is perhaps emphasised by Stenson's (2001) suggestion that the rise of the welfare state facilitated a separation of the social, as its own discipline of Social Policy, and obscured associations with issues of crime and control. It might therefore be appropriate to suggest that the various crisis narratives and explanations of contextual change (the globalisation and risk debates in the previous two chapters) facilitate a return to the disciplinary and controlling aspects of policy. As Wincup (2013) explained, there was a need to reconstitute social phenomena as governable problems; to render complex, wicked issues as matters of crime, so that governments are able to construct problems in ways that enable them to make an obvious intervention. If (as suggested by a range of neoliberal hybrid political ideologies) concepts of need are false demands driving political promises, and when state intervention is seen to be paving the road to serfdom, how does a state justify any intervention into welfare? Perhaps, we could argue, this results from identifying problems within a criminal discourse: amoral behaviours to be corrected. Here, the state can intervene, because failure to act will leave citizens vulnerable and at risk.

We know from previous chapters that policy narratives around the family, work ethic and undeservingness have come to dominate a range of policy debates. Concepts that determine entitlement have consequently changed; policy now seeks to focus on human capital, and the prudent citizen who is resilient in the face of change. Such developments require not only the potential threat of criminal behaviour but also the ability to emphasise citizen vulnerability and insecurity, associated with workless behaviours and irresponsible behaviour (or the danger posed by others exhibiting such traits), to further justify welfare reforms. Personal responsibility and active participation to address problems then becomes the central means to address problems, through either conditional forms of welfare support or methods of promoting responsibility.

In this context, Harrison and Sanders (2014) argued that narratives of a broken society (or social crisis) become important parts of political discourse. Although these are often ambiguous and vague, they allow for attention to be given to individual actions as the contributing factor to individual, community and social decline: a return to the moralistic arguments of the early development of state intervention. This can be illustrated in the Centre for Social Justice's *Breakdown Britain* report (2006), which sees poverty as caused by family breakdown; educational failure; economic dependency; worklessness; addiction to drugs and alcohol; and severe personal debt, and suggests that while each of these is individually damaging, when combined, they ensure poverty is a lived reality of households. The core protective factors against poverty, which should be established to prevent social breakdown and change lives, are: strong and stable families; inspiring education; a welfare system that rewards work; effective drug and alcohol prevention, enforcement and treatment; and efforts to prevent unmanageable levels of personal debt. Such arguments may appear difficult to critique, as these problems will be experienced by some who are in poverty. But they are also experienced by the non-poor. Drug addiction, debt or poor educational attainment can be risk factors, but being 'at risk' is not the same as being in poverty.

A number of arguments that promote criminal justice responses are embedded within this view. First (and as alluded to previously), new forms of conditionality of social security support can be introduced to require drug addicts or alcoholics to accept treatment, with failure to do so resulting in reduction or removal of social security support. Second, Brown (2014) suggests that the use of **vulnerability**, while aligning with ideas of social justice, also overlaps with the controlling intentions of the state. Problematic behaviours are identified among individuals and households to distinguish them from 'ordinary people', thereby allowing for increased use of selectivism in welfare interventions, which facilitate state intervention in tackling risk-avoiding behaviours. Vulnerability is used to highlight the *potential* of a social harm, rather than its *likelihood*. Being at risk of homelessness is not the same as being homeless. But state policy tends to identify certain groups as being at risk and requiring intervention in their personal (not socioeconomic) circumstances – such as the Troubled Families programme in the UK – requiring the implementation of new regulatory and assessment practices to ensure that identified individuals, households or communities take up their responsibilities and reduce their risk. As noted throughout this chapter, such views are based on particular accounts of what is an acceptable behaviour, which can be biased in favour of certain class values and powerful groups in society at the expense of the views and ideas of other citizens. This, in turn, links control with discussion of participation.

Summary

The foregoing adds to our exploration of key concepts to suggest that the pursuit of welfare, however defined, has been informed by a range of debates and considerations. Various forms of social control have often rested at the surface of policy discussions, but the influence of recent policy narratives regarding families, deservingness, responsibility and globalisation have generated a renewed focus on control in welfare debates. Efforts to secure citizen welfare have integrated attempts to control citizen behaviours, as well as the wider socioeconomic context. While the latter was seen to cause a range of social problems, the recent trend in policy debates has been to lay blame with the former: individual behaviours. This shift, for some, has been presented as an attempt to promote and defend capitalism and continued economic growth through the promotion of a disciplined labour force. As such, efforts to analyse welfare systems, entitlement and justifications of various uses of the mixed economy of welfare (MEW) must consider the cross-cutting nature of several debates, as illustrated in Figure 9.1. To this, we can add two further dynamics within the current interest in social control: citizen participation in, and empowerment from, welfare provision.

Figure 9.1: The development of welfare policies

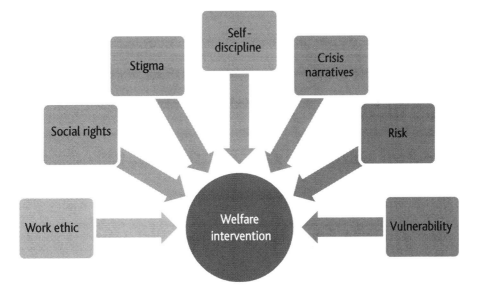

Participation

While it is possible to suggest that social policy has been about the control of certain groups within the population by those with power, there is an alternative argument that welfare policies are seeking to empower citizens. This section examines how welfare policy has a particular relationship with facilitating and encouraging participation. Design of policy interventions must consider the participation of the citizen in achieving the intended outcome. As a student, your teachers provide a curriculum, class activities, readings, assessments and so on to encourage and facilitate your learning. But this alone does not achieve the outcome: your best educational achievement. The outcome also requires effort by the recipient of the service. This is participation of a low order, and is usually expected when policy makers formulate policies. Other forms of participation may seek to generate citizen control over services. However, as will be shown, this can be pursued *either* in a way that ensures state-preferred practices and outcomes result from the engagement *or* as a true means of transferring power to citizens. As such, participation is a mechanism through which social control can be fostered or empowerment of citizens can be achieved. The focus on responsibility and self-help examined in the previous chapter could lend support to the former over the latter, although some forms of self-help may offer routes towards the latter (empowerment). To examine this debate in detail, we start by exploring what we mean by 'participation'.

What is 'participation'?

The concept of participation has grown in importance within welfare, and is often presented as a tool for addressing a number of challenges in contemporary society: improving democratic accountability, building social cohesion, aiding public service reform and creating personal (individual) benefits. It has also been promoted in welfare reform (Beresford, 2002a) to provide the basis for vibrant communities and generating social capital.

Participation can be developed in a number of different ways, but essentially involves engagement of citizens in some form of activity. Naturally, the discussion here focuses on participation in relation to government activity towards welfare provision, rather than participation in terms of engagement in the market, voluntary actions or family commitments (all sources of welfare provision). Thus, the term 'participation' encompasses wider forms of associational activity in both formal and informal contexts within civil society more broadly, and across these sector boundaries where the state facilitates market and third-sector provision. Brodie et al. (2009) highlight key drivers around the crisis of democracy and the need to develop new governance spaces, the promotion of civil society in solving social problems and increasing citizen action through technological developments and rising individualism. Combined, this creates a perceived democratic deficit, generating political interest in the need to promote participation within citizens to ensure accountability, and to promote and protect civil and political rights within society. Here, we can see how the participatory agenda has been promoted by a range of social movements in seeking to demand greater recognition and protection of their rights.

The efforts of social movements initially focused on promoting the civil and political rights of certain disadvantaged groups, highlighting the lack of (or limited) protection offered in law and appealing to notions of equality and justice to campaign for change. This has expanded into the realm of social rights. However, for some groups, such as the disability movement, this is not simply a demand for equal treatment but has essentially questioned the provision and suitability of social services for disabled people. Attention is often given to how these groups have sought to redefine notions of need so that, rather than top-down definitions determined by service providers, users of services have greater say in shaping and informing provision. In part, this initially led to the rise of representative forms of participation. Yet, Beresford and Campbell (1994) have suggested that the development of representative forms of participation may be limited. They appear to be an adequate response to demands for involvement, but may subtly shape participation practices and procedures to benefit providers, rather than service users. Rather, alternative participatory formats – such as self-organisation and the ability to direct service provision – are not easily reconciled with representative participation.

More recent developments can be found under the idea of **personalisation**, which Carr (2013:2) summarises as:

> starting with the person as an individual with strengths, preferences and aspirations and putting them at the centre of the process of identifying their needs and making choices about how and when they are supported to live their lives. It requires a significant transformation of adult social care so that all systems, processes, staff and services are geared up to put people first.

Personalisation seeks to promote a new form of user-led service, ensuring that greater control and choice is given to the citizen than the provider over the form of support offered. Service users can individually (or collectively) negotiate and organise the services they feel best suit their needs, and are often provided with the budget to arrange services. One contemporary development in relation to service provision that engages users has been the concept of co-production.

Co-production

Co-production is a recent example of an attempt to promote participatory forms of policy design and implementation. The term originated in the US in the 1980s, when a group of academics argued for citizen engagement to reform policy delivery during a time of economic constraint. The approach can be summarised as the joint effort of both service users and service providers in achieving service outcomes. Traditional views of welfare services presented the citizen as a passive recipient of a service and the target of an intervention, often overlooking the contribution citizens can make in achieving and enhancing service outcomes.

This early work tended to be focused on improving the economic efficiency of these services; what Gregory (2015) refers to as efficiency co-production. The term (and some rethinking of it) has since been found in academic discussions within the US and Europe. Retaining the acceptance that users and providers can provide 'inputs', the recent literature tends to focus on both sets of actors working together to achieve the aims (Gregory, 2015, refers to this as 'efficacy co-production', because it often requires an investment in service users to build up their confidence and capability to produce).

Early thinking in relation to co-production suggested inputs were separate (mostly) from the efforts of service providers. Parks et al. (1981) illustrated this though a discussion of community safety. The police can patrol a neighbourhood to promote safety, but local householders can be involved by installing locks on their front doors. It is also possible to work together, such as a Neighbourhood Watch scheme. The intentions behind this form of participation are to reduce the overall costs of service provision and improve the efficiency of the service offered. For efficacy co-production, however, the aim is the integration of citizens into a range of activities: from policy design and commissioning to implementation and evaluation. Bovaird (2007) offered a useful typology, distinguishing between provider-designed, provider-and-community-designed and community-designed services, and provider-delivered, provider-and-community-delivered and community-delivered services, developing a nine-square grid of different relationships (for example, provider designed and delivered, provider/community designed but provider delivered, and so on). He argued that seven of these nine relationships reflect different types of co-production because they involve both sets of actors in one or both activities; two are not co-production because the services produced are by the provider or community alone. The emphasis here is that co-production always involves joint activity of some form. Yet, as Gregory (2015) illustrates, this is not done only to improve the efficiency of services but also often attached to broader narratives of empowerment and the democratic notion of participation.

Beresford (2010) rightly suggested that user-involvement approaches to welfare service have been co-opted so that governments have more control and say over the type of participation possible. Part of his critique includes a discussion of co-production, which he claims facilitates government/agency control of participatory forms, because the term did not originate from service users themselves. Co-option *is* a concern for co-production (as I've discussed in detail elsewhere; see Gregory, 2015) – but not, I feel, in the way Beresford claimed. His argument did not distinguish between types of co-production; as such, he overlooks variation in co-production practices, and – like others (Ellison, 2011; Lister, 2011) – is in danger of criticising the term as defined in its *efficiency* form while overlooking *efficacy* co-production. Participation theory needs to ensure it is sensitive towards the starting points of participants regarding skills, knowledge and confidence, which are integral for successful participation. But not all citizens will have these in equal share; there will often be geographic and socioeconomic variations, resulting from longer historical differences in circumstances and contexts. Efficacy co-production can start with this realisation, utilise invited spaces to engage citizens, build up their ability to participate and shift to created spaces (Gregory, 2015). Other forms of co-production will not.

Before drawing this section to a conclusion, I want to comment further on co-option. This term refers to how mechanisms designed to achieve one thing are used to achieve another, and is vital in debates regarding participation. As we explored in the previous two chapters, the concepts of globalisation and risk suggest that welfare provision must change. In particular, these concepts have fostered a concern regarding risk-averse citizens, who should be supported to not only develop their human capital but also take greater responsibility for their welfare needs. Participatory practices therefore become more important, and can be drawn into debates regarding welfare provision through self-help, which seek not to support citizens but to relocate responsibility away from the central state. To an extent, this could be a positive move where it seeks to empower citizens (discussed shortly). It could also further less empowering practices that seek to foster citizen resilience – their ability to cope in adversity – rather than addressing the causes of those erroneous circumstances. Co-option refers to the process whereby the former aim is removed from a participatory practice and put towards the achievement of the latter.

Participation can therefore form part of a narrative for resilience as a means of producing support networks to ensure that individuals and communities are able to cope with the shocks and traumas experienced in day-to-day life. Often, however, such shocks are linked to the turbulent global context in which we live; these are beyond our individual control and (some argue) beyond the control of the nation state. Thus, self-help and participatory forms of collective action can be co-opted into a broader neoliberal account of social problems. Used to promote local activism, this is presented as empowering, while actually ensuring citizens remain victims of the circumstances into which they were born and grew up. While participation and self-help can be used to promote resilience to neoliberal praxis (see Gregory, 2014), participatory policies have often fostered the separation of communities from the structural and societal causes of social problems, despite efforts to locate these problems within the wider context (Bauman, 2001). This reflects the wider shift of neoliberal ideas filtering into key concepts and generating a subtle shift in discourse. In part, this relocates the locus of social problems onto the individual and/or community, rather than the wider social and economic context.

Summary

The participation and engagement of citizens is fundamental to the success of changes pursued by policies. Ultimately, these seek to promote the welfare of citizens; some forms of participation have also sought (through social movements) to secure the social rights of marginalised groups, especially along the lines of social divisions. However, even within efforts to promote participation, many of the themes explored in relation to control and policy narratives can be found, suggesting a different emphasis to participation efforts (see Figure 9.2). Exploring the meaning of participation in welfare provision requires that we pay attention (as ever), to how concepts are articulated and pursued through the design of welfare provision, for this will tilt the balance towards forms of social control that conflict with the concept of empowerment – the final focus of this chapter.

Figure 9.2: Tilting the balance of participation

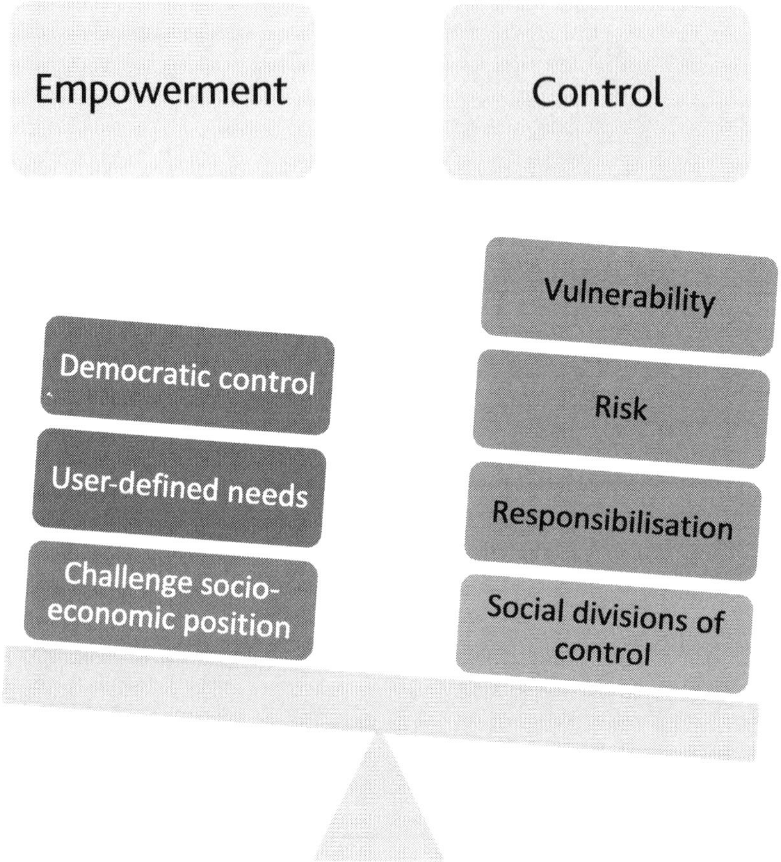

Empowerment

In the history of Social Policy, the term empowerment has received little overt attention; yet it underpins many of the conceptual debates implicitly. The concept of positive freedom (explored in Chapter 3) is about addressing social inequalities so that citizens are able to be and to do what they desire, despite the influence of one's circumstances of birth, and thus is about empowerment. As such, empowerment is nestled within a range of concepts we explored in earlier chapters: citizenship, freedom, equality and justice. Spicker's (2008) introductory text is one of few to give explicit attention to the concept, in contrast to Kennedy's (2013) useful dictionary of concepts, which only makes reference to empowerment in relation to other concepts (highlighting my initial point). Despite its ubiquitous nature in discussions of policy, empowerment appears more clearly in the participation, community and citizen engagement literatures.

Empowerment essentially refers to the process of transferring power to those who are relatively powerless. This suggests that power is transferred to individuals to pursue their (and, where relevant, their family's) welfare in order to reduce demand for state services. This can be questioned; it could be argued that state intervention to empower is not simply about reducing the demand per se, but rather about changing the socioeconomic structure, by removing the disadvantages generated by inequalities that limit life chances and hinder welfare. As such, it is not the management of social problems (as suggested in relation to responsibilisation and risk in the previous chapter) but the direct intervention into circumstance that causes diswelfare in a way that facilitates citizen control. The term can therefore also refer to collective action to empower previously disempowered groups; it need not be individualistic. Consequently, there is a distinction here, which is played out in the literature (and this section). One the one hand, participation as a mechanism for facilitating the process of empowerment can be tokenistic, giving merely the *illusion* of empowerment; on the other, participation structures that give a genuine voice in, and control over, services would achieve 'true' empowerment.

However, this requires we have some awareness of the counterfactual, as well as key elements required for empowerment to occur. In relation to the former, this introduces the concept of disempowerment, whereby individuals and groups are denied power to enable them to exercise control over their lives. This can emanate from an inability to communicate needs or circumstances effectively; or it may be a result of social isolation, stigma or lack of social networks. As such, many of the concepts we have examined can result in disempowerment; for example, Bradshaw's (2013) taxonomy of needs distinguished *felt* needs from *expressed* needs. Those facing inequality, discrimination or disadvantage as a result of wider socioeconomic structures will have little scope or means to transfer felt needs into expressed needs; they lack the power and means to transform their needs from a feeling to a political articulation of social rights. Thus, social movements have campaigned for equality and anti-discrimination, and have not only been effective in achieving policy change (to various extents) but also continue with ongoing campaigns to achieve these ends.

This leads us to consider what is required for empowerment to occur, and this returns us to the concept of participation. Deakin and Wright (1990) suggest six criteria that need to be incorporated into participatory structures if empowerment is to be secured:

1. *Accountability*: to ensure services are answerable to citizens;
2. *Representation and participation*: of service users to ensure their views carry some authority within services;
3. *Information*: required for citizens who participate to have opportunities to comment and control service design and delivery;
4. *Access*: to ensure all citizens are able to engage with participatory mechanisms;
5. *Choice*: over the options available in provision, and therefore influence over the outcomes of activity; and
6. *Redress*: the ability to limit the control of service providers and create formal opportunities for users to express their concerns.

This, however, can create complex and messy practices – especially as efforts to engage participation often rely on creating new relationships between service users and providers. As such, it is possible for conflict to arise between the two groups when their aims, interests and views do not align; here, power within the service is exposed to analysis. Additionally, there can be conflict between users themselves. Service users are not a homogeneous group; they are likely to have both similar and dissimilar views. Yet, resources are limited and services may not be able to accommodate such competing demands. Consequently, service users may compete with each other for a share of resources.

This also draws attention to professionalism and knowledge. An argument could be presented to suggest that service providers have specialist knowledge and skills, which should give them greater say. Using the example of type 2 diabetes, professional service providers will require patients to change their diet and exercise regime: a need that relates to medical circumstances to ensure their welfare. This returns us to our wants/needs debate (Chapter 3). The need to change diet and exercise regimes does not mean it is desired (a want) on the part of the citizen. So, whose voice should be loudest? Which of the two should influence policy and practice? From measurements of poverty to debates around user knowledge in healthcare, there has been a growing movement towards integrating both; for example, consensual methods for measuring poverty (Mack, 2017) and debates around lay knowledge (Williams and Popay, 2006). The foregoing has demonstrated that discussions of empowerment quickly move into an account of how participation is designed.

Is participation tokenistic or empowering?

Participation can take a number of forms, and there may be a tension between the service user and service provider in determining what form that participation will take. How empowering participation is for the user is generally open to debate, depending on the form of participation pursued. While arguments in favour of participation highlight its benefits – such as involving individuals in decision-making, generating cohesion and a sense of common purpose between citizens, reforming services and generating personal benefits, such as efficacy, self-esteem and confidence – these are often normative assumptions. Participation need not always be a positive experience. Often, examples can be found where local decision-making policies have been designed in ways that facilitate central government steering of local decision makers to make determinations in line with central government policy (Fussey, 2004). Additionally, participation as viewed by individuals and communities may not align with government/policy makers. As Mooney and Fyfe (2006) suggest, the normative assumptions around participation, active citizenship and social capital that governments support in policy documentation may not reflect the views of local citizens at the grassroots. Consequently, where government aims conflict with local communities and the latter organise against a government policy (thus reflecting their active citizenship), this will be at odds with government expectations of citizen behaviour and participation. Thus, we need to understand the varied possible forms of participation.

The most prominent typology offered has been Arnstein's (1969) ladder of citizen participation (see Figure 9.3), which focuses on intentionality and the associated approach of those who initiate participation. Arnstein uses the image of a ladder to illustrate different levels of participation, divided into three broad categories. The lower levels are 'nonparticipation', and focus on manipulation and therapy. The middle of the ladder covers 'tokenism', which consists of informing, consultation and placation. The top of the ladder, 'citizen control', consists of partnership, delegation and citizen control. Each of these is represented by a rung on the ladder, with manipulation being the lowest and citizen control being the highest. A key aim has been to draw out a distinction between citizen power and tokenism, providing an interesting lens through which to reflect on the intent and purpose behind government participation. For example, consultation on a policy proposal would be in the middle of the ladder, within the tokenistic spectrum; whereas citizen involvement in the creation and development could engage with any of the top three rungs within citizen control, depending on the nature of participation involved.

Lupton et al. (1998:48) links Arnstein's ladder to the three dimensions of power identified by Lukes:

> Forms of public participation may be established which appear to give people influence when viewed in terms of single-dimension explanations of power, but are actually used to prevent certain issues from being discussed. By channelling interaction to a limited agenda, attention can be diverted away from areas of potential conflict that those in power wish to avoid. Seen in this way, participatory mechanisms can serve as a means of social control by preventing challenges to the status quo. By engaging people and giving them responsibility in a particular area of policy or service, moreover, the process of public participation may also serve to contain criticism and unrest by helping

the public to appreciate the realities of government and/or implying public support for the actions taken.

Figure 9.3: Arnstein's ladder of participation

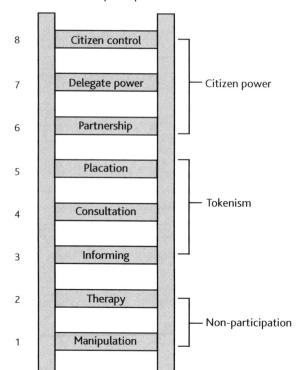

Source: Arnstein (1969). Reproduced with permission.

This illustrates why it is necessary to understand the various intentions and purposes on which participation is built into policy processes and practices. As noted in Chapter 8 in relation to self-help, there can be multiple intentions and aims behind policy designs, and these do not always easily align with Enlightenment ideas of social progress. Participation is a liberating and empowering concept, designed to engage citizens fully in policy and political processes at various levels of government. Yet, it can be a means by which citizens are controlled and directed to act and behave in certain ways.

Following this line of thought, Pretty's (1995, cited in Cornwall, 2008) typology of participation focuses on the users of the participatory process. He identifies tokenism (bad), consultation (better) and full participation. Functional forms are the most developed form found within state practices, and essentially require citizen participation in meeting the project objectives effectively and helping to reduce the costs of participation. These are essentially about improving efficiency.

However, these programmes are decided by external agents, not the participants. Additionally, Pretty's typology of participation includes interactive participation ('a "learning process" through which local groups take control over decisions, thereby gaining a stake in maintaining structures and resources') and self-mobilisation, 'where people take the initiative independently of external organizations, developing contacts for resources and technical assistance, but retaining control over these resources' (Cornwall, 2008: 271). This informs Cornwall's suggestion of the need to consider how citizens take up and use participatory practices to develop their own voice and empowerment. Thus, she contrasts between the spaces created *for* people ('invited spaces') and spaces created *by* people ('created spaces'). Invited spaces are structured and formed by service providers; here, the transfer of ownership is difficult, and the focus is on service access. Created spaces, however, are less structured; they allow people to come together because of something they share in common, and grant citizens control over the shape and nature of participation and activity involved. This is considered essential not only for those groups with limited voice but also because the space in which participation takes place is constructed by participants themselves.

Additionally, it should be noted that participation will uncover the diverse interests of those involved in the policy process or practice. These are important considerations within wider discussions of participation. Dinham (2006) suggested that citizens who experience disappointment in terms of participation and empowerment can experience negative impacts on their wellbeing, which in turn diminish any health, spiritual, social or psychological benefits. This becomes more complicated when we reflect on the discussion of self-help. If participation becomes 'do-it-yourself', then citizens may resist rather than embrace participation. Reflecting on the varied intentions of self-help schemes (see Chapter 8), it becomes apparent that participation will always include a variety of interests and ambitions for interaction, which may not align.

A further key division in the participation literature draws on the 'consumerist/ democratic' distinction set out by Beresford (2002b). 'Consumerist' approaches search for external input into service provision, but have preconceived ideas of the form input takes, resulting in no change in control or the distribution of power. Contrary to this, 'democratic' approaches ensured 'that welfare service users and other citizens have the direct capacity and opportunity to make change' (Beresford, 2002b:278). This model is associated with libertarian and transformative ideas, and can be brought together with Cornwall's (2008:275) aforementioned invited and created spaces, whereby the former reflect consumerist forms of participation and the latter reflect democratic participation. The distinction between types of co-production could also be shared across this divide – but with a note of caution. While provider-led forms of co-production would reflect invited spaces, this can be a starting point for building up citizens' confidence to start creating their own forms of participation and welfare provision. Additionally, citizen-designed services could invite service providers into joint-delivery activity, reflecting a further form of co-production but a reversal of the usual power differential discussed in welfare and participatory debates. What this illustrates is how participatory practice has to wrestle with the tension between participation as a form of empowerment, and participation as a more tokenistic or controlling practice seeking to foster controlled/disciplined citizens. We explore this tension in the final discussion of this chapter.

The blurred line between empowerment and control

If social policy is about control, will it always pursue forms of welfare support that seek to discipline citizens? The argument developing in relation to contemporary welfare provision suggests that the answer to this question is 'yes'. Explanations of contextual changes, as reviewed in Chapters 7 and 8, have created a new paradigm for welfare provision that places national competitiveness and individual responsibility (and resilience) at the core of social policy: not the eradication of causes of diswelfare. Thus, where welfare provision was once the compensation for the diswelfares of human progress (as noted by Titmuss), it is now a means by which citizens are disciplined to ensure economic progress is maintained. The use of a policy example is insightful here to illustrate how social control can inform the context in which participation occurs.

In her account of the Respect agenda, Gaskell (2008) explores how the notion of respect is utilised to facilitate government interventions, which seek to control the behaviours and actions of young people. Essentially, she argues that the Respect agenda built on earlier anti-social behaviour interventions to address disrespectful behaviours of young people; initially perceived as *causes* of crime, these soon became crimes themselves. This feeds into a narrative that childhood and youth are vulnerable times, in which misconduct can establish patterns of behaviour that persist into adult life, and therefore a legitimate area of state intervention. In a similar way to Troubled Families, this implies the idea of a 'public family' (Martin, 2014) and a 'public childhood', opening up personal lives to direct intervention and influence (and judgement) by the state. The policy cut across a range of government departments, particularly education and the Home Office, focusing practice around the idea that young people are authors of their own fate and fail because of personal behaviours and characteristics (ignoring the contribution of socioeconomic, structural factors). Thus, it clarifies that a group in society is particularly vulnerable, and in need of specific attention.

In terms of policy, the Respect agenda established a number of practices, such as dispersal orders, curfews, changes in powers for headteachers to expel students and introducing citizenship classes into the national curriculum. These formed parts of broader efforts to educate young people into moral behaviour and to shape their participation and engagement in society. Thus, regardless of whether they have transgressed social norms, all young people live their lives within educational, health and criminal justice systems. As we discussed in our review of selectivity (Chapter 5), the concept of active citizenship is relevant here. In schools, citizenship is something young people are educated *for* (rather than *about*); it focuses on their contributions and forms of participation in society. The Respect agenda established assessment criteria against which young people were assessed (including self-discipline, as outlined earlier), which can be transmitted through citizenship education and other forms of socialisation. However, such narratives of respect are government-imposed; they do not engage with young people's views of what respect involves and, as Gaskell shows, respect is demanded of young people while they feel disrespected by the policies they are subjected to.

While this illustrates how social control may influence the context of participation, it need not be as overt as this example illustrated. Nor must control always be punitive; efforts to facilitate control can pursue the notion of responsibilisation discussed in the previous chapter. Consequently, Harrison and Sanders (2014) adopt the social division of welfare structure offered by Titmuss (1974) to present a social division of control. They suggest that fiscal and occupational benefits (such as tax incentives for private pensions savings, or benefits attached to your terms of employment) offer more positive and supportive efforts to control. Social policy can be designed to support the welfare activities of the middle classes and respectably employed to take on personal responsibility for their welfare. This contrasts with the third part of the division (state welfare), targeted at lower-/no-income groups, which reflects the more punitive use of social control. Adopting overtly behaviourist, disciplinary and obtrusive forms of monitoring citizens (to promote stigma/shame), the intention is to discipline the unemployed or those on low incomes to act in ways deemed respectable for citizens. It can include monitoring the number of hours worked to determine if they are sufficient, monitoring attendance at training programmes as part of benefit receipt and removing or reducing support if attendance is lacking; all become more overt forms of control, which this chapter has addressed. The overarching aims Harrison and Hemingway (2014) suggest are conditional welfare support, a move towards social investment forms of welfare and the promotion of responsibilisation across policy domains as a response to the risk society narrative. Combined, this reduces the contemporary welfare setting's focus on citizens' needs and socioeconomic circumstances in favour of ensuring a social return on government investment.

This return on investment highlights both the language and the wider trends we have already commented on. In terms of the language, we can see the 'business speak' of neoliberalism having an influence here. Governments are investing in citizens and, as such, need to see a tangible outcome from this activity. In terms of wider trends, this investment is part of the wider narrative around national competitiveness in a global economy, a focus on 'good' forms of welfare expenditure and the fostering of greater responsibility by citizens (as discussed in previous chapters and throughout this one). Framed in this way, participatory practices retain a disciplinary dimension, which reflects social control arguments (whether around capitalist exploitation, patriarchy, ethnic discrimination and so on). The state plays a central role in this; while the government was identified as the locus of control early in the theoretical debate, Foucault's work broadens our analysis to consider a range of institutional practices and the influence on language in changing how citizens are regulated – and how they self-regulate.

Consequently, there is reason for concern for those who support welfare interventions as a means to empower citizens. As Squires (1990) illustrated in terms of anti-social policies, welfare interventions may not seek to radically change socioeconomic circumstances or to challenge the social inequities that impact on particular groups. Rather, as Gaskell (2008:225) explained, 'citizenship can be thought of in terms of a tool of state repression and control. Despite ideas about the decreasing importance of the nation state in an era of globalisation, the political institutions of the nation state continue to impact greatly upon citizens' everyday lives.'

As the state withdraws from intervention in the market, it seeks new forms of intervention in other domains of life, creating new 'public' spaces that are legitimate concerns of the state. Be these families, communities or young people, intervention is predicated on an identified moral slight – a potential vulnerability or behaviour that is incompatible with the ordinary, hard-working citizen – and it is the state's responsibility to intervene and help to correct this. In essence, this is the state seeking a social return on its own investment in citizens while retaining an underpinning desire to discipline them. Yet, it is important to remember that efforts to implement control will not always be negative; indeed, some aspects of control may be required in order to end human suffering. This is the double edge of the welfare sword. In a context of subtle narratives of control dressed up as citizen empowerment, we must not assume that the 'empowerment' pursued aligns with our earlier definition of the concept; that is, empowerment as a process of transferring power to those who are relatively powerless, not as a process of facilitating their resilience to achieve *successful management* of sources of diswelfare. True empowerment depends on *removing* those sources of diswelfare.

Summary

This section has sought to draw links between the ideas of empowerment and participation. While highlighting the significance of empowerment of citizens as part of the pursuit of welfare, the discussion explored how efforts to achieve this through participation face challenges in terms of how citizen involvement is facilitated. This overlaps with efforts to control the behaviours of citizens (as outlined in the earlier part of the chapter) while also forming part of the wider narrative for welfare reform generated by policy narratives around risk, globalisation and neoliberalism. This hints at associations with other key concepts integral to the pursuit of welfare, and returns attention to the design of policy itself. Just as the opening chapters on welfare, social rights, needs, equality and citizenship are drawn into debates around universalism and selectivism, the narratives of the previous chapters have been drawn into the debates around service design – in relation to control, participation and empowerment. Implicitly, this has sought to reiterate how concepts and debates inform the design of services, and the consequences this has in securing individual and societal welfare.

Chapter summary

Policy seeks to create change. It draws on a number of concepts to explain the context in which our lives and society exist, the rights, duties and entitlements that we have and the role of the state and wider MEW in delivering these. But the change it creates is also integrated into a conceptual debate about the way in which policy itself achieves this – in terms of not only social control and empowerment but also the participatory mechanisms that may be necessary. As this chapter has illustrated, there is a fine line between efforts to empower and efforts to control. While participation is presented within policy as a means to engage and empower, it can be used in tokenistic ways that offer not a genuine transfer of power to service users but rather the *illusion* of change. Other forms of participation offer more genuine means to empowerment, but are likely to be fraught with difficulties, as inflexible service designs, new ways of working and new power dynamics and voices seek to control the direction of policy and practice. As briefly noted, competing knowledge sources (professional and lay person) will not always align, resulting in debate in not only the design of services but also their intent and objectives; different interests and pressures on different actors will mix into these dynamics. Thus, how needs are defined (for example) will be open to debate (as Bradshaw's taxonomy in Chapter 3 illustrated) – although this could be the debate about how the basic needs (Doyal and Gough's personal autonomy and physical health) are *met*, rather than a debate of what our basic needs *are*.

However, the broader debate over social control impacts on the ability of welfare provision to address social problems, creating complex and messy processes – which might be the price to pay for genuine empowerment of citizens as part of wider social policy objectives. The opening quotes to this chapter demonstrate two core arguments. On the one hand, social policy is always about interventions into people's welfare – either directly into their personal lives or into the socioeconomic context in which they live. On the other, this overlaps with narratives of empowerment: how welfare facilitates citizens in pursuing their own personal welfare objectives. This is complicated by the conceptual debates this book has explored. Dependent on various conceptual and ideological positions, different welfare systems are designed to pursue various notions of welfare, which see empowerment and participation achieved through different means. For some, this can only be achieved through a free market, in which individual preferences are satisfied by the price mechanism. For others, this is problematic because it relies on having sufficient income to purchase those goods, when they should in fact be decommodified and, where appropriate, resources redistributed so all have an equal and fair chance to pursue their welfare objectives.

As Figure 9.4 illustrates, the nexus of welfare, control and empowerment is played out through participation. Different conceptual arguments will inform the design of participation initiatives to address welfare challenges. Some will result in the contemporary attempt to manage causes of diswelfare; others will seek to tackle and remove those causes. In particular, the accounts offered in Chapter 7 and 8, and in this chapter, illustrate how social control becomes the dominant outcome of welfare interventions in contemporary society. Various policy narratives have been drawn together, which fundamentally shifted the pursuit of welfare, as it was 'founded' during the post-Second World War period. Rather than pursuing the ambitious task of removing the causes of diswelfare and empowering citizens to pursue their welfare ambitions, policy fosters a disciplining of citizens to conform to the demands of the dominant political–economic paradigm (neoliberalism), while utilising the language of empowerment and participation in the form of a new 'common sense' regarding citizen responsibility and resilience. The concluding chapter draws out this overarching narrative, while exploring possibilities of pursuing alternative welfare practices.

Figure 9.4: Welfare, social control and empowerment

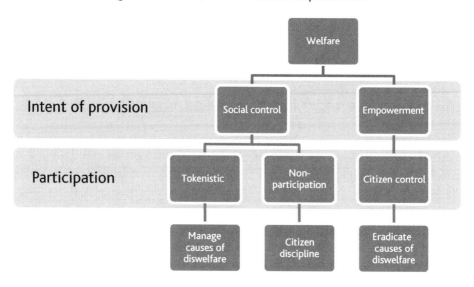

Critical thinking activity

Critically discuss the importance of participation as a tool for empowering citizens and reflect on the importance of this for securing freedom, social rights and self-determination.

Further reading

Arnstein, S.R. (1969) A Ladder of Citizen Participation. *Journal of the American Institute of Planners* 35 pp216–224.

Cornwall, A. (2008) Unpacking 'Participation': Models, Meanings and Practices. *Community Development Journal* 43 pp269–283.

Davies, J.S. and Pill, M. (2012) Empowerment or Abandonment? Prospects for Neighbourhood Revitalization Under the Big Society. *Public Money and Management* 32 pp193–200.

Squires, P. (1990) *Anti-Social Policy: Welfare, Ideology and the Disciplinary State*. New York and London: Harvester Wheatsheaf.

Don't forget to look at the companion website for more information.

10

Conclusion

In drawing this text to a conclusion, this chapter starts by reviewing the key concepts and debates outlined in the previous chapters. It draws out the general argument (especially in the second half of the text) that new policy narratives are shifting welfare systems away from state provision, and offers some thoughts on how to challenge this change. It then concludes with some reflections on where readers can go next in terms of developing their engagement with welfare and Social Policy debates.

Key concepts for exploring welfare

The approach adopted in this text has, to an extent, sought to break with traditional textbook practices. Rather than only providing an introduction to concepts, it has sought to do so through a particular narrative, to demonstrate the constant flux in how concepts are defined and integrated into welfare debates. This slow fluctuation is underpinned by social, political and economic shifts, altering perceptions of the purpose of welfare and change in the roles of both state and market (and the wider mixed economy of welfare (MEW)).

Consequently, the text has sought to achieve two main functions within its wider aim of introducing you to key concepts in social welfare. First, it has shown that there are no static definitions, no right or wrong articulations of concepts; just variations on the labels, underpinned by different ideological/philosophical positions. Second, it has demonstrated the complex web of interactions between concepts by focusing on a number of questions (reflected in the titles of Chapters 2 to 9) that inform interlinked debates about Social Policy. The intention here has been to ensure that these links are at the forefront of understanding rather than segmented. Combined, these two functions have started to draw out the influence of neoliberal thinking on key concepts and welfare debates.

Chapters 2 to 4, which can be viewed together in setting our historical context, mapped out the debate between welfare and wellbeing, explaining that the former term would be used in this text. They illustrated a range of philosophical debates that underpin these terms, and how some of these values and ideas came to the foreground and solidified into state support of welfare. This was associated with the idea of social rights and their centrality in the pursuit of welfare objectives. As part of a broader narrative of citizenship, the chapters discussed the universality of rights of citizens, and the need for the state to not only protect such rights but also create the context in which they can be realised by individuals. Table 10.1 offers an overview of the answers to these chapter questions.

Table 10.1: Answering key questions: the what, who and how of welfare

What is welfare and why pursue it?	Welfare is not a pejorative term used to identify those dependent on particular forms of support.
	Welfare can be defined as bare survival (thin notion of welfare) or human flourishing (thick notion of welfare).
	There is a debate regarding the extent of an objectively defined 'good life' and the pursuit of individual preferences.
	Wellbeing is a multidimensional concept concerned with a range of factors that contribute to our lives.
	Wellbeing is criticised for focusing on 'happiness' and reducing the importance of income/social inequalities.
	The pursuit of welfare rests on the identification of particular human and social rights.
	For Richard Titmuss, the provision of welfare was a price paid for human progress; it addressed the diswelfares generated by industrial change.
Who receives welfare support (and for what)?	Identification of social rights leads to two key debates: to whom are these rights attached, and what do they entail?
	Citizen status is associated with three sets of rights: civil, political and social.
	Concepts of citizenship tend to be biased in ways that privilege certain groups over others and therefore obscure diversity of citizens: we need to recognise difference.
	The contents of social rights are attached to needs, but these can be defined in terms of being inherent to all humans or interpreted through a range of social interactions.
	Debates around thick/thin needs offer a similar debate as thick/thin welfare.
	Equality is an important aspect of these debates, especially in terms of equal citizenship status and rights.
	Equality of opportunity and outcome are two polar debates in relation to this concept; while often separated out, in reality they are closely entwined.
Who provides welfare support?	There are varied sources of welfare, which can be illustrated through the idea of the MEW.
	The dominance of the state as a provider of welfare in many nations results from two trends: first, nation-building projects to create an imagined community around which national identity can form; second, the justification for welfare fosters a universal approach to welfare provision, which the state is the best placed to facilitate.
	But there are limitations and challenges to universal provision.

At the foreground of these discussions were a concern with human flourishing and the suggestion that rights and entitlements are the bedrock on which individuals can pursue their preferred end state. Social rights became a conceptual vehicle through which welfare interventions were justified in response to socioeconomic changes occurring through industrialisation, which required compensation for the diswelfares generated by change. Although these socioeconomic processes facilitated significant progress in living standards of whole nations, they created new social problems and consequences, which required new kinds of responses: through welfare provision.

Narratives regarding entitlement to welfare support were created around concepts of citizenship social rights. Such rights became part of a longer historical development of citizen rights alongside civil and political rights. Part of a wider nation–building narrative, citizenship is predominantly linked to territorial boundaries in which rights are articulated and protected. For some, this protection is dependent on the discharge of certain duties, which in turn facilitates the state's ability to protect rights. Furthermore, these nation–building narratives determine the characteristics of citizens, an implicit and explicit articulation of who is classified as a member of the nation, the challenges faced by the nation and how these can be responded to. Consequently, a totalising notion of the citizen is generated in policy debate, which suggests which rights and which duties should be included within the concept of a citizen.

This brings to the foreground a tension between rights and duties on the one hand and wider social divisions on the other. With regards to the former, there has been significant debate about the centrality of work, particularly in relation to care as an alternative activity. With regards to the latter, social divisions indicate that certain categories of citizens have diverse needs and experiences of the social world. Adopting a universal notion of the citizen, while ensuring all humans have the same fundamental rights, does not result in those rights being equally protected and accessible to different groups in society. Rather, existing social divisions illustrate how different citizens experience variation in their relationship with the state. Despite these differences, an altruistic attempt to provide welfare was pursued, which came under criticism for overlooking diversity in citizens' lives.

Adopting a totalising concept of citizens is not automatically a negative consequence of welfare provision; without a universal concept, we would not assume people are deserving of equal treatment, and nor would welfare provision seek to secure the needs of the wider citizenship. Rather, it highlights the importance of equal treatment across social divisions, and facilitates our ability to indicate when certain groups are disadvantaged: it provides a minimum standard all citizens should expect. Importantly for our interest in welfare, it also generated a recognition that social rights cannot always be met through the market; some form of state support/provision is required. Universal welfare provision was, and continues to be, an important dynamic in meeting not only individual needs but also societal needs. Universalism is fundamental to debates about welfare because it highlights two central considerations: altruism and non–stigmatising interventions. Altruism reflects the concern citizens have for the welfare of others and for society as a whole. Non–stigmatising practices, however, are essential if we are to ensure that citizens take up the welfare support they are entitled to as a right of citizenship without fear of derogatory treatment and experiences. In essence, universalism recognises that bare survival is not sufficient for welfare; there is a wider need to participate in the common life of your society as an integral part of achieving welfare ends.

Table 10.2: Answering key questions: rethinking the what, who and how of welfare

Is universal provision sustainable?	Universalism has never been the sole design feature of welfare services, nor is it likely to be. What is essential is how universalism is, or is not, located at the centre of welfare design.
	Selectivism has always had an influence on welfare provision, primarily in relation to targeting: some groups need additional support due to historic social inequalities.
	Means testing, however, has generated potentially stigmatising/shaming practices, which promulgate undeserving narratives of welfare provision. Conditionality as a design feature has furthered this transmission of undeservingness.
	Thus, a moral debate underpins welfare service design, which is not easily resolved.
	A further debate exists around socially diverse citizenry and the need to recognise diversity of needs.
	This need not require we abandon universalism, which can still be the central framing for welfare provision. But progressive universalism potentially allows us to engage diversity within a universal framework.
How does policy shape the experience of welfare support?	Particular narratives about citizens influence the design of welfare and can radically shape the experience of support.
	Stigma suggests a character failing of certain citizens. Shame reflects this, but generates a personal desire within the citizen to change their behaviours/character; they assume the source of shame to be correct.
	The family is one area in which these stigma/shame narratives can be found in policy narratives.
	Wider sociodemographic changes are explained in ways that privilege some family forms over others. These narratives influence policy design.
	Such designs potentially structure support in ways that ignore diversity of needs, or make use of conditional design, which demands behavioural change.
	This draws attention to whether rights remain the key mechanism for accessing welfare services, or if needs-based assessments (which potentially emphasise stigma) should inform welfare service design.

Our second set of questions (the topics of Chapters 5 and 6) questioned a number of these assumptions around not only universalism but also entitlement to welfare as a form of beneficial social progress. Table 10.2 offers a summary of the answers explored in relation to these two questions: the suitability of universal provision and the experience of welfare. It highlights, in particular, that welfare provision has never been (and likely never will be) only universal. There are good reasons for and against such universal provision, which need to be brought into our welfare debates.

Two general debates were explored in Chapter 5. First, that some forms of selective provision can be better suited to achieving welfare aims. We may know, for example, that health inequalities have an impact on certain geographical locations, resulting in shorter lives for some citizens. Targeted provision in a range of policy domains may be required to address such geographical differences. Interventions on this scale could retain an element of universalism (they are available to all in that particular locality) or be further targeted at those with a larger number of vulnerability factors. However, other forms of provision have moved towards targeting specific groups but including an element of conditionality to welfare provision, which requires citizens to discharge certain duties or actions to secure their support (eroding, one could argue, access to support as a social right). This debate overlaps with the discussion of stigma in Chapter 6, which we review later.

Second, the debate in Chapter 5 returned attention to social divisions and diversity of citizens' lives. Critiquing the universal and totalising assumptions that underpinned a number of forms of welfare provision, the chapter considered the possibility of securing universalism (retaining altruism and the fundamental significance of welfare provision across all citizens) while embracing difference. In relation to need, this is no different; but the concept of equality has drawn renewed attention to social inequalities – not only socioeconomic class (arguably the traditional focus of welfare interventions) but also gender, ethnicity, disability, sexuality and so on. Here, the concept of progressive universalism was introduced, despite a lack of theoretical development in relation to this concept. This discussion drew heavily on policy debates and examples to illustrate its significance. However, it drew attention to the potential means by which universalism and diversity can be drawn into one conceptual framework and offer a new approach to the design and delivery of welfare. Essentially, this framework seeks to reinvigorate not only entitlement to welfare support as a social right but also the understanding that welfare provision is not individualistic; rather, it contains important social functions, which are often overlooked in mainstream political debates about the provision of welfare services.

Progressive universalism may also be an important development when we consider how the design of welfare policy can generate stigma and shame (intentionally and unintentionally). Thus, the experience of receiving welfare support requires that we pay attention to particular narratives of what is and is not acceptable in terms of citizen behaviours and actions, and how this is framed in welfare debates. Such debates generate particular narratives around certain groups of citizens, with families used as an important example in this book.

Through the exploration of these broader narratives, we then started to explore how support for welfare interventions began to shift away from entitlements to social rights satisfaction, which guided welfare provision from the 1940s (if not the 1900s) onwards. Stigmatising explanations of social problems play a key role in developing a dual attack on welfare provision, generated by reframing both the cause of social problems and the economic context. Selectivism via means testing and conditionality, facilitated by the design of welfare in line with notions of deserving and undeserving citizens, reorientated the framing of social rights and citizenship so that individual fault (and a willingness to correct on the part of the citizen) justifies welfare provision. (These ideas were found in earlier reforms in the 1900s in the UK, but gradually lost their persuasive power). Thus, social rights are no longer protected as a common part of universal citizenship status;

rather, they are now conditional on completing certain tasks and activities, as defined by the state. Yet, debates around diversity and difference suggest that such selective approaches need not be presented in such negative and stigmatising narratives. We can contrast this with the progressive universal approach, which recognises that barriers to welfare satisfaction are not through individual fault (even where this may be a contributing factor) but originate in historic social inequalities and discriminations against particular groups of citizens. A common human endeavour requires we redress this situation.

Table 10.3: Answering key questions: reframing the what, who and how of welfare

Is the welfare state always in crisis?	A number of crisis paradigms suggest 'yes', but there is no agreement on the nature of the crisis.
	Economic crisis has dominated welfare provision debates, often from neoliberal and Marxist perspectives. Environmentalism offers a variation of this debate.
	The dominance of economic narratives in contemporary debate has resulted in the prominence of neoliberal economic theories.
	These have developed in parallel with the use of globalisation to explain significant change in nation-state power and practice.
	This, in turn, has generated a new nation-building project, where welfare should foster investment in citizens to ensure the nation is competitive in the global economy.
How does risk change the welfare state?	Risk promotion has replaced protection: citizens take risks to change their circumstances, rather than pool resources to protect whole populations.
	Arguments about dependency have been influential in suggesting the need for change (this overlaps with conditionality debates).
	Resilience to the new global economic context is to be fostered (this overlaps with the social investment approaches to welfare provision).
	Self-help, **re-familisation**, commodification and privatised provision become dominant forms of welfare provision; the state's own services are largely residual.
Is social policy about control?	Social policy has always been about the control of conditions that cause social problems, be these socioeconomic or behavioural.
	Forms of social control are focused on labour discipline: ensuring citizens comply with the needs of the economy.
	Control, however, can also be concerned with social cohesion and social functioning.
	Participation plays a key role here. The state encourages some forms of participation (such as contributions to a private pension), reflecting the responsibilisation agenda.
	Participation can also facilitate empowerment of citizens, but this depends on how participatory practices have been designed.
	Even where empowerment is sought, it can reflect social control. Thus, it is important to explore the conceptual arguments and subsequent design to uncover whether welfare services truly empower citizens.

A focus on policy narratives leads us to our final set of questions, explored in Chapters 7 to 9. The conceptual exploration started with a 'crisis of welfare' debate, demonstrating the dominance of economic narratives (perhaps unsurprisingly, as welfare provision is often focused on redistribution). Following a significant shift in economic thinking, changes were implemented in welfare provision to encourage greater use of the free market. Here, we saw how the rise of neoliberalism and the idea of globalisation (especially economic globalisation) gained sway over welfare debates. Combined, neoliberalism and globalisation discourses successfully shifted welfare provision away from the state, facilitating a change in welfare system design. Of importance here was the shift in conceptual arguments to justify the new welfare system. Table 10.3 summarises some of the key answers to these questions.

Combining the debates explored in Chapters 7 and 8, we find a powerful articulation of change in the context of welfare provision and human lives, especially in western nations. In particular, Chapter 8 explored the risk society thesis), how it has fundamentally reshaped welfare provision and how (despite critiques) it has successfully repositioned explanations of contemporary society and suitable forms of welfare support. Recognising that industrialisation and modernisation (as stages of development in human history) have ended, the theory suggested we are progressing towards a new reflexive modernity, which brings new risks and challenges to be addressed. As such, social welfare provision, recognising in part the contemporary global economic dynamics supposedly beyond the control of the state, requires risk-taking citizens and systems of welfare that do not foster dependency on a 'weakened' nation state. This requires fundamental change in how social policies are designed and implemented. Examples provided included a shift in focus from needs/poverty to social exclusion, and the rise to prominence of the term 'resilience'. Individual responsibility, rather than universal protection, becomes new forms of welfare provision, to be found across the western world.

Often, such developments are accompanied with narratives around participation and empowerment. Chapter 9 considered these concepts alongside the idea of social control, seeking to demonstrate how both social control and empowerment have been dual aims of welfare provision, both of which are achieved through efforts to enhance participation. On the one hand, citizen participation can be framed in tokenistic or predefined ways; this facilitates forms of control in which predefined expectations about behaviours and actions are shaped by policy makers, and often has a labour-market participation requirement. On the other hand, participation can facilitate greater power transfer to citizens, allowing them to influence their relationship with the state and to develop the services and support they require to achieve their own desired end state. This requires not only a willingness to transfer power but also acceptance that citizens can (and should) be the authors of their own welfare, through the removal of those historic social inequalities that have hindered many groups of citizens to date. This does potentially create new challenges; for example, can we retain equal welfare access if citizens play a greater role across various localities in shaping local services? This draws our attention to the necessity of retaining some of the core aspects of universalism, which underpin the common endeavour of supporting welfare needs, while encouraging empowerment of citizens.

As such, it is possible to draw out more questions about welfare support from the answers and reviews of debates this text has offered. But these are the debates and tensions you must think through for yourself, with your lecturers and fellow students, as you get to grips with the debates we have in Social Policy and the Social Sciences more broadly. For now, returning to our debate about empowerment, we can draw this particular review of the book to a conclusion by focusing on a broader account of why the state should, or should not, involve itself in welfare provision. If the state opts to facilitate the attainment of welfare, then the question remains as to how this is to be achieved. The argument drawn out here is that, post–1980s, there has been a gradual move away from a number of 'founding' justifications for welfare based around social rights and the entitlement triangle. Here, empowerment was framed in terms of intervention into the socioeconomic context to address social inequalities (initially around social class, but later across a range of social divisions). Post–1980s, a change in policy narratives and contextual concepts has shifted the notion of 'empowerment' so that it is presented in terms familiar to individualised, pathological explanations of social problems. Welfare policy must encourage responsibility, prudential citizens and risk-taking behaviours to change one's circumstances. Claimed dependency on the state fails to do this. Empowerment is therefore framed in a consumerist narrative, which offers little more than tokenistic engagement and conditionality, and ensures a disciplining of citizens to the needs of neoliberal economic practices. Citizens are 'empowered' to make a choice from existing options offered by welfare providers, not the ability to use one's voice to challenge and change how welfare was provided. Thus, the broader shifts in concepts outlined in much of this text result from the advancement of neoliberal economic theory across the globe, and the consequences of this theory integrating with national socioeconomic contexts and justifications of welfare provision.

Key debates for exploring welfare

As mentioned, the chapters of this book were intentionally set out to explore key concepts but also the interlinks between them. This is best illustrated by the front cover (naturally). Each concept is a thread, which combines with other threads in various ways to produce the whole: a notion of welfare and how it can be met. This entwining of concepts is influenced by a historical process: changes in the social, economic and political contexts in which concepts are articulated and drawn into policies to have a practical impact on our lives. At the core of changes in welfare provision post–1980 has been the rise of neoliberalism. This has fundamentally sought to not only reposition welfare systems but also question a number of key concepts in welfare provision. Presented as a new economic paradigm against which there are no alternatives, this has proven to be a powerful narrative for welfare reform.

How does neoliberalism influence concepts?

Conceptual debates about welfare emanate from broader ideological understandings of human nature and the state–market relationship. Yet, the advent of global neoliberal **hegemony** results in significant repositioning of welfare problems and solutions, fundamentally changing some of the key founding principles of the welfare state outlined in foregoing chapters. This section reviews the changes that have occurred.

The different sectors of the MEW have been drawn on to create different welfare systems to secure human welfare. The welfare state is one such system, which, while not found in all western nations, has become the typical model of Social Policy discussion. Built on a notion of universal ideas of citizenship in which welfare provision was to be based around social rights, need and equality, Titmuss (in Titmuss et al., 1997) has suggested that these efforts are built around an altruistic core, which ensures that universal provision is predominantly provided through the state. As mentioned a number of times, this was seen as a necessary and appropriate compensation for the costs of human progress. This provision seeks to promote equal life chances within a framework of achieving societal needs, alongside each individual's potential to flourish towards their own preferred end state. Yet, as previous chapters have shown, this is not always so clear-cut. The recession of the 1970s saw a shift in dominant economic theory, from Keynesian to neoliberal, and a move away from how some of these core concepts of welfare were articulated within political discourse.

Langan (1998) argues that this crisis precipitated the politicisation of need. Economic crisis narratives have generated arguments about the state's provision of welfare, alongside a critique of Keynesian economic theory. In its place, neoliberal economic theory was integrated into social policy activity, suggesting a need for reform based on economic efficiency, the emergence of permanent mass unemployment, increasing demand for welfare support, increasing insecurity and social malaise and dissatisfaction with the style of provision of state welfare (it did not meet the particular requirements of the 'modern–day consumer'). Neoliberalism offered a paradigm that suggested the state no longer had at its command the resources necessary to provide expansive welfare provision; indeed, it was argued that it never did. Rather, there was an ambitious expansion of welfare provision, driven by the infinite demand of citizens to have certain needs met and the willingness of politicians to promise to meet these needs to secure electoral success.

A number of perceived barriers to welfare provision encouraged the development of momentum for change: increased economic globalisation, an ageing population and technological advances. These changes combined with popular expectations and selfish wants, create new challenges and dependencies to which the state could provide no acceptable solution. The state, it was argued, no longer had adequate economic resources for provision, could not deliver as efficiently as the market *and* was being hollowed out in the new global order. This renewed understanding of the socioeconomic context was needed to promote welfare reform; this, in turn, required a rearticulating of concepts to underpin new explanations of social problems and solutions, relying on a change in narratives around welfare entitlement and how it was to be delivered.

On the one hand, this was achieved through presenting social problems as generated by individual behaviours and actions, combined with a claim that state welfare did not address these behaviours but rather created dependency. Images of 'dole scroungers', 'irresponsible parents' and 'bogus asylum seekers' were set up as the 'other'. These were positioned as abusers of the welfare state, creating an imagery of welfare provision that fostered support for selectivity and a move towards market provision to allow 'consumers' to make their own welfare demands, which, in turn, would drive economic production. These cultural explanations can be best illustrated in sentiments such as:

> A high and rising proportion of children are being born to mothers least fitted to bring children into the world. ... Some are of low intelligence, most of low educational attainment. They are unlikely to be able to give children the stable emotional background, the consistent combination of love and firmness ... They are producing problem children ... The balance of our human stock, is threatened. (Keith Joseph, in Halcrow, 1989:83)

This quotation blends narratives of stigma with those of responsibilisation. It was insufficient to just present the behaviours of some as inappropriate and damaging to the individual and society; there was also a need to articulate how a citizen should behave. Openly questioning the deservingness of certain citizens in this way makes it possible to expand this analysis further. Ideas of **welfare tourism** and the presentation of migrants as the new scroungers, claiming benefits despite not contributing to the system, have been recent prominent articulations of undeservingness. The slight irony here is that migrants are also blamed for taking jobs, and (as noted in Chapter 5) the dominant narrative regarding welfare services rests on being either in work or on welfare: a binary distinction that, in this particular skewed analysis, migrants seem to straddle. In the US, a similar image was presented with the label 'welfare queens' – a key part of Reagan's electoral campaign and a means of depicting (predominantly) women as engaging in fraudulent welfare claims to secure excessive welfare support. The aim here is an overt return to distinctions between deserving and undeserving and the promotion of the moral underclass discourse (Levitas, 1998), which presents social problems as being about culture and behaviours to be corrected and controlled. Such attitudes remain prevalent in policy; for example, a UK Department for Work and Pensions (2015, emphasis added) press release highlighting changes to the official measure of child poverty said: 'The government will also develop a range of other measures and indicators of *root causes* of poverty, including family breakdown, debt and addiction, setting these out in a children's life chances strategy'.

Three trends can be drawn out here: first, the presentation of needs as unreasonable desires; second, that those generating these needs are unwilling to take responsibility for themselves and their futures – unlike those willing to make their own provision to become self-sufficient; and third, the identification of responsible citizens. Combined, these have provided a powerful impetus for policy change. This final trend, a focus on responsibility, found its influence in the idea of individual resilience. Conceptually, this facilitated a repositioning of the state as a tool for social investment welfare provision, but sought to relocate responsibility onto the individual.

The concept of risk also underpins the development of this social investment approach. It is important to recognise three different ways of using the idea of risk. First, risk factors refer to certain circumstances or characteristics identified as being potential contributors to social problems. This is not the same as being poor, but it does equate to being vulnerable. This underpins the two further ways in which risk can be used to explain those risk factors. Thus, second, risk factors are embedded in the socioeconomic context, and are beyond the influence of the individual and their community and require wider collective protection at the level of the nation state. The fact that living in certain geographical locations results in people living shorter lives (due to historic deprivation and poverty) suggests the need for the state to intervene through a number of economic and policy initiatives to change the health-influencing context. However, and third, causes of ill health can be portrayed as individual risks resulting from health-damaging behaviours: smoking, drinking alcohol, lack of exercise and inappropriate diets. Addressing risk factors, therefore, relies not on the state but on the individual changing their behaviours; the wider socioeconomic context is sidelined.

The dominant neoliberal paradigm recognises and promotes this third use of the term 'risk', suggesting that behaviours need to change by challenging the risk-averse natures of those dependent on welfare. It proposes that globalisation has reduced the state's ability to control economic forces, and so individuals and communities need to become resilient to global economic tides. It recommends that responsible citizens make their own preparations to protect themselves from the uncertainty of the contemporary globalised world. General trends in social policy around risk have promoted new approaches in social provision built around notions of responsibilisation and **financialisation** (Finlayson, 2009). Taking responsibility to be resilient, especially through self-provision in the market or self-help in the community, is essential if we are to move from a 'passive' to an 'active' welfare state (Giddens, 1998). This has been most evident in UK social security reforms (Seymour, 2012), which drew lessons from US experimentation with welfare policies (Peck, 1998).

Generally speaking, this underpins a shift in notions of entitlement. Hayek's (1979) critique of social rights, and the suggestion that they are dependent on financial considerations, gains credence. The notion of equality of opportunity continues to dominate, to the demise of interest in outcomes, as meritocracy becomes a more vocal notion in welfare reform (especially education and the idea of social mobility). And, as noted, the idea of need is challenged and repositioned as creating welfare dependency and risk-averse natures. Consequently, the notion of citizenship is altered to emphasise duties over rights. This results in a change in how welfare is provided; here, means testing to provide residual welfare and support, conditional on the performance of certain duties, starts to filter into welfare reforms. Despite claims of creating freedom for citizens, empowering them as consumers within the welfare markets, elements of social control are integrated into the redesign of welfare. From conditionality within residual state provision to the subtle designs of other sources of welfare, the social division of control is implemented to its full extent within the new paradigm. Social rights as the basis of access to welfare are changed; your rights now reflect those of a consumer – where you behave in the appropriate manner (those who do not need correction).

The global financial crisis of 2008 created a renewed economic urgency to further cut and restrict welfare. Although this austerity agenda has been presented as an urgent truth that must be accepted, there is growing critique of this claim. For Clarke and Newman (2012:300), the UK response demonstrated how the focus of debate has shifted 'from an economic problem (how to "rescue" the banks and restore market stability) to a political problem (how to allocate blame and responsibility for the crisis): a reworking that has focused on the unwieldy and expensive welfare state and public sector'. As I have argued previously (Gregory, 2014:172):

> This shift reflects both Galbraith's (1958) suggestion that when countries experience financial crises, the public sector is usually targeted with the blame, and Farnsworth's (2011) view that public expenditure cuts are pursued to facilitate a redistribution of resources from the poorest to the rich. Consequently, the repositioning of the causes of the financial crisis impacts on the perceived solutions, creating a discursive space in which the notion of austerity is presented to secure public support for the proposed cuts.

This revisits the moral and economic case for welfare reform, using terms such as 'resilience' to promote new forms of self-help. More broadly, this is part of a change in policy along the lines suggested by Harrison and Sanders (2014) in their aforementioned discussion of the social divisions of control. Thus, it could be suggested that a class bias persists in the design of welfare, so that certain forms of control are applied to particular groups of citizens. On the one hand, the middle classes are encouraged to continue to act as prudential citizens through incentives to save and foster self-help. On the other, the working classes are exposed to conditional welfare designed to change their behaviours. Part of a new conventional wisdom, this has become the commonly accepted face of welfare provision – an agenda actively pursued under the pretence of no alternatives and the 'national good'.

Are there alternative narratives?

Whether there are alternatives depends on your view. Some readers will be supportive of the changes and arguments briefly sketched out in this chapter; others, if not most, will be starting to question some of the common assumptions they held before starting to read the text (or starting their degree), and may need time for further reflection. Another group may find themselves in agreement because this speaks to their own critical understanding of contemporary welfare debates. Regardless of where you are placed on these divides, I wish to consider how it *is* possible, if desired, to challenge these current configurations of welfare and its supportive systems.

This requires a brief move away from the dominant economic paradigm – justified because, as I have suggested, welfare has a number of different sources. Gibson-Graham (1993) illustrated the existence of a vast amount of activities outside of the market, which reflect different values and practices that go against the grain of neoliberal interpretations of the social and economic worlds. The challenge, however, is that it is difficult to convince people of these alternatives when neoliberal explanations both seem plausible and have become deeply ingrained in how we think. Gibson-Graham contended that it is the presentation of capitalism (we could say 'neoliberalism'), through a range of discursive practices, which makes change difficult. It is made to appear that there is no peer or equivalent; that capitalism exists in a category of its own, and that all other forms of exchange and value are inferior and can be said to have failed in the past.

We can illustrate this in relation to concepts. For example, Titmuss was critiqued for assuming that altruism was at the core of social provision, and embedding this at the core of the welfare state. Rather, as Le Grand noted, a range of human motivations exist. Such motivations require different forms of welfare provision, which are beyond the state. Markets and quasi-markets are therefore presented as the modern, enlightened approach to fit the new context. The state must create conditions for welfare pluralism, and (some would then argue) punish those not willing to conform to the new expectations of citizenship – determined by the state, not by public will. While progressive universalism has received some attention, it is often presented as a means by which economic inequality could be addressed to facilitate equality of opportunity. Its wider potential, as a means of accepting diversity within a universal framework, is underdeveloped in policy debate. Thus, in a way, the provision of welfare is relocated into the language of capitalism: markets, efficiency of allocation and so on. These are not necessarily ideas to ignore in welfare debates, but are just one part of a wider picture.

The articulation of alternatives must therefore break through these influential arguments, which insist on the use of market ideas and practices across all aspects of social life. There is a need to challenge the new 'common-sense' understandings of the modern world, human behaviour and the role of the state. This requires a new language for framing welfare debates. I hope it is clear to you by this point that this language for alternatives already exists; it is embedded in the concepts we use to debate the why, what and how of welfare. Understanding concepts is the first task; searching for evidence to support your argument comes next. Developing a convincing account of not only welfare reform but also the context of welfare provision is integral to success. This is complex – it is something you will likely spend most of your degree starting to unpick and understand – but we do not need to grasp everything the first time we come across it. The complexity rests in how the alternatives can be articulated. For some, the debate is around how to retain capitalism without its neoliberal dimension, such as the '**varieties of capitalism**' argument (Schröder, 2013). For others, there is a broader analysis that seeks to promote alternative notions of citizenship or measures of value in relation to human activities (Bryson, 2007; Gregory, 2015).

Afoko and Vockins (2013:2) suggest that framing has been integral in promoting austerity as a permanent feature of neoliberal praxis post-2008. These frames have been drawn into an effective story regarding the economic context, who to blame (the public sector) and the consequential need for reform. Although their analysis is UK-specific, its relevance is much broader. Of the seven frames, four are relevant here:

1. *Austerity is a necessary evil*: there is no economic alternative to spending cuts (a modern-day 'TINA');
2. *Big bad government*: the bloated, inefficient and controlling government is getting in the way of progress, interfering in people's lives and rewarding the undeserving;
3. *Welfare is a drug*: like drug addiction, state support is tempting but ultimately dangerous, and benefit claimants are weak, reckless, undeserving and addicted to handouts; and
4. *Strivers and skivers*: there are two kinds of people in Britain – hard-working strivers and lazy skivers – and we each choose which to be.

These points illustrate themes explored throughout this text. Points 1 and 2 relate to crisis narratives that have dominated contemporary welfare debates; the third draws attention to risk-averse citizens, generated by state support, which contributes to the wider economic problem; and the final point draws out the stigmatising, pathological explanations of social problems, which the media and citizens uncritically accept.

Combined, such arguments generate a powerful narrative, which limits scope for change. But, as Afoko and Vockins (2013) argued, this does not mean change is impossible. Rather, there is need to develop an effective story – a counterclaim

– which requires a new series of frames. Some of those listed by Afoko and Vockins include the suggestion that neoliberalism creates a **casino economy** based on the instability of high-stakes gambling, that nations stuck in a neoliberal frame fail to progress (reversing the 'end of history' narrative, which positions neoliberalism as the pinnacle of historical development) and that austerity is a smokescreen, which uses the public deficit to justify policy change that seeks to prevent critique of the consequences of such change. This reframing also draws attention to the fact that yes, there are people who work hard; however, their opposites are not 'skivers' but the 'big guys', who have money and power and play by their own rules, leaving the 'little guys' to suffer the consequences of the social harms generated by inequality in the wider social context. Thus, Afoko and Vockins (2013:30) conclude that '[t]he battle for the economic narrative will be won with stories, not statistics. Armed with facts alone, opponents of austerity stand little chance against a story that is well developed, well told and widely believed'.

Creating such stories *is* possible, and concepts will form an integral part of this endeavour. Yet, the complex knot in our welfare thread, which is implicit in this chapter, is that the articulation of alternatives is exceptionally difficult. The dominance of neoliberal economics presents certain values and principles as a correct interpretation of the social and economic worlds, and argues that we must accept these as they are. To seek change is to question fundamental truths about the nature of both the social and the economic spheres. This is the integral role of the Social Policy student; as I stated in Chapter 1, our task is to find alternative futures towards which society can travel to secure human welfare.

Where next? The role of policy analysis

This is not the end of your engagement in Social Policy concepts. As Drake (2001) highlights, concepts are highly relevant to policy analysis. He opens his text by highlighting three key questions that emerge from a discussion of principles and values:

1. What values and principles does a government use to guide the formulation of its policies?
2. What principles have been declared, or may be discerned by observation?
3. What is the scope of these principles: are they closely circumscribed within specific areas of action, or do they enunciate more general objectives above and beyond the substantive matters in hand? (Adapted from Drake, 2001:134)

The first two questions are clear not only in purpose but also in relation to concepts. Concepts are the building blocks of welfare policies. Underpinned by differing political ideologies, we have seen how concepts can be defined and interpreted in a number of ways, which have significant consequences for the types of policies they produce and varied impacts on our lives. The third question reflects on how the specific principles of the policy relate to broader social goals; these overarching aims are themselves constructed through the concepts we have explored. It is about how different definitions and ideas come together to form the ambitions of a government – and, therefore, the policies they wish to pursue.

Through the exploration of key concepts, we can start to unpick how governments perceive notions of equality or justice, citizenship, and the pressures and challenges facing governments in seeking to provide welfare services. Essentially, we get insight into how certain governments, or at least key actors, think – as well as the ideas of those outside of government who support or oppose a particular policy. Subsequently, we can explore how governments navigate tensions between equality and liberty, absolute and relative needs, and obligations and rights. Additionally, concepts can be used as lenses through which policies can be assessed. Issues of social control are rarely overt elements of government narratives, but policy is inherently about some level of control. This is why, as Social Policy students, you should always ask the four fundamental questions of any students of welfare:

1. *What* is being delivered through the welfare system to achieve human welfare?
2. *How* is this being delivered?
3. *Why* is this being pursued?
4. *Is* this the right approach to take?

The first two questions draw attention to the mechanical aspects of social policies: those aspects tied into an investigation of welfare system design and implementation. The third and fourth questions require a more explicit understanding of concepts. The third rests on the articulation of concepts offered by policy makers. The fourth depends on the analyst's interpretation of the appropriateness of the answers found in relation to the previous three questions. If feminist scholars, for example, had not asked whether the Beveridge social security design was appropriate, its gendered assumptions and the resulting practices may never have been challenged. As students of Social Policy, your ability to ask the final question should be done in this way, through your understanding of key concepts. This book has sought to offer you the starting point for developing this critical analysis.

A beginning, not an end

Entering into these debates, this text has sought to encourage you to think critically about not only current developments in welfare provision but also the concepts that underpin welfare services. Rather than accepting the arguments of policy makers at face value, you should question the appropriateness and suitability of all policy interventions that (directly or indirectly) seek to pursue welfare objectives. This final chapter has sought to bring the key concepts and debates together, and to provide a framework for you to start your own critical exploration of welfare and Social Policy. This book has sought to introduce you to a range of tools to assist you in this analysis, and so it concludes with one of the opening comments of the book; that is, to fully appreciate these debates, you need to engage in the original texts from which these arguments developed. This book has sought to provide you with sufficient familiarity with these ideas for you to begin your own investigation of key concepts and explore these welfare debates for yourself.

Further reading

Gibson-Graham, J.K. (1993) Waiting for the Revolution, or How to Smash Capitalism While Working at Home in Your Spare Time. *Rethinking Marxism* 6 pp10–24.

Jordan, B. (2010) *What's Wrong with Social Policy and How to Fix It*. Cambridge: Polity Press.

Don't forget to look at the companion website for more information.

Bibliography

Adams, J. and Schmueker, K. (Eds.) (2005) *Devolution in Practice 2006: Public Policy Differences Within The UK*. London: IPPR.

Adger, W.N. (2000) Social and Ecological Resilience: Are They Related? *Progress in Human Geography* 24 pp347–364.

Adorno, T. (2001) Free Time, in T. Adorno, *The Culture Industry*. London: Routledge.

Afoko, C. and Vockins, D. (2013) *Framing the Economy: The Austerity Story*. New Economics Foundation. Available at: http://b.3cdn.net/nefoundation/a12416779f2dd4153c_2hm6ixryj.pdf

Alcock, P. (1996) *Social Policy in Britain: Themes and Issues*. Basingstoke: Palgrave Macmillan.

Alcock, P. (2008) *Social Policy in Britain* (3rd edn.). Basingstoke: Palgrave Macmillan.

Alcock, P. (2006) *Understanding Poverty* (3rd edn.). Basingstoke: Palgrave Macmillan.

Alcock, P. (2012) *The Big Society: A New Policy Environment for the Third Sector?* Available at: /www.birmingham.ac.uk/generic/tsrc/documents/tsrc/working-papers/working-paper-82.pdf

Alcock, P. (2016) *Why We Need Welfare: Collective Action for the Common Good*. Bristol: Policy Press.

Alcock, P. and May, M. (2014) *Social Policy in Britain* (4th edn.). Basingstoke: Palgrave.

Alcock, P., Erskine, A. and May, M. (Eds.)(2002) *The Blackwell Dictionary of Social Policy*. Oxford: Blackwell.

Alford, J. (2002) Defining the Client in the Public Sector: A Social-Exchange Perspective. *Public Administration Review* May/June 62 pp337–346.

Anders, B. (2016) *Imagined Communities: Reflections on the Origins and Spread of Nationalism*. London: Verso.

Anderson, B. (2016) *Imagined Communities: Reflections on the Origins and Spread of Nationalism* (Revised edn.). London: Verso.

Annetts, J., Law, A., McNeish, W. and Mooney, G. (Eds.) (2009) *Understanding Social Welfare Movements*. Bristol: Policy Press.

Anthias, F. (2001) The Material and the Symbolic in Theorizing Social Stratification: Issues of Gender, Ethnicity and Class. *The British Journal of Sociology* 52 pp367–390.

Arnstein, S.R. (1969) A Ladder of Citizen Participation. *Journal of the American Institute of Planners* 35(4) pp216–224.

Ashford, E. (2006) The Inadequacy of our Traditional Conception of the Duties Imposed by Human Rights. *Canadian Journal of Law and Jurisprudence* 19(2) pp 217-35.

Atkinson, W., Roberts, S. and Savage, M. (2012) Introduction: A Critical Sociology of the Age of Austerity; in W. Atkinson, S. Roberts and M. Savage (Eds.), *Class Inequality in Austerity Britain: Power, Difference and Suffering.* Hampshire: Palgrave Macmillan pp1–12.

Bagilhole, B. (2010) *Understanding Equal Opportunities and Diversity: The Social Differentiations and Intersections of Inequality.* Bristol: Policy Press.

Baker, J., Lynch, K., Cantillon, S. and Walsh, J. (2004) Dimensions of Equality: A Framework for Theory and Action; *Equality: From Theory to Action.* London: Palgrave Macmillan UK pp21–46.

Baldock, J. (2012) Social Policy, Social Welfare, and the Welfare State; in J. Baldock, L. Mitton, N. Manning and S. Vickerstaff (Eds.), *Social Policy* (4th edn.). Oxford: Oxford University Press pp7–26.

Bambra, C. (2007) Defamilisation and Welfare State Regimes: A Cluster Analysis. *International Journal of Social Welfare* 16 pp326–338.

Bandura, A. (1994) Self-Efficacy; in V.S. Ramachandran (Ed.), *Encyclopaedia of Human Behaviour.* San Diego, CA: Academic Press pp71–81.

Barr, N. (2012) *Economics of the Welfare State* (5th edn.). Oxford: Oxford University Press.

Bartolini, S., Bilancini, E., Bruni, L. and Porta, P.L. (Eds.) (2016) *Policies for Happiness.* Oxford: Oxford University Press.

Bastagli, F. (2009) Conditionality in Public Policy Targeted to the Poor: Promoting Resilience? *Social Policy and Society* 8 pp127–140.

Bauman, Z. (2001) *Community: Seeking Safety in an Insecure World.* Cambridge: Polity.

Baumberg, B., Bell, K. and Gaffney, D. (2012) *Benefits Stigma in Britain.* Turn2Us. Available at: www.turn2us.org.uk/T2UWebsite/media/Documents/Benefits-Stigma-in-Britain.pdf

Bean, P., Ferris, J. and Whynes, D. (1985). *In Defence of Welfare.* London: Routledge.

Beck, U. (1992) *Risk Society.* London: Sage.

Beck, U. and Beck-Gernsheim, E. (2002) *Individualization: Institutionalized Individualism and its Social and Political Consequences.* London: SAGE.

Becker, S., Dearden, C. and Aldridge, J. (2000) Young Carers in the UK: Research, Policy and Practice. *Research, Policy and Planning* 8 (2) pp3–22.

Béland, D and Lecours, A. (2008) *Nationalism and Social Policy: The Politics of Territorial Solidarity.* Oxford: Oxford University Press.

Bennett, F. and Daly, M. (2014) *Poverty Through a Gender Lens: Evidence and Policy Review on Gender and Poverty.* Oxford: Department of Social Policy and Intervention.

Beresford, P. (2002a) Thinking about 'Mental Health': Towards a Social Model. *Journal of Mental Health* 11 (6) pp581–584.

Beresford, P. (2002b) Participation and Social Policy: Transformation, Liberation or Regulation?; in R. Sykes, C. Bochel and N. Ellison (Eds.), *Social Policy Review 14: Developments and Debates: 2001–2002.* Bristol: Policy Press pp265–290.

Beresford, P. (2010) Service Users and Social Policy: Developing Different Discussions, Challenging Dominant Discourses; in I. Greener, C. Holden and M. Kilkey (Eds.), *Social Policy Review 22: Analysis and Debate in Social Policy*. Bristol: Policy Press pp227–252.

Beresford, P. and Campbell, J. (1994) Disabled People, Service Users, User Involvement and Representation. *Disability and Society* 9 (3) pp315–325.

Berlin, I. (1958) *Two Concepts of Liberty: An Inaugural Lecture Delivered Before the University of Oxford on 31 October 1958*. Oxford: Clarendon Press.

Best, S. (2005) *Understanding Social Divisions*. London: Sage.

Blakemore, K. and Warwick-Booth, L. (2013) *Social Policy: An Introduction* (4th edn.). Berkshire: Open University Press.

Bonanno, G.A. (2008) Loss, Trauma, and Human Resilience: Have We Underestimated the Human Capacity to Thrive after Extremely Aversive Events? *Psychological Trauma: Theory, Research, Practice, and Policy* 59(1) pp101–113.

Bottomore T. (1979) *Political Sociology*. London: Hutchinson and Co.

Bould, S. (2006) The Need for International Family Policy. *Marriage and Family Review* 39 pp75–98.

Boulding, K.E. (1967) The Boundaries of Social Policy. *Social Work* 12 pp3–11.

Bourdieu, P. (1986) The Forms of Capital; in J.G. Richardson (Ed.), *Handbook of Theory and Research for the Sociology of Education*. New York: Greenwood Press.

Bovaird, T. (2007) Beyond Engagement and Participation: User and Community Coproduction of Services. *Public Administration Review* 67 (5) pp846–860.

Bradshaw, J. (2013) The Concept of Social Need; in R. Cookson, R. Sainsbury and C. Glendinning (Eds.), *Jonathan Bradshaw on Social Policy: Selected Writings 1972–2011*. York: University of York pp1–12. Available at: https://www.york.ac.uk/inst/spru/pubs/pdf/JRB.pdf

Bradshaw, J., Kemp, P., Baldwin, S. and Rowe, A. (2004) *The Drivers of Social Exclusion: A Review of the Literature*. Breaking the Cycles Series. London: Social Exclusion Unit, Office of the Deputy Prime Minister.

Briggs, A. (1961) The Welfare State in Historical Perspective. *European Journal of Sociology / Archives Européennes de Sociologie* 2 pp221–258.

Brodie, E., Cowling, E. and Nissen, N. with Paine, A.E., Jochum, V. and Warburton, D. (2009) 'Understanding Participation: A Literature Review'; in *Pathways Through Participation*. Available at: http://pathwaysthroughparticipation.org.uk.

Brown, K. (2014) 'Beyond Protection: "The Vulnerable" in the Age of Austerity'; in M. Harrison and T. Sanders (Eds.), *Social Policies and Social Control: New Perspectives on the 'Not-So-Big Society'*. Bristol: Policy Press pp39–54.

Bryson V. (2007) *Gender and the Politics of Time: Feminist Theory and Contemporary Debates*. Bristol: Policy Press.

Burchardt, Tania (2006) Happiness and Social Policy: Barking up the Right Tree in the Wrong Neck of the Woods; in L. Bauld, Linda, T. Maltby and K. Clarke (Eds.), *Analysis and Debate in Social Policy, 2006. Social Policy Review: 18*. Bristol: Policy Press pp209-230

Burns, D. and Taylor M. (1998) *Mutual Aid and Self-Help.* Bristol: Policy Press.

Butler, I. and Drakeford, M. (2005) *Scandal, Social Policy and Social Welfare.* Bristol: Policy Press.

Butler, P. (2015) Thousands Have Died After Being Found Fit for Work, DWP Figures Show; *The Guardian*, 27 August. Available at: www.theguardian.com/society/2015/aug/27/thousands–died–after–fit–for–work–assessment–dwp–figures.

Cabinet Office (2011) *Giving White Paper.* London: The Stationery Office.

Calder, G. (2016) *How Inequality Runs in Families: Unfair Advantage and the Limits of Social Mobility.* Bristol: Policy Press.

Cameron D. (2009) *The Big Society.* Speech. 10 November. Available at: www.conservatives.com/News/Speeches/2009/11/David_Cameron_The_Big_Society.aspx.

Cameron, D. (2011). *Full transcript David Cameron speech on troubled families* [Online]. Available at: http://www.newstatesman.com/uk–politics/2011/12/troubled-families-family [Accessed 23 May 2013].

Cameron, D. (2014) *David Cameron on Families.* Speech, 18 August. Available at: www.gov.uk/government/speeches/david-cameron-on-families.

Canavan, M. (1996) *Nationhood and Political Theory.* Cheltenham: Edward Elgar Publishing.

Carabine, J. (2001) Constituting Sexuality through Social Policy: The Case of Lone Motherhood 1834 and Today. *Social and Legal Studies* 10 pp291–314.

Carabine, J. (Ed.) (2009) *Sexualities.* Milton Keynes: Open University Press.

Carr, E.H. (1949) The Rights of Man; in UNESCO (Ed.) *Human Rights: Comments and Interpretations.* Westport, CT: Greenwood Press pp19–23.

Carr, S. (2013) *Personalisation: A Rough Guide* (Revised edn.). Transition Info Network. Available at: https://www.scie.org.uk/personalisation/introduction/rough-guide

Carroll, L. ([1865] 1982) *Lewis Carroll's Alice's Adventures in Wonderland* / illustrated by Barry Moser. London: University of California Press.

Carter, J. (1998) Studying Social Policy after Modernity; in J. Carter (Ed.), *Postmodernity and the Fragmentation of Welfare.* London: Routledge.

Casey, L. (2012) *Listening to Troubled Families.* Available at: www.gov.uk/government/uploads/system/uploads/attachment_data/file/6151/2183663.pdf.

Centre for Social Justice (2006) *Breakdown Britain.* London: Centre for Social Justice.

Chaney, P. and Drakeford, M. (2004) The Primacy of Ideology: Social Policy and the First Term of the National Assembly for Wales; in N. Ellison, L. Bauld and M. Powell (Eds.), *Social Policy Review.* Bristol: Policy Press pp121–142.

Chen F-l, Yang, P.-S. and Wang, L.L.-R. (2010) The Changing Profile of the Taiwanese Family and the Governmental Response. *Journal of Asian Public Policy* 3 pp135–145.

Chorley, J. (2012) IoS Exclusive: Problem Families Told – 'Stop Blaming Others'; *The Independent*, 9 June. Available at: www.independent.co.uk/news/uk/politics/ios-exclusive-problem-families-told-stop-blaming-others-7834235.html.

Chriss, J.J. (2013) *Social Control: an Introduction* (2nd edn.). Cambridge: Polity Press.

Clarke, A. and Monk, S. (2011) Residualisation of the Social Rented Sector: Some New Evidence. *International Journal of Housing Markets and Analysis* 4 pp418–437.

Clarke, J. (2000) A World of Difference? Globalization and the Study of Social Policy; in G. Lewis, S. Gewiritz and J. Clarke (Eds.), *Rethinking Social Policy*. London: Sage pp201–206.

Clarke, J. (2001) 'Social Problems: Sociological Perspectives'; in M. May, R.M. Page and E. Brunsden (Eds.), *Understanding Social Problems*. Oxford: Blackwell. pp3-17

Clarke, J. (2004) *Changing Welfare, Changing States: New Directions in Social Policy*. London: Sage.

Clarke, J. and Newman, J. (2012) The Alchemy of Austerity. *Critical Social Policy* 32 pp299–319.

Clarke, J., Langan, M. and Williams, F. (2001) 'Remaking Welfare: The British Welfare Regime in the 1980s and 1990s'; in A. Cochrane, J. Clarke and S. Gewirtz (Eds.), *Comparing Welfare States* (2nd edn.). London: Sage pp72-111

Clarke, J., Newman, J., Smith, N., Vidler, E. and Westmarland, L. (2007) *Creating Citizen–Consumers: Changing Publics and Changing Public Services*. London: Sage.

Clayton, S. (1983) Social Need Revisited. *Journal of Social Policy* 12 pp215–234.

Coffey A. (2004) *Reconceptualising Social Policy*. Maidenhead: Open University Press.

Cohen, S. (2002) *Folk Devils and Moral Panics: The Creation of The Mods and Rockers*. London: Routledge.

Coleman, J. (1990) *Foundations of Social Theory*. Cambridge, MA: Harvard University Press.

Connor, S. (2013) *What's Your Problem? Making Sense of Social Problems and the Policy Process*. Northwich: Critical Publishing.

Cornwall, A. (2008) Unpacking 'Participation': Models, Meanings and Practices. *Community Development Journal* 43 (3) pp269–283.

Danson, M., MacLeod, G. and Mooney, G., (2012) Devolution and the Shifting Political Economic Geographies of the United Kingdom. *Environment and Planning C: Government and Policy* 30 (1) pp1–9.

Daly, M. (2008) Whither EU Social Policy? An Account and Assessment of Developments in The Lisbon Social Inclusion Process. *Journal of Social Policy* 37 (1) pp1-19.

Daly, M. (2011) *Welfare*. Cambridge: Polity.

David, M. (2000) New Labour's Post-Thatcherite Modernisation Project: A Third Way? *Journal of Social Policy* 29 pp143-146.

Davidson, N. McCafferty, P. and Miller, D. (Eds.) (2010) *Neoliberal Scotland: Class and Society in a Stateless Nation*. Cambridge: Cambridge Scholars Press.

Davies, J. (Ed.) (1993) *The Family: Is It Just Another Lifestyle Choice?* London: IEA Health and Welfare Unit.

Davies, J.S. and Pill, M. (2012) Empowerment or Abandonment? Prospects for Neighbourhood Revitalization under the Big Society. *Public Money and Management* 32 pp193–200.

Davies, W. (2016) *The Happiness Industry: How the Government and Big Business Sold Us Well-Being.* London: Verso.

Deacon, A. (2002) *Perspectives on Welfare: Ideas, Ideologies and Policy Debates.* Buckingham: Open University Press.

Deakin, N. and Wright, A. (Eds.) (1990) *Consuming Public Services.* London: Routledge.

Dean, H. (2008) Social Policy and Human Rights: Re-thinking the Engagement, *Social Policy and Society* 7 (1) pp1–12

Dean, H. (2010) *Understanding Human Need.* Bristol: Policy Press.

Dean, H. (2012) *Social Policy* (2nd edn.). Cambridge: Polity.

Dean, H. (2015) *Social Rights and Human Welfare.* Oxon: Routledge.

Dean, H. and Melrose, M. (1999) *Poverty, Riches and Social Citizenship.* Basingstoke: Macmillan.

Denham, J. (2009) Just Deserts; in T. Hampson and J. Olchawski (Eds.), *Is Equality Fair? What the Public Really Think About Equality – and What We Should Do About It.* London: Fabian Society pp19–26.

Department of Work and Pensions (2015) *Government to Strengthen Child Poverty Measure.* Press release, 1 July. Available at: www.gov.uk/government/news/government-to-strengthen-child-poverty-measure.

Dermott, E. and Pantazis, C. (2014) Gender and Poverty in Britain: Changes and Continuities between 1999 and 2012, *Journal of Poverty and Social Justice* 22(3) pp253–269.

Dickens, C. ([1843] 1992) *A Christmas Carol.* Oxford: Oxford University Press.

Dingwall, R. (1999) 'Risk Society': The Cult of Theory and the Millennium? *Social Policy and Administration* 33 pp474–491.

Dinham, A. (2005) Empowered or Over-Powered? The Real Experiences of Local Participation in the UK's New Deal for Communities. *Community Development Journal* 40 (3) pp301–312.

Dinham, A. (2006) Raising Expectations or Dashing Hopes? Well-Being and Participation in Disadvantaged Areas. *Community Development Journal* 41 (2) pp181–193.

Donati, P. (1987) Traditional Political Theories and New Social Option: Replies to the Crisis of the Welfare State; in A. Evers, H. Nowotny and H. Wintersberger (Eds), *The Changing Face of Welfare.* Aldershot: Gower Publishing Company pp24-45

Dower, N. and Williams, J. (Eds.) (2002) *Global Citizenship: A Critical Reader.* Edinburgh: Edinburgh University Press.

Doyal, L. and Gough, I. (1984) A Theory of Human Needs. *Critical Social Policy* 4 pp6–38.

Drake, R.F. (2001) *The Principles of Social Policy*. Hampshire: Palgrave.

Drakeford, M. (2000) *Privatisation and Social Policy*. Harlow: Longman Press.

Drakeford, M. (2007) Social Justice in a Devolved Wales. *Benefits* 15 (2) pp171–178.

Driver, S. and Martell L. (2002) New Labour, Work and the Family. *Social Policy and Administration* 36 pp46–61.

Dryzek, J. (2008) The Ecological Crisis of the Welfare State, *Journal of European Social Policy* 18 (4) pp334–337.

Dwyer, P. (2002) Making Sense of Social Citizenship. *Critical Social Policy* 22 pp273–299.

Dwyer, P. (2004) *Understanding Social Citizenship*. Bristol: Policy Press.

Eagleton-Pierce, M. (2016) *Neoliberalism: The Key Concepts*. London: Routledge.

Ellingsæter, AL (2003) The Complexity of Family Policy Reform: The Case of Norway. *European Societies* 5 pp419–443.

Ellison N. (2011) The Conservative Party and the 'Big Society'; in C. Holden, M. Kilkey and M. Ramia (Eds.), *Social Policy Review 23: Analysis and Debate in Social Policy*. Bristol: Policy Press pp45–62.

Esping-Andersen, G. (1990) *The Three Worlds of Welfare Capitalism*. Princeton, NJ: Princeton University Press.

Evers, A. and Wintersberger, H. (1994) Introduction; in A. Evers, H. Nowotny and H. Wintersberger (Eds.), *The Changing Face of Welfare*. Aldershot: Gower.

Farazmand A. (1999) Globalization and Public Administration. *Public Administration Review* 559 pp509–522.

Farnsworth, K. (2004) *Corporate Power and Social Policy in a Global Economy*. Bristol: Policy Press.

Farnsworth, K. and Irving, Z. (2011) *Social Policy in Challenging Times: Economic Crisis and Welfare Systems*. Bristol: Policy Press.

Ferrera, M. (2005) *The Boundaries of Welfare: European Integration and the New Spatial Politics of Social Protection*. Oxford: Oxford University Press.

Field, F. (1989) *Losing Out: The Emergence of Britain's Underclass*. Oxford: Basil Blackwell.

Finlayson, A. (2008) Imagined Communities. *The Blackwell Companion to Political Sociology*. Oxford: Blackwell Publishing Ltd.

Finlayson, A. (2009) Financialisation, Financial Literacy and Asset-Based Welfare. *The British Journal of Politics and International Relations* 11 pp400–421.

Fitzpatrick, T. (2001a) *Welfare Theory: An Introduction*. London: Palgrave.

Fitzpatrick, T. (2001b) Before the Cradle: New Genetics, Biopolicy and Regulated Eugenics. *Journal of Social Policy* 30 pp589–612.

Fitzpatrick, S., Watts, B. and Johnsen, S. (2014) *Conditionality Briefing: Social Housing*. Welfare Conditionality. Available at: www.welfareconditionality.ac.uk/wp-content/uploads/2014/09/Briefing_SocialHousing_14.09.10_FINAL.pdf.

Fives, A. (2007) *Political and Philosophical Debates in Welfare*. Basingstoke: Palgrave.

Flanigan, D. and Hosie, A. (2016) Human Rights and Equality; in P. Alcock, T. Haux, M. May and S. Wright (Eds.), *The Student's Companion to Social Policy*. Sussex: Wiley pp34–40

Forder, A. (1974) *Concepts in Social Administration*. London: Routledge and Kegan Paul.

Foucault, M. (1990) *The History of Sexuality, Vol. 1: An Introduction*. Harmondsworth: Penguin.

Foucault, M. (1991) *Discipline and Punish: The Birth of the Prison*. London: Penguin.

Fourcade-Gourinchas, M. and Babb, S.L. (2002) The Rebirth of the Liberal Creed: Paths to Neoliberalism in Four Countries. *American Journal of Sociology* 108 (3) pp533–579.

Fox Harding, L. (1996) *Family, State and Social Policy*. Hampshire: Macmillan Press.

Fraser, M.W., Galinsky, M.J. and Richman, J.M. (1999) Risk, Protection, and Resilience: Toward a Conceptual Framework for Social Work Practice. *Social Work Research* 23 pp131–143.

Fraser, N. (2003) From Discipline to Flexibilization? Rereading Foucault in the Shadow of Globalization. *Constellations* 10 pp160–171.

Frayne, D. (2015) *The Refusal of Work*. London: Zed Books.

Freedland J. (2010) There's a Good Idea in Cameron's 'Big Society' Screaming to Get Out; *The Guardian*, 20 July. Available at: www.guardian.co.uk/commentisfree/2010/jul/20/good-idea-camerons-big-society-screaming-get-out.

Freeman, M. (2011) *Human Rights* (2nd edn.). Cambridge: Polity Press.

Freeman, R. (1992). 'The Idea of Prevention: A Critical Review'; in S. Scott, G. Williams, S. Platt and H. Thomas (Eds.), *Private Risks and Public Dangers*. Aldershot: Avebury pp34–56

Friedman, M. with the assistance of Rose D. Friedman (2002) *Capitalism and Freedom* (40th anniversary edn.). Chicago, IL: Chicago University Press.

Fukuyama, F. (1992) *The End of History and The Last Man*. London: Hamish Hamilton.

Furlong, A and Cartmel F. (1997) *Young People and Social Policy: Individualization and Risk in Late Modernity*. Buckingham: Open University Press.

Fussey, P. (2004) New Labour and New Surveillance: Theoretical and Political Ramifications of CCTV Implementation in the UK. *Surveillance and Society* 2 (2/3) pp251–269.

Galbraith, J.K. (1958) *The Affluent Society*. London: Penguin Books.

Garland, D. (1981) The Birth of the Welfare Sanction. *British Journal of Law and Society* 8 (1) pp29–45.

Garland, D. (1996) The Limits of the Sovereign State: Strategies of Crime Control in Contemporary Society. *British Journal of Criminology* 36 pp445–471.

Gaskell C. (2008) 'But They Just Don't Respect Us': Young People's Experiences of (Dis)respected Citizenship and the New Labour Respect Agenda. *Children's Geographies* 6 pp223–238.

Gellner, E. (1983) *Nations and Nationalism*. Oxford: Blackwell.

Genschel, P. (2004) Globalization and the Welfare State: A Retrospective. *Journal of European Public Policy* 11 pp613–636.

George, V. and Wilding, P. (1976) *Ideology and Social Welfare*. London: Routledge.

George, V. and Wilding, P. (1984) *The Impact of Social Policy*. London: Routledge and Kegan Paul.

George, V. and Wilding, P. (1994) *Welfare and Ideology*. London: Harvester Wheatsheaf.

Gibson-Graham, J.K. (1993) Waiting for the Revolution, or How to Smash Capitalism while Working at Home in Your Spare Time. *Rethinking Marxism* 6 pp10–24.

Giddens, A. (1992) *The Transformation of Intimacy: Sexuality, Love and Eroticism in Modern Societies*. Cambridge: Polity.

Giddens, A. (1998) *The Third Way*. Cambridge: Cambridge University Press.

Giddens, A. (2002) *The Runaway World: How Globalisation is Reshaping Our Lives*. London: Profile.

Gilder, G. (1981) *Wealth & Poverty*. London: Buchan & Enright.

Ginsburg, N. (1992) *Divisions of Welfare: A Critical Introduction to Comparative Social Policy*. London: Sage.

Glennerster, H. (2003) *Understanding the Finance of Welfare*. Bristol: Policy Press p25.

Goffman, E. (1963) *Stigma: Notes on the Management of Spoiled Identity*. Middlesex: Penguin.

Goode, E. and Ben-Yehuda, N. (2010) *Moral Panics: The Social Construction of Deviance*. Chichester: John Wiley and Sons.

Goodin, R.E.A. (1988) *Reasons for Welfare: The Political Theory of the Welfare State*. Princeton, NJ: Princeton University Press.

Goodin, R.E., Parpo, A. and Kangas, O. (2004) The Temporal Welfare State: The Case of Finland. *Journal of Social Policy* 33 pp531–552.

Gordon, D. (2011) *Consultation Response: Social Mobility and Child Poverty Review*. Poverty and Social Exclusion. Available at: www.poverty.ac.uk/system/files/WP%20Policy%20Response%20No.%202%20Consultation%20Resp%20Social%20Mobility%20and%20Child%20Poverty%20%28Gordon%20Oct%202011%29.pdf.

Gough, I. (1979) *The Political Economy of The Welfare State*. Hampshire: Macmillan.

Gough, I. (2011) From Financial Crisis to Fiscal Crisis; in K Farnsworth and Z. Irving (Eds.), *Social Policy in Challenging Time: Economic Crisis and Welfare Systems*. Bristol: Policy Press pp65–80.

Gouldner, A.W. (1956) Explorations in Applied Social Science. *Social Problems* 3 pp169–181.

Greco, M. and Stenner, P. (2013) Happiness and the Art of Life: Diagnosing the Psychopolitics of Wellbeing. *Health, Culture and Society* 5(1) pp1–19.

Greer, S. (2014) Structural Adjustment Comes to Europe: Lessons for the Eurozone from the Conditionality Debates. *Global Social Policy* 14 pp51–71.

Gregory, L. (2009) Change Takes Time: Exploring the Structural and Development Issues of Time Banking. *International Journal of Community Currencies* 13 pp19–36.

Gregory, L. (2010) An Opportunity Lost? Exploring the Benefits of the Child Trust Fund on Youth Transitions into Adulthood. *Youth and Policy* 106 pp78–94.

Gregory, L. (2012) Time and Punishment: A Comparison of UK and US Time Bank Use in Criminal Justice Systems. *Journal of Comparative Social Welfare* 28 pp195–208.

Gregory, L. (2014) Resilience or Resistance? Time Banking in the Age of Austerity. *Journal of Contemporary European Studies* 22 (2) pp171–183.

Gregory L. (2015) *Trading Time: Can Exchange Lead to Social Change?* Bristol: Policy Press.

Gregory, L. and Drakeford, M. (2011) Just Another Financial Institution? Tensions in The Future of Credit Unions in The United Kingdom. *Journal of Poverty and Social Justice* 19 pp117–129.

Gregory, L. and Joseph, R. (2015) Big Society or Welfare Failure: How Does Food Insecurity Reflect the Future of Welfare Trends?; in L. Foster, A. Brunton, C. Deeming and T. Haux (Eds.), *In Defence of Welfare II*. Bristol: Policy Press pp114–116.

Greve, B. (2015) *Welfare and the Welfare State: Present and Future*. Oxon: Routledge.

Grice, A. (2009) 'Big Society' is the Solution to Poverty, Declares Cameron; *The Independent*, 11 November. Available at: www.independent.co.uk/news/uk/politics/big-society-is-the-solution-to-poverty-declares-cameron-1818209.html.

Grimshaw, D. and Rubery, J. (2012) The End of the UK's Liberal Collectivist Social Model? The Implications of the Coalition Government's Policy During the Austerity Crisis. *Cambridge Journal of Economics* 36 pp105–126.

Grint, K. and Nixon, D. (2015) *The Sociology of Work* (4th edn.). Cambridge: Polity Press.

Gwatkin, D.R. and Ergo, A. (2010) Universal Health Coverage: Friend or Foe of Health Equity? *The Lancet* 377 (9784) pp2160–2161.

Halcrow, M. (1989) *Sir Keith Joseph: A Single Mind*. London: Macmillan.

Hall, C. (2002) 'A Family for Nation and Empire'; in G. Lewis (Ed.), *Forming Nation, Framing Welfare*. London: Routledge pp9–48.

Hall, S. (1980) *Drifting in to a Law and Order Society*. London: The Cobden Trust.

Hall S. (2005) New Labour's Double-Shuffle. *Review of Education, Pedagogy, and Cultural Studies* 27 pp319–335.

Harrison, M. with Hemingway, L. (2014) Social Policy and the New Behaviourism: Towards a More Excluding Society; in M. Harrison and T. Sanders (Eds.), *Social Policies and Social Control: New Perspectives on the 'Not-So-Big Society'*. Bristol: Policy Press pp23–38.

Harrison, M. and Sanders, T. (2014) Introduction; in M. Harrison and T. Sanders (Eds.), *Social Policies and Social Control: New Perspectives on the 'Not-So-Big Society'*. Bristol: Policy Press pp3–22.

Harvey, D. (2007) *A Brief History of Neoliberalism*. Oxford: Oxford University Press.

Hayek, F.A. (1944) *The Road to Serfdom*. London: Routledge.

Hayek, F. (1979) *Law, Legislation and Liberty, Vol. 3: The Political Order of a Free People*. London: Routledge and Kegan Paul.

Heins, E. and Deeming, C. (2015) Welfare and Well-being: Inextricably Linked; in L. Foster, A. Brunton, C. Deeming and T. Haux (Eds.), *In Defence of Welfare 2*. Bristol: Policy Press pp.13–15

Hewitt, M. (1994) Social Policy and the Question of Postmodernism; in R. Page and J. Baldock (Eds.), *Social Policy Review 6*. Canterbury: Social Policy Association.

Heywood, A. (2007) *Political Ideologies: An Introduction* (4th edn.). London: Palgrave Macmillan.

Hills, J., Sefton, T. and Stewart, K. (Eds.) (2009) *Towards A More Equal Society? Poverty, Inequality and Policy Since 1997*. Bristol: Policy Press.

Hills, J., Brewer, M., Jenkins, S., Lister, R., Lupton, R., Machin, S., Mills, C., Modood, T., Rees, T. and Riddell, S. (2010) *An Anatomy of Economic Inequality in the UK: Report of the National Equality Panel*. London: Government Equalities Office.

Hillyard, P. and Watson, S. (1996) Postmodern Social Policy: A Contradiction in Terms? *Journal of Social Policy* 25 pp321–346.

Hiroko T. (2008) The Political Economy of Familial Relations: The Japanese State and Families in a Changing Political Economy. *Asian Journal of Political Science* 16 pp196–214.

Hirst, P. and Thompson, G. (2004) *Globalisation in Question*. Cambridge: Polity Press.

HM Treasury (2002) *Pre-Budget Report 2002*. HM Stationery Office. Available at: http://webarchive.nationalarchives.gov.uk/20100407010852/www.hm-treasury.gov.uk/prebud_pbr02_repindex.htm.

Holden, C. (2003) Decommodification and the Workfare State. *Political Studies Review* 1 pp303–316.

Hort, S.E.O. (2014) *Social Policy, Welfare State and Civil Society in Sweden: Vol. I. History, Policies, and Institutions 1884–1986*. Lund: Arkiv Academic Press.

Jencks, C. (1992) *Rethinking Social Policy: Race, Poverty and the Underclass*. Cambridge, MA: Harvard University Press.

Jensen, T. and Tyler, I. (2015) 'Benefits Broods': The Cultural and Political Crafting of Anti-Welfare Commonsense. *Critical Social Policy* 35 pp470–491.

Jessop B. (1995) Towards a Schumpeterian Workfare Regime in Britain? Reflections on Regulation, Governance, and Welfare State. *Environment and Planning A* 27 pp1613–1626.

Jessop, B. (2004) Comments on 'New Labour's Double-Shuffle. Available at: eprints.lancs.ac.uk/236/01/E-2004e_Hall-Shuffle.doc [Accessed 1 November 2007].

Johnson, N. (1990) *Reconstructing the Welfare State: A Decade of Change*. London: Harvester Wheatsheaf.

Jordan, B. (2008) *Welfare and Well-being: Social Value in Public Policy.* Bristol: Policy Press.

Jordan, B. (2010) *What's Wrong with Social Policy and How to Fix It.* Cambridge: Polity Press.

Karger, H.J. and Stoesz, D. (1990) *American Social Welfare Policy: A Pluralist Approach* (2nd edn.). White Plains, NY: Longman.

Kemshall, H. (2002) *Risk, Social Policy and Welfare.* Buckingham: Open University Press.

Kendall, J. and Knapp, M. (1994) A Loose and Baggy Monster: Boundaries, Definitions and Typologies; in J. Davis Smith, C. Rochester and R. Hedley (Eds.), *An Introduction to the Voluntary Sector.* London: Routledge pp66–95.

Kennedy, P. (2013) *Key Themes in Social Policy.* London: Routledge.

Kevles, D.J. (1997) *In the Name of Eugenics: Genetics and the Uses of Human Heredity.* Cambridge, MA: Harvard University Press.

Klein, R. and Maybin, J. (2012) *Thinking About Rationing.* The Kings Fund. Available at: https://www.kingsfund.org.uk/sites/default/files/field/field_ publication_file/Thinking-about-rationing-the-kings-fund-may-2012.pdf.

Kneale, D., Majoribanks, D., and Sherwood, C. (2014) *Relationships, Recession and Recovery: The Role of Relationships in Generating Social Recovery.* Relate. Available at: www.relate.org.uk/policy-campaigns/publications/relationships-recession- and-recovery-role-relationships-generating-social-recovery.

Kotz, D. M. (2009) The Financial and Economic Crisis of 2008: A Systemic Crisis of Neoliberal Capitalism. *Review of Radical Political Economics* 41 pp305–317.

Krager, H.J. and Stoesz, D. (1990) *American Social Welfare Policy: A Pluralist Approach* (2nd edn.). White Plains, NY: Longman.

Kuhn, T. (1970) *The Structure of Scientific Revolutions* (2nd edn.). Chicago, IL: University of Chicago Press.

Land, H. (2012) Altruism, Reciprocity and Obligation; in P. Alcock, M. May and S. Wright (Eds.), *The Student's Companion to Social Policy.* West Sussex: John Wiley and Sons pp55-62.

Land, H. and Rose, H. (1985) Compulsory Altruism for Some or an Altruistic Society for All?; in P. Bean, J. Ferris and D. Whynes (Eds.), *In Defence of Welfare.* London: Tavistock Publications pp74–122

Langan, M. (1998) The Contested Concept of Need; in M. Langan (Ed.), *Welfare: Needs, Rights and Risks.* London: Routledge pp3-34.

Lansley, S. (no date) *Redefining Poverty?* Poverty and Social Exclusion. Available at: www.poverty.ac.uk/analysis-poverty-measurement-life-chances-government- policy/redefining-poverty#_edn19.

Lansley, S. (2009) We All Think We're in the Middle; in T. Hampson and J. Olchawski (Eds.), *Is Equality Fair? What the Public Really Think About Equality – and What We Should Do About It.* London: Fabian Society pp27–34.

Larner, W. (2005) Neoliberalism in (Regional) Theory and Practice: The Stronger Communities Action Fund in New Zealand. *Geographical Research* 43 pp9–18.

Lawrence, J. (2000) The Indian Health Service and the Sterilization of Native American Women. *American Indian Quarterly* 24 (3) pp400–419.

Legarde, C. (2014) *The Global Economy in 2014 by Christine Lagarde, Managing Director, International Monetary Fund*. Speech. 15 January. Available at: www.imf.org/external/np/speeches/2014/011514.htm.

Le Grand, J. (1992) *The Strategy of Equality: Redistribution and the Social Services*. London: George Allen and Unwin.

Le Grand, J. (1997). Knights, Knaves or Pawns? Human Behaviour and Social Policy. *Journal of Social Policy* 26 pp149–169.

Le Grand, J., Propper, C. and Robson, R. (1992) *The Economics of Social Problems*. London: Macmillan.

Leitner, S. (2003) Varieties of Familialism: The Caring Function of the Family in Comparative Perspective. *European Societies* 5 pp353–375.

Levin, P. (1997) *Making Social Policy: The Mechanisms of Government and Politics, and How to Investigate Them*. Buckingham: Open University Press.

Levitas, R. (1988) Competition and Compliance: The Utopias of the New Right; in R. Levitas (Ed.), *The Ideology of the New Right*. Cambridge: Polity Press.

Levitas, R. (1998) *The Inclusive Society? Social Exclusion and New Labour*. Basingstoke: Macmillan.

Levitas, R., Pantazis, C., Fahmy, E., Gordon, D., Lloyd, E. and Patsios, D. (2007) *The Multi-Dimensional Analysis of Social Exclusion: Report Prepared for the Social Exclusion Unit*. Bristol: University of Bristol.

Lewis, G. (2002) *Forming Nation, Framing Welfare*. London: Routledge.

Lewis, G. (Ed.) (2004) *Citizenship*. Milton Keynes: Open University Press.

Lewis, J. (1997) Gender and Welfare Regimes: Further Thoughts. *Social Politics: International Studies in Gender State and Society* 4 pp160–177.

Lewis, O. (1966) The Culture of Poverty. *Scientific American* 215 (4) pp19–25.

Liddard, M. and Mitton, L. (2012) 'Social Need and Patterns of Inequality'; in J. Baldock, L. Mitton, N. Manning and S. Vickerstaff (Eds.), *Social Policy* (4th edn.). Oxford: Oxford University Press pp81–99.

Lister, R. (1997) *Citizenship: Feminist Perspectives*. Hampshire: Macmillan.

Lister, R. (2004) *Poverty*. Cambridge: Polity.

Lister, R. (2010) *Understanding Theories and Concepts in Social Policy*. Bristol: Policy Press.

Lister, R. (2011) The Age of Responsibility: Social Policy and Citizenship in the Early 21st Century; in C. Holden, M. Kilkey and M. Ramia (Eds.), *Social Policy Review 23*. Bristol: Policy Press pp63–84.

Local Government Act (1998) Available at: www.legislation.gov.uk/Ukpga/1988/9/Contents

Lupton, C. Peckham, S. and Taylor, P. (1998) *Managing Public Involvement in Health-care Purchasing*. Buckingham: Open University Press.

Lynch, J., Due, P., Muntaner, C. and Davey Smith, G. (2000) Social Capital: Is it a Good Investment Strategy for Public Health? *Journal of Epidemiology and Community Health* 54 pp404–408.

MacCallum, G. C. (1967) Negative and Positive Freedom. *The Philosophical Review* 76 pp312–334.

Mac Cárthaigh, S. (2014) Need and Poverty. *Policy and Politics* 42 pp459–473.

Mack, J. (2017) *Consensual Method*. Poverty and Social Exclusion. Available at: www.poverty.ac.uk/Definitions-Poverty/Consensual-Method.

Macpherson, W. (1999) *The Stephen Lawrence Inquiry: Report of an Inquiry by Sir William Macpherson of Cluny*. London: The Stationery Office.

Manis, J.G. (1976) *Analysing Social Problems*. New York: Praegar.

Marmot, M. (2005) *Status Syndrome*. London: Bloomsbury.

Marshall, T.H. (1992) *Citizenship and Social Class*. London: Pluto Press.

Marsland, D. (1996) *Welfare or Welfare State: Contradictions and Dilemmas in Social Policy*. London: Macmillan Press.

Martin, D. (2014) Young People, Education, Families and Communities: Marginalised Hopes and Dreams?; in M. Harrison and T. Sanders (Eds.), *Social Policies and Social Control: New Perspectives on the 'Not-So-Big Society'*. Bristol: Policy Press pp101–116.

Marx, K. (1990). Capital [electronic resource]: A Critique of Political Economy. Volume One; in B. Fowkes (Ed.). London: Penguin Books in association with New Left Review.

Maslow, A. H. (1943) A Theory of Human Motivation. *Psychological Review* 50(4) pp370–96.

Mason, T. (1993) *Social Policy in the Third Reich: The Working Class and the 'National Community'*. Oxford: Berg.

Matsaganis, M. (2012) Social Policy in Hard Times: The Case of Greece. *Critical Social Policy* 32 pp406–421.

Mauss, M. (1950) *The Gift*. London: Routledge.

Maxwell, D., Sodha, S. and Stanley, K. (2006) *An Asset Account for Looked After Children: A Proposal to Improve Educational Outcomes for Children in Care*. IPPR. Available at: www.ippr.org/publications/an-asset-account-for-looked-after-children-a-proposal-to-improve-educational-outcomes-for-children-in-care.

May, J., Cloke, P. and Johnsen, S. (2005) Re-phasing Neoliberalism: New Labour and Britain's Crisis of Street Homelessness. *Antipode* 37 pp703–730.

McGhee, D. (2003) Joined-Up Government, 'Community Safety' and Lesbian, Gay, Bisexual and Transgender 'Active Citizens'. *Critical Social Policy* 23 pp345–374.

Mckenzie, L. (2015) *Getting By: Estates, Class and Culture in Austerity Britain*. Bristol: Policy Press.

Mead, L. (1986) *Beyond Entitlement: The Social Obligations of Citizenship*. New York: The Free Press.

Meil, G. (2006) The Evolution of Family Policy in Spain. *Marriage and Family Review* 39 pp359–380.

Miller, D. (2005) What is Social Justice?; in N. Pearce and W. Paxton (Eds.), *Social Justice: Building a Fairer Britain*. London: IPPR pp21–61.

Mishra, R. (1984) *The Welfare State in Crisis: Social Thought and Social Change.* Sussex: Open University Press.

Mishra, R. (1999) *Globalization and the Welfare State.* Cheltenham: Edward Elgar.

Mitchell, M., Beninger, K., Rahim, N. and Arthur, S. (2013) *Implications of Austerity for LGBT People and Services.* London: Natcen Social Research.

Modood, T. (2007) *Multiculturalism: A Civic Idea.* Cambridge: Polity.

Mooney, G. and Fyfe, N. (2006) New Labour and Community Protests: The Case of the Govanhill Swimming Pool Campaign, Glasgow. *Local Economy* 21 (2) pp136–150.

Mooney, G. and Scott, G. (Eds.) (2005) *Exploring Social Policy in the 'New Scotland'.* Bristol: Policy Press.

Morel, N., Palier, B. and Palme, J. (Eds.) (2012) *Towards A Social Investment Welfare State? Ideas, Policies and Challenges.* Bristol: Policy Press.

Morris, A. (2015) The Residualisation of Public Housing and its Impact on Older Tenants in Inner-City Sydney. *Australia Journal of Sociology* 51 pp154–169.

Morris, L. (1994) *Dangerous Classes: The Underclass and Social Citizenship.* London: Routledge.

Mouffe, C. (1992) Democratic Citizenship and the Political Community; in C. Mouffe (Ed.), *Dimensions of Radical Democracy.* London: Verso pp225–239.

Muir, R. and Cooke, G. (2012) *The Relational State: How Recognising the Importance of Human Relationships Could Revolutionise the Role of the State.* IPPR. Available at: www.ippr.org/publications/the-relational-state-how-recognising-the-importance-of-human-relationships-could-revolutionise-the-role-of-the-state.

Mulgan, G. (2012) Government with the People: The Outlines of a Relational State; in G. Cooke and R. Muir (Eds.), *The Relational State: How recognising the Importance of Human Relationships could Revolutionise the Role of the State.* Online only. Available at: https://www.ippr.org/publications/the-relational-state-how-recognising-the-importance-of-human-relationships-could-revolutionise-the-role-of-the-state

Muncie, J. and Wetherell, M. (1995) Family Policy and Political Discourse; in J. Muncie, M. Wetherell, M. Langan, R. Dallos and A. Cochrane (Eds.), *Understanding the Family.* London: Sage pp39–80.

Muncie, J., Wetherell, M., Langan, M., Dallos, R. and Cochrane, A. (1995) *Understanding the Family.* London: Sage.

Murdock, G.P. (1949) *Social Structure.* New York: Macmillan.

Murray, C. (1996) *The Emerging British Underclass.* London: IEA Health and Welfare Unit.

National Economic and Social Council (2009) *Well-being Matters: A Social Report for Ireland* 119 (1 & 2). Dublin: National Economic and Social Council.

Nelson, J.M. (1996) Promoting Policy Reforms: The Twilight of Conditionality? *World Development* 24 pp1551–1559.

New Economics Foundation (2008) *Triple Crunch.* London: NEF.

New Economics Foundation (2012) *Happy Planet Index: 2012 Report. A global index of sustainable wellbeing.* New Economics Foundation. Available at http://b.3cdn.net/nefoundation/d8879619b64bae461f_opm6ixqee.pdf

Ngok, K. and Kwan Chan, C. (2015) *China's Social Policy: Transformation and Challenges.* London: Routledge.

Norris, F.H., Stevens, S.P., Pfefferbaum, B., Wyche, K.F. and Pfefferbaum, R.L. (2008) Community Resilience as a Metaphor, Theory, Set of Capacities, and Strategy for Disaster Readiness. *American Journal of Community Psychology* 41 (1–2) pp127–150.

Nozick, R. (1973) Distributive Justice. *Philosophy and Public Affairs* 3 pp45–126.

Nussbaum, M. (2011) *Creating Capabilities: The Human Development Approach.* London: Belknap Press.

Obama, B. (2016) *Remarks of President Barack Obama: State of the Union Address as Delivered.* Speech. 12 January. Available at: www.whitehouse.gov/the-press-office/2016/01/12/remarks-president-barack-obama-%E2%80%93-prepared-delivery-state-union-address.

O'Connor, J. (1973) *The Fiscal Crisis of the State.* New York: St. Martin's Press.

O'Connor, J.S. (1993) Gender Class and Citizenship in the Comparative Analysis of Welfare States: Theoretical and Methodological Issues. *British Journal of Sociology* 44(3) pp501–19.

O'Neill, M. (2010) Talk of fairness is hollow without material equality: Greater socioeconomic equality is indispensable if we want to realise our shared commonsense values of societal fairness; *The Guardian*, 12 October.

O'Neill, O. (2005) Agents of Justice; in A. Kuper (Ed.), *Global Responsibilities: Who Must Deliver on Human Rights?* New York: Routledge pp37-52.

Offe, C. (1984) *Contradiction of the Welfare State.* London: Hutchinson and Co.

Office of National Statistics (2016) *United Kingdom Population Mid-Year Estimates.* Available at: https://www.ons.gov.uk/peoplepopulationandcommunity/populationandmigration/populationestimates/timeseries/ukpop/pop.

Oliver, D. and Heater, D. (1994) *The Foundation of Citizenship.* London: Harvester Wheatsheaf.

Page, R. (1984) *Stigma.* London: Routledge and Kegan Paul.

Page, R. (1996) *Altruism and the British Welfare State.* Aldershot: Avebury.

Parks, R.B., Baker, P.C., Kiser, L, Oakerson, R., Ostrom, E., Ostrom, V., Percy, L., Vandivort,.M.B., Whitaker, G.P. and Wilson, R. (1981) Consumers as Coproducers of Public Services: Some Economic and Institutional Considerations. *Policy Studies Journal* 9 (7) pp1001–1011.

Parry-Jones, B. and Soulsby, J. (2001) Needs–Led Assessment: The Challenges and the Reality. *Health and Social Care in the Community* 9 pp414–428.

Parsons, T. (1991) *The Social System.* London: Routledge.

Pascall G. (2012) *Gender Equality in the Welfare State?* Bristol: Policy Press.

Paterson, L. (1994) *The Autonomy of Modern Scotland.* Edinburgh: Edinburgh University Press.

Payne, G. (Ed.) (2013) *Social Divisions.* Basingstoke: Palgrave Macmillan.

Peck, J. (1998) Workfare in the Sun: Politics, Representation, and Method in US Welfare-to-Work Strategies. *Political Geography* 17 (5) pp535–566.

Peck J. (2004) Geography and Public Policy: Constructions of Neoliberalism. *Progress in Human Geography* 28 pp392–405.

Peck, J. and Tickell, A. (2002) Neoliberalizing Space. *Antipode* 34 pp380-404

Pemberton, S. (2015) *Harmful Societies: Understanding Social Harm*. Bristol: Policy Press.

Phillips, A. (2004) Defending Equality of Outcome. *Journal of Political Philosophy* 12 (1) pp1–19.

Piachaud, D. (2008) Social Justice and Public Policy: A Social Policy Perspective; in G. Craig, T. Burchardt and D. Gordon (Eds.), *Social Justice and Public Policy: Seeking Fairness in Diverse Societies*. Bristol: Policy Press pp33–52

Pierson, C. (2006) *Beyond the Welfare State? The New Political Economy of Welfare*. Cambridge: Polity.

Pierson, P. (1996) The New Politics of the Welfare State. *World Politics* 48 pp143–179.

Pierson, P. (1998) Irresistible Forces, Immovable Objects: Post-Industrial Welfare States Confront Permanent Austerity. *Journal of European Public Policy* 5 pp539–560.

Pilisuk, M. and Pilisuk, P. (1976) *How We Lost the War on Poverty*. New Brunswick, NJ: Transaction Books.

Pilkington, A. (1992) Is there a British Underclass? *Sociology Review* February pp29–32.

Pinker, R. (2006) From Gift Relationships to Quasi-Markets: An Odyssey Along the Policy Paths of Altruism and Egoism. *Social Policy and Administration* 40 pp10–25.

Pinker, R.A. (1971) *Social Theory and Social Policy*. London: Heinemann.

Pinker, R.A. (1985) *The Idea of Welfare*. London: Heinemann.

Plant, R. (1984) *Equality, Markets and the State*. London: Fabian Society.

Plant, R. (1992) Citizenship, Rights and Welfare; in A. Coote (Ed.), *The Welfare of Citizens: Developing New Social Rights*. London: River Oram Press pp15–39.

Platt, L. (2013) Poverty; in G. Payne (Ed.), *Social Divisions* (3rd edn.). Basingstoke: Palgrave Macmillan pp303-331.

Powell, M. (1999) Introduction; in M. Powell (Ed.), *New Labour, New Welfare State?* Bristol: Policy Press pp1–27.

Powell, M. (2007) *Understanding the Mixed Economy of Welfare*. Bristol: Policy Press.

Priestly, M. (2016) Disability; in P. Alcock, T. Haux, M. May and S. Wright (Eds.), *The Student's Companion to Social Policy*. Sussex: Wiley pp439–444.

Putnam, R.D. (2001) *Bowling Alone*. New York: Simon and Schuster.

Rae, D. (1981) *Equalities*. London: Harvard University Press.

Rapport, F.L. and Maggs, C.J. (2002) Titmuss and the Gift Relationship: Altruism Revisited. *Journal of Advanced Nursing* 40 pp495–503.

Rawls, J. (1999) *A Theory of Justice*. Oxford: Oxford University Press.

Rees, T. (2006) *Mainstreaming Equality in the European Union*. London: Routledge.

Rex, J. and Moore, R. (1979) *Race, Community and Conflict: A Study of Sparkbrook.* Oxford: Oxford University Press.

Riches, G. and Silvasti, T. (Eds.) (2014) *First World Hunger Revisited: Food Charity or the Right to Food?* (2nd edn.). London: Palgrave Macmillan.

Rieger, E. and Leibfried, S. (1998) Welfare State Limits to Globalization. *Politics and Society* 26 (3) pp363–390.

Robertson, D. and Smyth, J. (2009) Tackling Squalor? Housing's Contribution to the Welfare State; in K. Rummery, I. Greener and C. Holden (Eds.), *Social Policy Review 21: Analysis and Debate in Social Policy.* Bristol: Policy Press pp87–106.

Rodger, J.J. (2000) *From a Welfare State to a Welfare Society: The Changing Context of Social Policy in a Postmodern Era.* Hampshire: Macmillan.

Room, G. (1995) Poverty in Europe: Competing Paradigms of Analysis. *Policy and Politics* 23 pp103–113.

Rose, N. (1996) The Death of the Social? Re-Figuring the Territory of Government. *International Journal of Human Resource Management* 25 pp327–356.

Roseneil, S. (2004) Why We Should Care about Friends: An Argument for Queering the Care Imaginary in Social Policy. *Social Policy and Society* 3 pp409–419.

Rowlingson, K. and McKay, S. (2012) *Wealth and The Wealthy: Exploring and Tackling Inequalities between Rich and Poor.* Bristol: Policy Press.

Rowntree, B.S. (2000) *Poverty: A Study of Town Life* (Centennial Ed.). Bristol: Policy Press.

Rubington, E. and Weinberg, M.S. (1995) *The Study of Social Problems: Seven Perspectives.* Oxford: Oxford University Press.

Saggar, S. (1993) The Politics of 'Race Policy' In Britain. *Critical Social Policy* 13 pp32–51.

Sassen, S. (2000) The Need to Distinguish Denationalized and Postnational. *Indiana Journal of Global Legal Studies* 7 (2) pp575–584.

Sassen, S. (2002) Towards Post-National Citizenship; in E. Isin and B. Turner (Eds.), *Handbook of Citizenship Studies.* London: Sage pp277–292.

Schmueker, K. and Lodge, G. (Eds.) (2010) *Devolution in Practice 2010.* London: IPPR.

Schröder, M. (2013) *Integrating Varieties of Capitalism and Welfare State Research: A Unified Typology of Capitalisms.* Hampshire: Palgrave Macmillan.

Scrivens, E. (1980) Towards a Theory of Rationing; in R. Leaper (Ed.), *Health, Wealth and Housing.* Oxford: Blackwell pp223–239.

Seeley, C. (2015) *Social Policy Simplified: Connecting Theory with People's Lives.* London: Palgrave.

Sen, A. (1999) *Commodities and Capabilities.* Delhi: Oxford University Press.

Sennett, R. and Cobb, J. (1993) *The Hidden Injuries of Class.* New York: WW Norton.

Seyfang, G. (2004) Working Outside the Box: Community Currencies, Time Banks and Social Inclusion. *Journal of Social Policy* 33 pp49–71.

Seymour, R. (2012) Lord Freud on Welfare: Making the Poor Pay for the Risk-Taking of the Rich; *The Guardian*, 23 November. Available at: www.guardian.co.uk/commentisfree/2012/nov/23/lord-freud-welfare-poor-risk.

Shildrick, T. and MacDonald, R. (2013) Poverty Talk: How People Experiencing Poverty Deny Their Poverty and Why They Blame 'The Poor'. *The Sociological Review* 61 pp285–303.

Sky News (2107) Stateless Seven-Year-Old's Goal of Football Stardom at Risk. Available at: https://news.sky.com/story/stateless-seven-year-olds-goal-of-football-stardom-at-risk-10765226

Smart, C. (2007) *Personal Life: New Directions in Sociological Thinking*. Cambridge: Polity Press.

Spicker, P. (1988) *Principles of Social Welfare: An Introduction to Thinking About the Welfare State*. London: Routledge.

Spicker, P. (2008) *Social Policy: Themes and Approaches*. Bristol: Policy Press.

Squires P. (1990) *Anti-Social Policy: Welfare, Ideology and the Disciplinary State*. London: Harvester Wheatsheaf.

Starr, C. (2014) *Health 2015: A Conversation with Davidson Gwatkin on Progressive Universalism*. Results for Development, 25 February. Available at: http://r4d.org/blog/2014-02-25/health-2015-conversation-davidson-gwatkin-progressive-universalism.

Stears, M. (2012) The Case for a State that Supports Relationships, not a Relational State; in G. Cooke and R. Muir (Eds.), *The Relational State: How Recognising the Importance of Human Relationships could Revolutionise the Role of the State*. Online only. Available at: https://www.ippr.org/publications/the-relational-state-how-recognising-the-importance-of-human-relationships-could-revolutionise-the-role-of-the-state

Stedman Jones, D. (2014) *Masters of the Universe: Hayek, Friedman, and the Birth of Neoliberal Politics*. Princeton, N.J.: Princeton University Press.

Stenson, K. (2001) The New Politics of Crime Control; in K. Stenson and RR Sullivan (Eds.), *Crime, Risk and Justice: The Politics of Crime Control in Liberal Democracies*. Cullompton: Willan pp15-28.

Stevenson, N. (2000) *Culture and Citizenship*. London: Sage.

Stiglitz, J., Sen, A. and Fitoussi, J. (2008) *Report of the Commission on the Measurement of Economic Performance and Social Progress*. Available at: www.stiglitz-sen-fitoussi.fr/en/.

Tawney, R.H. (1921) *The Acquisitive Society*. Charleston, SC: Bibliobazaar.

Taylor, D. (2015) Well-being and Welfare under the U.K. Coalition: Happiness is not Enough; in L. Foster, A. Brunton, C. Deeming and T. Haux (Eds.), *In Defence of Welfare II*. Bristol: Policy Press pp16-20.

Taylor, M. (2011) Community Organising and the Big Society: Is Saul Alinsky Turning in his Grave? *Voluntary Sector Review* 2 pp257–264.

Taylor-Gooby, P. (1985) *Public Opinion, Ideology and State Welfare*. London: Routledge and Kegan Paul.

Taylor-Gooby, P. (1994) Postmodernism and Social Policy: A Great Leap Backwards? *Journal of Social Policy* 23 pp385-404.

Taylor-Gooby, P. (2001) Risk, Contingency and the Third Way: Evidence from the BHPS and Qualitative Studies. *Social Policy and Administration* 35 (2) pp195–211.

Taylor-Gooby, P. (2016) Equality, Rights and Social Justice; in P. Alcock, T. Haux, M. May and S. Wright (Eds.), *The Student's Companion to Social Policy*. Sussex: Wiley pp27–33.

Taylor-Gooby, P., Dean, H., Munro, M, and Parker, G. (1999) Risk and the Welfare State. *The British Journal of Sociology* 50 pp177–119.

Telegraph, The (2012) Welfare Minister: Dreadful Benefits System Gives People a Lifestyle on the State; *The Telegraph*, 23 November. Available at: www.telegraph. co.uk/news/politics/9697983/welfare-minister-dreadful-benefits-system-gives-people-a-lifestyle-on-the-state.html.

Testart, A. (1998) Uncertainties and the 'Obligation to Reciprocate': A Critique of Mauss; in W. James and N.J. Allen (Eds.), *Marcel Mauss: A Centenary Tribute*. New York: Berhahn Books pp97–110.

Thompson, S. and Hoggett, P. (1996) Universalism, Selectivism and Particularism: Towards a Postmodern Social Policy. *Critical Social Policy* 16 pp21–42.

Titmuss, R.M. (1967) The Welfare State: Images and Realities; in P. Alcock, H. Glennerster and A. Oakley (Eds.) (2001), *Welfare and Wellbeing: Richard Titmuss's Contribution to Social Policy*. Bristol: Policy Press pp49–58.

Titmuss, R.M. (1971) *Commitment to Welfare*. London: George Allen and Unwin.

Titmuss, R.M. (1974) *Essays on 'The Welfare State'*. London: Unwin University Books.

Titmuss, R.M., Ashton, J. and Oakley, A. (1997) *The Gift Relationship: From Human Blood to Social Policy*. New York: New Press.

Townsend, P. (1976) *Sociology and Social Policy*. Middlesex: Penguin.

Townsend, P. (1979) *Poverty in the United Kingdom*. Middlesex: Penguin.

Trench, A. and Lodge, G. (2014) *Devo More and Welfare: Devolving Benefits and Policy for a Stronger Union*. IPPR. Available at: www.ippr.org/publications/devo-more-and-welfare.

Twine, F. (1994) *Citizenship and Social Rights*. London: Sage.

Utting, D. (2009) *Contemporary Social Evils*. Bristol: Policy Press.

Waddell, G. and Burton, A.K. (2006) *Is Work Good for your Health and Wellbeing?* London: The Stationery Office.

Wahl, A. (2011) *The Rise and Fall of the Welfare State*. London: Pluto Books.

Waine, B. (1991) *The Rhetoric of Independence: The Ideology and Practice of Social Policy in Thatcher's Britain*. Oxford: Berg Publishers Limited.

Walker, R. (2014) *The Shame of Poverty*. Oxford: Oxford University Press.

Wapshott, N. (2011) *Keynes Hayek: The Clash That Defined Modern Economics*. New York: W.W. Norton & Company, Inc.

Ward, C. (1996) *Social Policy: An Anarchist Response*. London: Freedom Press.

Wearden, G. and Elliott, L. (2013) Angela Merkel tells Davos Austerity must Continue; *The Guardian*, 24 January.

Webb, S. (2006) *Social Work in a Risk Society: Social and Political Perspectives.* Hampshire: Palgrave Macmillan.

Weber, M. (1946) Politics as a Vocation; in M. Weber (trans. H.H. Gerth and C. Wright Mills), *From Max Weber: Essays in Sociology.* Oxford: Oxford University Press pp77–128.

Weiss, L. (1998) *The Myth of the Powerless State.* Cambridge: Polity.

Welshman, J. (2013) 'Troubled Families': the lessons of history, 1880–2012. *History & Policy.* Available at: http://www.historyandpolicy.org/policy-papers/papers/troubled-families-the-lessons-of-history-1880-2012

Wetherly, P. (1996) Basic Needs and Social Policies. *Critical Social Policy* 16 pp45–65.

White, M.D. (2014) *The Illusion of Well-being: Economic Policymaking Based on Respect and Responsiveness.* Hampshire: Palgrave.

Whiteford, M. (2010) Hot Tea, Dry Toast and the Responsibilisation of Homeless People. *Social Policy and Society* 9 pp193–205.

Wilby, P. (2007) A New Revolutionary Slogan; *New Statesman*, 18 October. Available at: www.newstatesman.com/uk-politics/2007/10/poor-families-brown-children.

Wilding, P. (Ed.) (1986) *In Defence of the Welfare State.* Manchester: Manchester University Press.

Wilding, P. (1992) The British Welfare State: Thatcherism's Enduring Legacy. *Policy & Politics* 20 pp201-212.

Wilkinson, H. (1999) Celebrate the New Family; *New Statesman*, 9 August. Available at: https://www.newstatesman.com/node/198112

Wilkinson, H. (Ed.) (2000) *The Family Business.* London: Demos.

Wilkinson, R.G. (1997) Comment: Income, Inequality and Social Cohesion. *American Journal of Public Health* 87 pp1504–1506.

Wilkinson, R.G. and Pickett, K.E. (2007) The Problems of Relative Deprivation: Why Some Societies Do Better Than Others. *Social Science and Medicine* 65 pp1965–1978.

Williams, F. (1989) *Social Policy: A Critical Introduction.* Cambridge: Blackwell.

Williams, F. (1992) Somewhere Over the Rainbow: Universality and Diversity in Social Policy; in N. Manning and R. Page (Eds.), *Social Policy Review 4.* London: SPA pp200–219.

Williams, G. and Popay, J. (2006) Lay Knowledge and the Privilege of Experience; in D. Kelleher, J. Gabe and G. Williams (Eds.), *Challenging Medicine* (2nd edn.). Oxon: Routledge pp118–139

Wincup, E. (2013) *Understanding Crime and Social Policy.* Bristol: Policy Press.

Wintour, P. (2008a) We Need International Regulation to Protect Global Economy, Brown Tells World Leaders; *The Guardian*, 25 September. Available at: www.theguardian.com/politics/2008/sep/25/gordonbrown.marketturmoil.

Wintour, P. (2008b) Minister Persists with Plans to Link Housing with Work; *The Guardian*, 21 March. Available at: www.theguardian.com/society/2008/mar/21/housing.labour.

Wright Mills, C. (1959) *The Sociological Imagination*. Oxford: Oxford University Press.

Wronka, J. (1998) *Human Rights and Social Policy in the 21st Century*. Langham, MD: University Press of America.

Yeates, N. (Ed.) (2008) *Understanding Global Social Policy*. Bristol: Policy Press.

Young, M. (1979) *The Rise of the Meritocracy*. Middlesex: Penguin Books.

Index

Note: Page numbers in *italics* indicate figures and tables.

Printed in Great Britain
by Amazon

66282562R00160